Public Sector Management

Norman Flynn

FIFTH EDITION

⑤ SAGE Publications

London ● Los Angeles ● New Delhi ● Singapore

First edition published by Harvester Wheatsheaf 1990
Second and third editions © Prentice Hall UK Limited 1993, 1997
Fourth edition © Pearson Education Limited 2002

This edition © Norman Flynn 2007

First published 2007

SAGE Publications Ltd
1 Oliver's Yard
55 City Road
London EC1Y 1SP

SAGE Publications Inc.
2455 Teller Road
Thousand Oaks, California 91320

SAGE Publications India Pvt Ltd
B 1/I 1 Mohan Cooperative Industrial Area
Mathura Road, New Delhi 110 044
India

SAGE Publications Asia-Pacific Pte Ltd
33 Pekin Street #02-01
Far East Square
Singapore 048763

British Library Cataloguing in Publication data

A catalogue record for this book is available from the British Library

ISBN 978-1-4129-2992-9
ISBN 978-1-4129-2993-6 (pbk)

Library of Congress Control Number: 2006904389

Typeset by C&M Digitals (P) Ltd., Chennai, India
Printed in Great Britain by The Alden Press, Witney
Printed on paper from sustainable resources

Dedication

For Rachel, Mickaela, Letrishka, and Alastair

Contents

Personal acknowledgements

Since the first edition, many people have contributed ideas and experience to this book. Thanks are especially due to Carole Ballardie, Richard Common, Michael Connolly, Ashley Dowlen, Michael Flynn, Peter Hall, Dominic Hurley, Veronica James, Peter Jones, Andrew Likierman, Stephanie Macauley, Elizabeth Mellon, Clive Miller, Janet Newman, Sandra Nutley, Alice Perkins, Andrew Puddephatt, Ellie Scrivens, John Stewart, Ted Unsworth, (late) Kieron Walsh, Stuart Wilks-Heeg, Andy Wynne.

Acknowledgements

We are grateful to the following for permission to reproduce copyright material:

Figures 1.1 and 1.2 from Trends in Public Sector Employment, *National Statistics Feature*, December (ONS, 2005); Table 1.2 from *Local Government Finance Key Facts: England* (ODPM, 2005); Table 1.3 from *Local Government Financial Statistics, 2005–6* (ONS, 2006); Table 1.4 from *Civil Service Staffing, 1 April 2004* (ONS, 2004); Figures 3.1 and 3.2 from *Comprehensive Spending Review* (HM Treasury, 2005); Table 3.1 after Table in *Public Expenditure: Statistical Analyses 1996–7* Cm 3201 (HM Treasury, 1997) and Table in *Public Expenditure: Statistical Analyses 2000–2001* Cm 4601 (HM Treasury, 2001); Table 3.2 after Figures in *Comprehensive Spending Review* (HM Treasury, 1999); Table 3.3 after Table in *Public Expenditure Statistical Analysis* (HM Treasury, 2005); Figure 3.3 from *2005–6 Projections* (HM Treasury, 2005); Table 3.4 after Tables in *Pre-Budget Reports* (HM Treasury, 1995; 2000; 2005); Figure 4.1 and Table 4.1 after Figures in *Modern Social Services 9th Annual Report* (Social Services Inspectorate, 2000); Table 4.2 from *Community Care Services* (ONS, 2006); Table 4.3, Figures 4.2, 4.3 and 4.4 from *Social Trends 36* (ONS, 2006); Table 4.4 after Tables in *Social Trends 26, 31 and 35* (ONS, 1996; 2001; 2005); Table 4.5 after Tables in *Social Trends 31* (ONS, 2001); Figure X and Table C1 from *Understanding Government Output and Productivity* (ONS, 2003); Table Y from *Average Earnings Index 2000–2005* (ONS, 2006); Table 5.1 from *British Crime Survey 2004* (ONS, 2004); Table 5.2 from *British Crime Survey 2005* (ONS, 2005); Figures 5.3 and 5.4 from *Performance Targets* (Department for Education & Skills, 2005); Figures 5.5 and 5.6 from *Performance Targets* (Department of Health, 2005); Figure 6.2 after Figures in *Report on the Evaluation of the Public Service Excellence Programme* (Cabinet Office, 2000); Figure 7.1 from *Best Value Inspection* (Audit Commission, 1999); Figure 8.3 from *Making a Difference: Effective Implementation of Cross-cutting Policy* (Scottish Executive, 2000); Table 11.1 from HM Treasury website (HM Treasury, 2005); Figure 11.1 from *PFI: Meeting the Investment Challenge* (HM Treasury, 2003); Figures in Appendix from *Performance Index*, HM Treasury website (HM Treasury, 2005), all Crown Copyright material reproduced under the terms of the Click-Use Licence; Figure 6.1 from 'A spectrum of consumer/citizen control' in *Public Money and Management*, July-September, Blackwell Publishers (Skelcher, C.K., 1993) reprinted with permission from Blackwell; Figures 8.4 and 8.5 from Capita Group plc unpublished presentation, reprinted with permission from The Capita

Group plc; Table 8.1 from Capita Profile, figures for 2000, in *Hoover's Company Profiles,* reprinted with permission from Hoover's Inc.; Figure 10.1 from *Markets and Hierarchies,* The Free Press (Williamson, O., 1975), reprinted with permission from Simon & Schuster; Figures 11.2, 11.3 and 11.4 from *London Underground and the PPP: the second year 2004/2005,* reprinted with permission from Transport for London; Table 11.2 from 'Private Finance and "Value for Money" in NHS Hospitals: a policy in search of rationale' in *The British Medical Journal,* volume 324 (Pollock, A.M. et al, 2002), reprinted with permission from BMJ Publishing; Extract from 'The Managerialisation of Prisons – Efficiency Without a Purpose?'in *Criminal Justice Matters, No 40* (Bryans, S., 2000), reprinted with permission from The Centre for Crime and Justice Studies.

We are indebted to HMSO for the reproduction of an extract from HM Inspector of Prison's report on Wandsworth, published in October 1999.

While every effort has been made to trace the owners of copyright material, in a few cases this has proved impossible and we take this opportunity to offer our apologies to any copyright holders whose rights we have unwittingly infringed.

Companion Website

Visit the SAGE Companion Website for Public Sector Management 5th Edition at www.sagepub.co.uk/flynn to find valuable resources including extensive thematically organized weblinks and downloadable figures and diagrams from the book for use in lectures and presentations.

Part One

Introduction

This is a book about management in the public sector in the United Kingdom. Successive governments have restructured, reformed, privatized, reorganized, outsourced and modernized public services so that managers and workers are subject to permanent change. This book is designed to help anyone who is working in or studying the public sector to understand and cope with the changes. It does so by analysing policy and management in the context of the history of the welfare state. Ideas about how to run public services have a habit of coming around more than once, and understanding the development of management and control systems can help put this year's initiatives into perspective.

What is the public sector?

The boundary between the public and private sectors is neither clear nor permanent. In some cases the boundary is well defined: assets get transferred from the public to the private sector through privatization; assets that remain in state ownership are clearly public. The process of outsourcing, whereby private companies provide all or part of services, makes the boundary less clear. If the IT services of a core function such as tax collection are outsourced, the employees are not public servants. When companies finance, build and maintain assets, such as schools, prisons and hospitals and lease them to government, the ownership of the assets is less clearly defined and may revert to the state at the end of the contract. Within functions that are traditionally thought of as core state activities, such as the provision of defence, various arrangements for the supply of buildings, equipment and services involve companies and their employees: invasions are carried out by a mixture of publicly employed military personnel and contractors.

Even after privatization, there may be strong public interest and state involvement in the services. The national railway was privatized but the state continued to subsidize the system and have an interest in its performance. Water and sewerage services are similarly mostly in private hands but subject to regulation. Bus services are privatized but variously subject to subsidy and regulation.

The public sector that this book addresses is those parts of the economy that are either in state ownership or under contract to the state, plus those parts that are regulated and/or subsidized in the public interest. It does not include all those parts that are subject to competition policy, as that would be close to the whole economy, but does include competition policy in what used to be called the public utilities.

The public services that are provided by state employees account for about 20% of the economy and the labour force. If we add all transfer payments such as social security benefits and pensions and subsidies, public spending adds up to about 40% of the amount of Gross Domestic Product.

What is management?

Management in the public sector means many different things. First, there is a distinction between administration and management, the former involving the orderly arrangement of resources to follow previously defined procedures and rules, the latter involving discretion in the management of resources to achieve a set of objectives. In practice, both activities occur in public services: many activities require administration rather than management, and many managers are engaged in both.

Management, in the sense of exercising some discretion, requires that managers think and act to find the best ways of achieving some target or objective, using and directing other people's skills. In this sense, the managers become distinct from the various professions in the public sector, such as teachers, doctors, nurses, social workers, engineers, lawyers and accountants, who use their own professional skills and knowledge to produce results. The distinction between a manager and a professional has been promoted by those who believe in management and by the professionals, who like to remain different from managers. Professionals try to keep their knowledge and skills within the profession and look after the resources put at their disposal using their own ideas about how to work.

In this sense management is 'the management', or a group of people who are separate from those doing the work, whether of a professional, technical or manual kind. 'The management' has some formal authority as well carrying out a set of activities, such as planning, budgeting, performance measurement, setting up organizational arrangements, through which they direct and control the others. While such managers may previously have been technicians, workers or professionals, once they are put into a managerial position their role and activities change.

To be able to do this, and to keep themselves in a position of authority over the others, they have to acquire a set of techniques, skills and language which give their claim to authority some legitimacy. Managers develop or learn them as a way of maintaining control. The techniques include strategic planning, budgeting, project management, marketing, personnel management, performance management, quality procedures and the whole apparatus of contracting. The language is sometimes only understood by a select few, although often there is a normal word which would be a good substitute. For example, 'delayering' would be understood by most people as sacking middle management, 'downsizing' as sacking management and workers, 'business process reengineering' as doing things differently, 'quality circles' as groups of workers discussing how to do things better, 'network organization' as a group of subcontractors, and 'mission statement' as understanding what staff are supposed to do. New governments bring new lexicons. The introduction of competition brought with it the language of cost accounting, asset-sweating and customer focus. Experiments in getting agencies to co-operate were introduced with the language of partnership, joined-up government and pathfinders. Publication of performance measures comes with beacons, red and green lights and league tables.

In the public sector, politicians also claim a legitimacy to manage, along with the right to introduce new language. After all, if they are elected to positions of authority and are held accountable for the money spent on public services, they have a right to influence how they are run. The distinction between policy and management is not always clear. Managers and professionals have views about what are the most effective services and therefore which should be provided. At the same time, politicians will have views about the best way to manage, either from their experience or from beliefs about management which they have developed or acquired though politics.

Ideas about management are not technical and free of values. Many of the main ideas about how organizations should be run are based on beliefs about people's motivation, how they relate to each other, the use of authority, and the extent to which people can be trusted. In other words, management itself can be ideological. Indeed 'managerialism' or the pursuit of a particular set of management ideas has itself been described as an ideology.

In many cases where activities have been contracted out to the private sector, the management activity of public sector managers does not consist of directly managing resources. Rather, the task is how to specify services and make sure that contractors provide them in accordance with the specification. For many this has meant that they have had to acquire skills in contract writing, negotiating and supervising another organization's work.

The structure of the book

This book is in two parts. Part One is concerned with the institutional, political, financial and policy environment in which managers work. The scale, scope and organization of the public sector, the amount of money devoted to public services and the main developments in policy towards the welfare state and other aspects of state activity all create the conditions within which services are delivered.

Chapter 1 describes the scale, scope and functions of the public sector in the United Kingdom. It shows that after a long period of financial constraint and employment cuts, budgets and staffing levels increased from 1999, especially in the education and health sectors. The decline and constant low level of capital spending was also reversed. The institutions are introduced, as are the relationships between them and central government. While there is devolved government in Scotland and Wales, and periodically in Northern Ireland, there are tight and detailed controls over local government and strict hierarchy, assisted by administered markets, in the National Health Service. The service delivery functions of the Civil Service are carried out by the Executive Agencies and other departments working under the same style of control, working to performance contracts. Outside these institutions there is a large collection of quangos, run by Boards appointed by government. Overall, the institutional framework is a highly centralized system of government and service delivery.

Chapter 2 covers the politics of the public sector. It briefly describes the development of the public sector over four periods: the formation of the institutions after the second world war; the period during which Margaret Thatcher was Prime Minister; the years of John Major's premiership and Prime Minister Tony Blair's three terms of office. Each government had its own philosophy about what the state should do and responded to the economic, social and political environment in its own way.

The level and distribution of public spending is an important element of policy towards the public sector. Chapter 3 traces the trends in spending over a forty-year period and covers recent developments in more detail. It then analyses the process of budgeting at central and local government level and in the NHS. It shows that while there is tight central policy control, detailed financial management is decentralized.

The development of social policies has a big impact on how the institutions of the state are run. Chapter 4 discusses how policy has developed in the main sector of social policy: income maintenance; health services; community care; education; housing; criminal justice. It shows that there have been common themes of policy development running through all the sectors.

Part Two is about how services are managed. The first four chapters are mostly concerned with services provided by directly employed personnel. The following three chapters are about services provided by companies and others, either contracted to or regulated by the government. An introduction to Part Two appears after Chapter 4 on page 117.

A companion website for this book can be found at www.sagepub.co.uk/flynn.

1

The public sector in the United Kingdom

Introduction

This chapter introduces the scale, scope and functions of the public sector in the United Kingdom. What is private and what is public varies between countries, and with time within countries. We start by asking whether users of services or workers are concerned about whether the organizations providing services are in public or private ownership, and conclude that people are probably more concerned with quality and accessibility of services as users, and income and security as workers, than with the ownership of the assets. In any case, the distinctions are no longer very clear. Private companies using state-owned assets are providing public services. The state is leasing assets owned and managed by private companies. Workers in the state sector may be employed on casual or temporary contracts and be badly paid.

One characteristic makes the management of public services different in principle from managing private services: the fact that they are not usually sold to people at a price that yields a profit and are not withheld from people who cannot afford them. While even this definition is not inclusive of all public services it is the most important in thinking about the differences in the way in which they are run. In private services marketing is designed to attract customers. Strategies of market segmentation are designed to distinguish between types of customer and offer them different services at different prices. Good service is offered to persuade people to come back. In the public sector, the problem is often one of rationing, not marketing, considerations of equity require that all service users are treated similarly, and pricing, where it is done, is not normally to maximize profit. The whole purpose of public services is not to make money but to collectively provide protection, help, restraint, education, recreation and care outside market relationships.

The chapter describes the scale and scope of the public sector, including the Civil Service, local government, the NHS and 'quangos' or quasi-non governmental organizations with which the rest of the book is concerned.

It concludes by asking whether the United Kingdom is different from other countries. On one dimension, spending on social protection, the United Kingdom is close to the European average. A main difference is that the UK state is more centralized than that of most other countries, despite the genuine devolution to Scotland and to a lesser extent Wales.

What is a public service? The boundary between the public and private sectors

A premise of this book is that managing public services is not the same as managing services in the private sector. It is important to be clear about what the differences and similarities are, so that good ideas and ways of working from both sectors can be applied in the public sector.

A public view

A public opinion survey commissioned by the Trades Union Congress during the last Conservative government's term of office[1] produced answers that surprised people working in public services. The respondents made no distinction between services provided to the public by public institutions and those provided by companies. Banks were linked in people's minds with hospitals and social security. This was not a result of ignorance but of concern: people were concerned with good service, not with the ownership of the facilities or the employment contracts of the service providers. Who knows or cares whether the staff at their local leisure centre are employed by the local authority or a leisure management company? Or that their income tax or council tax form is processed on a computer operated by a private sector employee? Or, more obscurely, that the hospital in which they are being treated is owned by a PFI contractor and leased for 30 years, serviced, to the NHS Trust?

The exceptions were the public utilities, especially gas and water where opinion surveys showed that people resented the combination of higher charges, poor service and the publicity given to the very large salary increases for senior management. This seemed not to be an objection in principle to privatization but to the practice of a few people getting rich at the public's expense. This reaction also produced a majority against the privatization of the railways and the Post Office. The catastrophic record of track maintenance following the privatization of the railway and its division into many separate operating companies shows that public opinion was probably correct.

At the same time, surveys have shown that citizens do not have a clear idea about the distribution of functions among the institutions of the state. 'The social' refers to social security and social services; few people have a clear idea about the distribution of functions between the tiers of local government, where these still exist. A survey[2] of residents living in 'two-tier' boroughs showed a high degree of confusion about the distribution, more people thinking that the District rather than the County was responsible for social services and road and streetlight maintenance, for example. Accountability to the public is difficult under these circumstances and contributes to the low levels of participation in local elections, which was below 30% in 1998 and 2000.[3]

The employees' view

Employees may have a different opinion. Surely a 'proper job' is more likely to be found in the Civil Service or other public services than in a company with a short-term contract with the government or local authority. Traditionally jobs with local authorities were considered secure, if not very well paid. People who preferred security or were at a stage in their life where security was most important could find stable employment, usually with provision for an occupational pension. Now there is great variation. If you are a casual cleaner, employed on a weekly contract with an office cleaning company, then your terms and conditions of employment are probably much worse than a previous position in which cleaners were employed directly, with sick pay and holiday pay. The change from public to private is not just a matter of benefits and pay; it is also a question of affiliation to the institution. In the cases of both hospital and school cleaners, there was often a rapport between the cleaners and the patients and children, benefiting both sides in the relationship: a (usually) friendly representative of an otherwise daunting institution getting satisfaction from personal contact in an otherwise tedious job. Once cleaning is contracted out, staff are moved from one site to another with no time to stop and say hello, so both sides lose those benefits.

If you are a home carer, working as a self-employed person for a homecare agency, you are probably earning the minimum wage and in a less secure job than when you used to be employed by the social services department. Contracting out low-paid jobs such as these has resulted in lower pay, fewer benefits and less security, especially for women workers.

However, if you are a clerical worker on a short-term contract with Jobcentre Plus, you may well have less security than if you had been employed as a programmer by a company running one of the Agency's computer applications. Certainly if you are employed as a leisure centre worker by a leisure company with a three-year contract with a local authority, you are probably better off than a casual worker taken on by the same authority. In an extreme case, that of management consultants or directors of IT companies contracted to the government, the benefits are much higher than those of a civil servant, as the numerous civil servants who made the transition discovered. People resigned from government departments, under policies of staff reductions, joined a consulting firm and were hired back at three to four times their cost and paid twice their previous salary. In other words, security is not a necessary result of working for public authorities, nor is it necessarily the case that employment in companies contracted to the public sector is less secure than a public sector job. The unskilled and low paid, whether in the clerical or manual operations, are increasingly insecure with both employers.

Public goods and public services

There are four elements to the distinction between private and public services. The first is that certain things are 'public goods'. One feature of such goods and services is that they produce 'externalities', or benefits that accrue to people other than those who benefit directly. For example, education is said to benefit everyone living in a society of skilled and educated people. The other feature is that people cannot be excluded from certain benefits. Everyone benefits from clean air or street lighting. Because no one can be excluded, people should pay for such services collectively rather than individually. Even those politicians who believe that the state should do the minimum possible are normally willing to concede that these categories of services should be carried out by the public sector. Some people believe that no services are better provided by government and that even clean air is best achieved by property rights in air.

As a *justification* for the public sector, the 'public goods' argument suggests that the public sector should provide services where the market fails to do so, and the goods or services are required collectively, a decision made through the political process. As an *explanation* of what is public and what is private it is less convincing, since different services are in the public and private sectors in different societies and at different stages of development. Examples of the differences include the extensive provision of education through religious organizations but financed by the state in the Netherlands, the private provision of ambulances and fire protection in Denmark, public ownership of airlines in various countries. History and politics have more convincing explanations than a theory about public goods. Britain went through a period in which the ruling Conservative Party had an instinctive suspicion of public provision and preference for markets and the private sector. The Labour party abandoned its belief in state ownership as part of its modernization programme and claims to be pragmatic in its approach to what should be private and what should be public.

The second distinction is how services are financed. Services are public services if they are financed mainly by taxation, rather than by direct payments by individual customers. One characteristic of most public services is that they are not available for sale and people cannot necessarily have more if they pay more. Even those services that are 'commercial', in the sense that money is exchanged at the point of consumption, are still public services in the sense that they are controlled through the political process and accountability for service delivery is through politicians to the public rather than to shareholders.

The distinction is no longer absolute. People who receive homecare, for example, may pay for extra hours beyond those which they are assessed as needing. School children who do not pay for school visits may be left at school. Some public services are subject to charging: leisure facilities and car parks are normally charged for at cost or close to it. The NHS has charged for drugs since 1952 and patients pay about 10% of the cost of drugs to the NHS.[4] NHS Trusts have private wings in which patients who pay may receive quicker treatment and better facilities than NHS patients. A high proportion of public services are 'free', at least at the point at which they are used: most of education and health, social security, criminal justice.

A third difference is who owns the facilities and by whom the service providers are employed. Traditionally public services were provided by public employees using publicly owned assets. Again, such a distinction is not absolute, after a period of contracting out and privatization. Take public transport. In the United Kingdom outside London, bus transport is privately owned and deregulated. But there are still public service features. Everyone benefits from there being a public transport system, even car users whose freedom to drive is enhanced by other travellers taking buses. In London, buses are privately owned, but the routes are regulated by Transport for London and some routes are subsidized. Or take refuse collection. Where private companies have won the right to collect rubbish, their employees are not public employees, the vehicles may or may not be owned by the local authorities but the details of the service are determined by the local authority.

The main defining characteristic is whether goods and services are sold only to people who pay for them and whether anyone with money can access them while other people are excluded. For people running and providing the services this distinction is important. In a business, the task is to attract customers, persuade them to pay a price that produces a profit and satisfy them enough to persuade them to remain customers. Public services have to attract people to use them, but they also have to enforce eligibility criteria where scarce resources have to be rationed in a way which does not apply in the private sector where scarce services are rationed by price. In the public sector, resources are rarely deliberately rationed by price. Prescription charges for drugs may deter poor people from taking medication, but there are safeguards to try to ensure that people in need do not have to pay and are not deterred. Nor do the managers and workers of public services have to satisfy people enough to persuade them to return. In those cases where the service is a monopoly, the service users have no choice. Even if they have a choice, it is not always the case that attracting more service users creates benefits for the organization or its workers: often it just means more work. The motivation for satisfying customers is not to persuade them to return and generate more profit, but the value of public service.

It is really this last feature, the lack of a direct connection between ability to pay and access to the service and the fact that there is not always a direct benefit from attracting customers, that makes management in the public sector distinct: marketing to generate sales is mostly irrelevant, unless artificial markets are created. Customer satisfaction as expressed by repeat business is not a relevant measure of success, nor is profitability. Motivations for good service are not themselves based on profit.

If these differences did not exist, then managing in the private and public sectors would be identical. Of course there are similarities: people's motivations in both sectors may have no connection with the well-being of the organization or its customers; services in both sectors need to be designed and managed in similar ways; organizations have to be created to support the service process. Underlying these techniques, however, are the important differences in values and definitions of success.

The scale of the public sector

The Conservative governments from 1979 reduced the scale of the public sector through a series of privatizations, initially the sale of nationalized industries, such as Cable and Wireless and British Aerospace (1981). Then came oil (British Petroleum first shares in 1983) and telecommunications (British Telecom 1984). The utilities were privatized in the late 1980s (gas 1986, water 1989 and electricity 1990).

Apart from these 'denationalizations', privatization has been implemented in other ways. Local authorities, the National Health Service and central government have outsourced many services. In these cases, the state retains responsibility for the function, but has the work carried out by contractors. Sometimes the contracting-out process is carried out by organizing a competition between the existing employees and private companies, in a tendering process. In other cases, there is a competition without a bid from the in-house employees. In yet other cases, there is no competition, rather a negotiation between the government department and a preferred supplier. In central government, the competition policy was set out in a White Paper in 1991, 'Competing for Quality'. Departments and agencies were expected to subject a proportion of their work either to 'market testing', i.e. inviting a competition between the private sector and the in-house teams to bid for existing work, or to what was known as 'strategic contracting', i.e. an invitation to outside firms to tender for work without an in-house bid. The Labour government slightly changed this policy for the civil service through its Better Quality Services initiative and a new office to oversee procurement, but continued with the outsourcing programme.

Another form of privatization was the Private Finance Initiative/Public Private Partnerships, under which private companies were invited to design, build, finance and operate facilities which would then be leased to public authorities, a process which is discussed in more detail in Chapter 11.

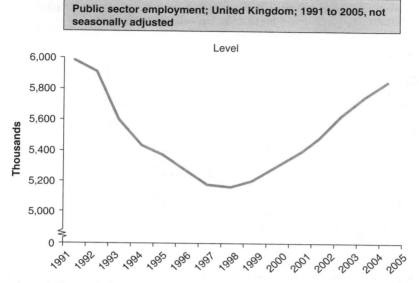

Figure 1.1   Trends in public sector employment 1991–2005

Source: Hicks, 2005

From 1981 to 1998 the number of people employed in the public sectors fell from over 7 million to around 5 million, mainly through privatization. Of those reductions 1,355,000 were in the nationalized industries. Local government lost 321,000, mainly because of the transfer of outsourced jobs, education lost 250,000, almost all because schools and colleges were redefined as private when they became corporate bodies. The civil service shrank by 200,000 and the armed forces by 114,000. Only the sale of nationalized industries involved the state withdrawing from activities because of a political view about the role of the state. The reduction of the scale of the armed forces was the result of the end of the Cold War. The other reductions involved contracting out or the redefinition of the sector.

The Labour governments reversed this trend and employee numbers started to increase again. Figure 1.1 shows United Kingdom public sector employment numbers from 1991 to 2005. From 1998 public sector employment rose every year to stand at 5,882,000 in December 2005. This was 719,000 higher than in June 1998, but still below the levels of 1991 and 1992.

Figure 1.2 shows the sectors in which this growth took place. The biggest increase, over 300,000, was in the National Health Service, followed by education and public administration.

This trend reflects Labour policy towards the public sector: a willingness to spend money and employ people (although 'investment' was commonly used to describe

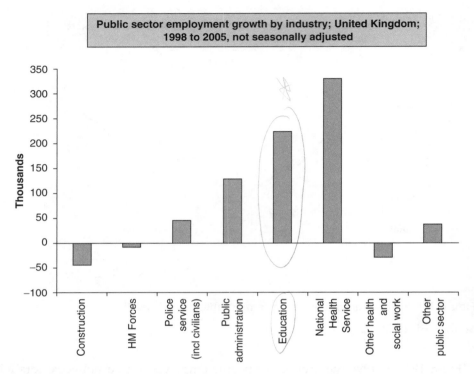

Figure 1.2   Public sector employment growth by sector 1998–2005

Source: Hicks, 2005

the spending). It also forms the background to many of the management initiatives taken by the government, anxious that the extra spending should show demonstrable results in improvements in the volume and quality of public services.

The institutions of the state

The public sector employs just under 6 million people out of a total workforce of 27 million and spends about 40% of GDP, if we include the payment of pensions and benefits, or about 20% of GDP if we exclude them.[5] The main institutions are the local authorities, still the largest public sector employer, the Civil Service, including both its policy aspects and its service delivery functions, and the National Health Service. Within these institutions there are public bodies with various statutory forms and status, many set up to have relatively autonomous operational management, such as school boards, hospital trusts and various entities which are run by people appointed by ministers, whether in England or the devolved administrations.

Devolved government

Constitutional change was an important part of the Labour government's agenda, including changes in the membership of the House of Lords, trying to change the institutions of government in Northern Ireland and creating national assemblies in Scotland and Wales. Scotland and Wales have different devolution arrangements, more powers being devolved to Scotland.

Scotland has a Scottish Parliament and an Executive consisting of Ministers drawn from members of the Scottish Parliament. The Scottish Consolidated Fund has about £20 billion per year. Scotland also has 19 Executive Agencies:

Accountant in Bankruptcy	Scottish Agricultural Science Agency
Communities Scotland	Scottish Building Standards Agency
Fisheries Research Service	Scottish Court Services
General Register Office for Scotland	Scottish Fisheries Protection Agency
Historic Scotland	Scottish Prison Service
HM Inspectorate of Education	Scottish Public Pensions Agency
Mental Health Tibunal for Scotland	Social Work Inspection Agency
National Archives of Scotland	Students Awards Agency for Scotland
Office of the Scottish Charity Regulator (OSCR)	Transport Scotland
Registers of Scotland	

While the Act of Union is still in place, Scotland has developed distinctive policies since the Parliament was established in 1999, especially in education and health and social care. Organizational forms in Scotland also have their own distinct character, with the Scottish Executive, a different NHS structure, and public ownership of the water industry.

Wales has the National Assembly for Wales and a Cabinet. The functions on which it can make policy are:

agriculture	industry
ancient monuments and historic buildings	local government
culture	social services
economic development	sport and leisure
education and training	tourism
the environment	town and country planning
health and health services	transport and roads
highways	the Welsh language
housing	

Wales has two Executive Agencies, for historic monuments and European funding.

Table 1.1   *Local government in the United Kingdom*

England	Wales
46 Unitary authorities in urban areas	22 Unitary authorities
36 Metropolitan District Councils	**Scotland**
32 London Boroughs and the Corporation of the City of London	32 Unitary authorities
34 County Councils in rural areas	**Northern Ireland**
238 District Councils in rural areas plus Parish and Town Councils	26 District Councils
1 Greater London Authority	9 Area Boards for Health and Social Services

Both countries have had significant powers and responsibilities devolved to them and are developing distinctive policies and ways of working.

Local authorities

The structure of local government was changed by the Local Government Review, implemented between 1995 and 1998. The distribution of authorities is set out in Table 1.1.

In those areas of England which do not have unitary authorities, the main functions of County Councils are education and social services, main roads, strategic planning. District Councils are responsible for housing, local planning, refuse collection, council tax collection. The Parish and Town Councils do not have many service functions but are important as representative bodies. In Wales and Scotland and the Metropolitan and urban areas of England the unitary authorities are responsible for all local authority services. Expenditure by service is shown in Table 1.2.

Relationships between central and local government

There has always been tension between local and national governments, especially when the central and local government have been controlled by different parties, as they frequently have been. Throughout the period of Conservative rule, local authorities spent as much energy trying to evade central government control as central government spent trying to subjugate them. Despite these efforts, local authorities clung on to a surprising degree of autonomy and difference.[6]

Funding

Local authority spending is almost all directly controlled by central government. There is a formula by which the Department of Environment calculates a spending level for each service for each local authority, the amount which the government says would provide a standard level of service (the Standard Spending

Table 1.2   *Budgeted net current expenditure by service 2006–07*

	Net Current expenditure £ million	% of total
Education	36,998	36.8
Highways and transport	5,336	5.3
Social services	17,767	17.7
Housing (excluding Housing Revenue Account)	2,361	2.3
Culture, environment and planning	9,379	9.3
Police	10,828	10.8
Fire	2,086	2.1
Courts	59	0.1
Central services	3,419	3.4
Other	248	0.2
Mandatory rent allowances	7,676	7.6
Mandatory rent rebates	593	0.6
Rent rebates granted to HRA tenants	3,485	3.8
Total net current expenditure	100,535	

Source: Department for Communities and Local Government. Statistical Release. 7 June 2006. Local Authority Revenue Expenditure and Financing, 2006–07 Budget

Assessment or SSA). This level is then used to distribute the business rate, which is aggregated nationally and redistributed, the revenue support grant and the amount of council tax which authorities are expected to raise. Council Tax accounts on average for about 30% of local authority spending. Business rates are collected locally but pooled and redistributed according to population size. Revenue Support Grant is allocated on a formula and there are various grants dedicated to particular services, such as the Standards Fund for education and monies for such things as services for asylum seekers. Less than 10% of the total central government support is ear-marked in this way. Capital expenditure is subject to direct control, through a process of application, approval and now competition.

The Labour government tried to raise the amount of central government support for local government spending. Support had been declining in real terms in the last 3 years of the previous government and the incoming government announced plans to make it grow by 4% per year. Some of the money came with strings attached. Local authorities that achieve their Best Value targets are allowed extra central government support of up to 2.5% of their budget. The revised financial régime also includes a three-year planning period and a formula to limit annual changes in the formula allocated grant in an attempt to produce more pre-dictability and stability. Table 1.3 shows the sources of revenue for local government in 2005, in England.

Table 1.3   *Local Government sources of revenue 2005–6 England*

	£million	%
Revenue support grants	26,663	37.8
Council tax	21,320	30.2
Business rates redistributed	18,004	25.5
Police grant	4,353	6.2
GLA grant	37	0.1
Other	104	0.1
	70,481	100.0

Source: Office for National Statistics 2005

Direct controls

As well as control over spending, there are many aspects of policy and management through which central government controls local authorities. The compulsory competitive tendering legislation, in place until 1998, determined the answer to one of the questions any organization has to ask: how much of what we do should we consider contracting out? Changes in education legislation determined the proportion of the budget that education authorities can spend on activities other than that which goes on inside schools. Planning controls have been weakened by a process of upholding a greater proportion of appeals against local authority planning decisions. House building by local authorities has virtually stopped and housing management is subject to outsourcing.

These direct controls have affected the way in which local authorities are managed. As individual departments and services are to a large extent controlled by regulations, managers have low discretion and are increasingly concerned with implementing national policies rather than managing the interface between local politicians and their organizations. In turn this leads to fragmentation of decision-making within the authorities.

Overall allocation of resources among the services is still subject to some local discretion. While SSAs are published for each service, these figures are only indicative. Within services decisions are circumscribed and this means that there is a reduced possibility for overall planning and management of the organization as a corporate whole, which in any case is fragmented as a result of outsourcing. Contracts operate for a variety of services, whether they are carried out by the private sector or an in-house team. The contracting process makes the contracted parts relatively independent and subject to specific constraints. For example, if there is a five-year contract which specifies how a service is to be delivered, it is difficult to make any fundamental decisions about that service until the contract is up for renewal. The competition process also sets constraints. If the price for the contract is set through competition, management must ensure that costs are at or below the contract price. This has implications for staffing levels, wage and salary levels and, often, conditions of service: some of the major areas of managerial discretion are therefore dictated by the market, itself created by legislation and regulations.

As well as these financial, policy and managerial controls, central government ultimately has the power to create and abolish local authorities. The Local Government Review, completed in 1995, caused great uncertainty in those areas where the authorities' boundaries and functions were subject to change. Management and political effort was diverted away from service delivery towards campaigning and lobbying for survival. Local government is subjected to such fundamental change approximately once a decade. London government was reorganized in 1965, the rest of England, Scotland and Wales in 1974/5, the metropolitan areas and London had their upper level of authority abolished in 1985. The 1995 review completely reorganized Scottish and Welsh local authorities, while leaving London and the Metropolitan areas of England unchanged. In 2006 it was proposed that the police authorities be reorganized into much larger, regional forces to produce economies of scale in dealing with serious crime and terrorism.

Modernizing local government

Local government was 'modernized' by the Labour government. A White Paper[7] in July 1998 was followed by a Bill. This time the intervention was not to be concerned with boundaries and functions but with internal political and management arrangements. The White Paper had a long list of diagnoses of local government's ailments: it was inefficient and inward-looking; there were variations in service quality; some councils had failed badly in particular services; some members and officers put self-interest before the public interest; there were corruption and wrong-doing because of a lack of scrutiny and openness; voters could not be bothered to vote in local elections; councillors were unrepresentative of the people in their area; previous initiatives had caused demoralization; committee structures were opaque and inefficient; voting methods were old-fashioned (ballot-boxes); local accountability for local taxation was weak; personal conduct and ethics had reduced public confidence; there was insufficient partnership with and influence by local businesses.

The proposed changes started at the top: new political management arrangements were demanded, with a choice of three options: directly elected mayor with a cabinet; cabinet and leader; directly elected mayor and appointed council manager. Whichever option was chosen by authorities, the change implied that fewer people would be involved in decision-making and the rest of the councillors would be relegated to a back-bench role, much like the relationship between central government and Parliament.

The lack of interest by voters was to be cured by making voting easier. This was probably a forlorn proposal, since voting arrangements for general elections are identical to those for council elections and people manage to find the polling station on the relevant day. Freeing local government from central control to make the elections meaningful was not an option considered in the White Paper. While capping of local spending was stopped, reserve powers were retained to make sure local spending decisions were taken within nationally set constraints.

There was also to be a new ethical framework policed by Standards Committees and Standards Board, designed to raise standards and improve public confidence. Partnerships were to be encouraged, rather than direct service delivery, now considered to be 'old-fashioned'. John Prescott's introduction to the White Paper was blunt:

> ...councils need to break free from old fashioned practices and attitudes. There is a long and proud tradition of councils serving their communities. But the world and how we live today is very different from when our current systems of local government were established. There is no future in the old model of councils trying to plan and run most services. It does not provide the services which people want, and cannot do so in today's world. (p. 6)

A significant change was the establishment of a 'Best Value' régime. The old rules about compulsory competitive tendering were scrapped and a new set of rules installed. These were very similar to a previous set of rules in central government, known as the 'Prior Options'. Councils were to ask fundamental questions about whether their services were necessary and then whether the ways in which they were delivered were the best option. Competition was no longer to be compulsory for any service but fair competition had to be considered as an option for all of them. The whole process was to be documented and monitored in annual performance plans and reviews.

Many of the policies towards local authorities involved removing the authorities' discretion, either by setting out in detail how they should carry out their functions and the funds they should have, or bypassing them and making more local institutions more independent of their local authorities. This devolution of powers from the local authorities was labelled 'new localism', especially by David Miliband. Schools were subject to less local authority influence, housing was mostly transferred to Registered Social Landlords, community care budgets were ring-fenced and prescribed. At the same time, efforts were made to co-ordinate services at local level across all services, through Local Strategic Partnerships. Various capital budgets were devolved to special partnership bodies. Combined with the increase in central control over local authorities, the 'new localism', transferring powers to lower levels of control, further diminished the autonomy of local authorities. In 2004, the Office of the Deputy Prime Minister produced 'The Future of Local Government',[8] setting out proposals to reverse the decline in local engagement and participation at the local, 'neighbourhood' level. Whatever the new institutions were to be, as Tony Travers pointed out, 'local government (in its traditional form) would have to be the local agent to create the new arrangements'.[9]

Table 1.4   *Civil Service permanent staff, full time equivalent, by department or agency: 1 April 2004*

Total staff in all departments and agencies	523,580
of whom:	
Executive agencies	275,570
Department for Work and Pensions	125,170
of whom	
Department for Work and Pensions (excl. agencies)	19,300
Child Support Agency	10,570
JobCentre Plus	76,760
The Pension Service	17,790
The Rent Service	750
Inland Revenue and Customs and Excise	97,910
Defence	91,430
HM Prison Service	45,280
Home Office	24,010
Department for Transport	15,760
Department for Environment, Food and Rural Affairs, total	9,690
Department of Trade and Industry	9,640
Foreign and Commonwealth Office, total	5,970
Department for Education and Skills	5,130
Office for Standards in Education	2,520
Security and Intelligence Services	4,490
Health	4,180
Health and Safety Executive	3,860
Cabinet Office, total	2,090
HM Treasury	1,030
Culture, Media and Sport	730
Scottish Executive	12,140
The National Assembly for Wales	4,290

Source: Office for National Statistics

Civil Service and the agencies

Table 1.4 shows where civil servants worked in 2004. The biggest employer was the Department of Work and Pensions and its agencies, at 125,000 employees; the Inland Revenue and Customs and Excise with nearly 98,000, and the Ministry of Defence, which at 91,000 employees has one civil servant for every two members of the armed forces.

The Civil Service is divided into Departments and Executive Agencies, just over half of civil servants working in the Agencies, plus Revenue and Customs and Excise which operates on the same principles and management methods. The

Agencies are founded on the principle that management of service delivery is better if policy formulation is separated from management. Agencies are given explicit performance targets and a defined framework of managerial discretion in which to operate. The staff are part of the Civil Service but the responsibility for their management, including pay and grading, is with the agency rather than the Civil Service as a whole.

Expenditure by department, including their Agencies, is shown in Table 3.3, Chapter 3 (p. 51). Of total public spending of around £500 billion, the biggest items are Work and Pensions, around £120 billions, Health, £100 billion, local government services, £50 billion and education and defence at about £35 billion each.

National Health Service

The NHS has been reviewed and reorganized many times since it was founded. Organizational form has been used to solve many continuing dilemmas: what should be controlled locally and what centrally? How should local people be represented in decision making? Should the doctors be controlled by somebody other than doctors, and if so how should this be done? How can access be organized so that people have the same chances of getting treated wherever they live? How should resources be allocated, to populations or to hospitals and other services? Resource allocation has always struggled with the fact that hospitals and doctors have been concentrated in the cities while the population is more dispersed, and many formulas have been designed to preserve or correct that imbalance.

The answers to these questions have been varied. There have been hierarchies of health authorities and various other bodies between the Department of Health and the patients. Local people have been represented on health authorities, although never through direct elections, and on community health councils. The two mechanisms that have been used to control the doctors have been some form of management through which someone other than a doctor has tried to tell them what to do, changes to doctors' contracts and administered markets.

Currently the UK has four different organizational forms for health care, one for each of Northern Ireland, Scotland, England and Wales. Each was based on its own White Paper or consultation paper complete with catchy title: 'Fit for the Future' in Northern Ireland, 'Designed to Care' in Scotland, 'The New NHS, Modern, Dependable' in England and 'Putting Patients First' in Wales. The structures are shown in outline in Figures 1.3–1.7.

All four systems have 'trusts'. Northern Ireland stands out because of its long-standing integration of health and social services. This is replicated to some extent in the arrangements for care commissioning at local level in the other jurisdictions. England has a longer hierarchy, including Strategic Health Authorities. The division of responsibilities among the various bodies is similar in each case. Trusts, which can be for acute services in hospitals, for integrated services, community services or mental health, enter long-term agreements with the bodies

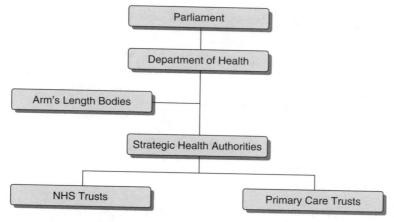

Figure 1.3   NHS in England

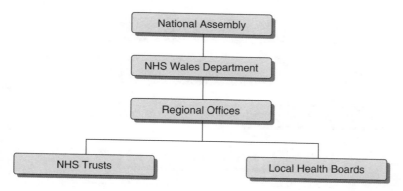

Figure 1.4   NHS in Wales

responsible for commissioning services. These bodies have different names and compositions in the different places but mostly consist of general practitioners and other health care professionals and representatives of social services in a district. In addition there is a body (Council, Board or Authority) whose job is public health and health policy. Around one million people are employed in the NHS.

Quangos

Quango, or quasi non-governmental public body, is a term used to define those public bodies which are not elected, which are technically independent but whose members are appointed either directly or indirectly by government.

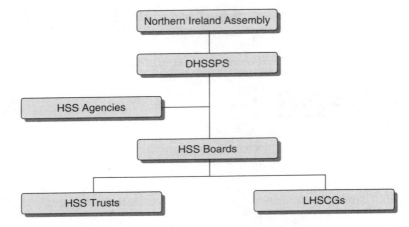

Figure 1.5   Northern Ireland: Health and Social Services

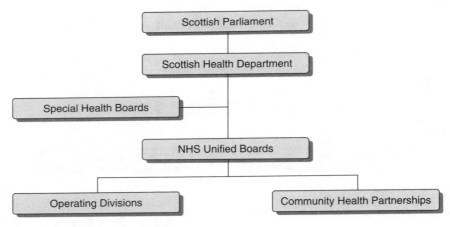

Figure 1.6   NHS in Scotland

The Cabinet Office defined one category of such organizations: 'A non-departmental public body is a body which has a role in the processes of national government, but is not a government department or part of one, and accordingly operates to a greater or lesser extent at arm's length from Ministers'.[10] They include 211 executive Non-Departmental Public Bodies (NDPBs), 458 advisory NDPBs and 42 tribunals. As well as these, the category of quango includes 26 NHS bodies and 861 NDPBs, none of which are elected, plus school boards of governors (about one thousand grant-maintained schools, accountable to the Department for

Organisation	England	Wales	Scotland	NI
Government Department	DH	NHSD	SEHD	DHSSPS
Strategic Direction	SHAs	Regional Offices	NHS Unified Boards	HSS Boards
Primary Care Management	PCTs	LHBs	Primary Care operating division	LHSCGs
Hospital Management	NHS Trusts	NHS Trusts	Secondary Care Operating divisions	HSS Trusts
Community Care Management	PCTs and NHS Trusts	NHS Trusts	Operating divisions	HSS Trusts
Social Services Management	Local Authorities	Local Authorities and LHBs	SEHD and Local Authorities	HSS Trusts

Figure 1.7   Overview of the structure of the NHS in the UK, 2004. The Structure of the NHS.

Source: Royal College of General Practitioners (2004) Information Sheet No.8

Education and Employment (DfEE)) and the 650 boards of further and higher education colleges and universities. Around 21,000 people are appointed to these non-elected bodies.

In many cases the quango is legally established as a company but carries out functions which would otherwise have been carried out by a department or by local authorities. Housing Action Trusts refurbish housing and estates. The use of companies for these functions has eroded local democracy in the sense that people are appointed rather than elected; it also fragments the actions taken by the state at local level since each body carries out its own mandate.

These arrangements have important implications for managers. One results from the authority and accountability of board members. Local authority members are directly elected and have a legitimacy as a result. Paid officials are accountable to them and understand where responsibility for decisions lies. Similarly the relationship between civil servants and ministers may cause occasional problems but generally people understand who is responsible for what. When working for an appointed board, the relationships are not so clear. Board members may be removed by ministers, for example, so a manager must take account of the minister's wishes as well as the board's. In some cases the boards are very part-time and have no legitimacy which comes from professional expertise. Their relationship with the managers is therefore not hierarchical, as between a company board and company managers: it

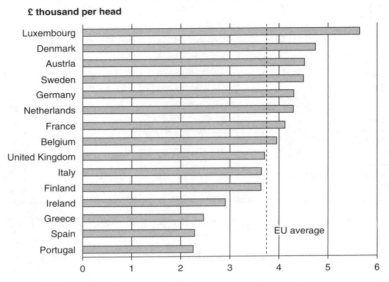

Figure 1.8   Expenditure on Social protection benefits per head: EU Comparison, 2000

[1]Before deduction of tax, where applicable, Tax credits are
generally excluded. Figures are purchasing power parities per inhabitant.

Source: Eurostat

can be more advisory, with the paid managers having most of the power. Some school boards have this relationship with head teachers.

Is the United Kingdom different?

If we look at expenditure on what in Europe is called 'social protection', including social security and health care, we see that the United Kingdom spends slightly less than the European Union average. Figure 1.8 shows the figures for 2000.

The UK was ninth out of the 15 members of the EU in 2000. The range of spending on social protection as a proportion of GDP in the EU was from 18% in the Republic of Ireland to 34% in Sweden. The figure for the United Kingdom was 27%. A significant difference in spending has been the proportion of the GDP spent on health care, the UK proportion being historically around 5% compared with Germany and France's 8–9%, a difference the Prime Minister committed the government to removing.

The most obvious difference between the United Kingdom and the rest of Europe and the United States of America is the degree of centralization of the public sector, with the exception of the devolved administrations. Other states have more autonomous local and provincial levels of government. In the cases of Germany, Switzerland and Austria, regional and local governments are protected by the constitution from interference by the federal or central governments, as they are in the United States of America. The protection includes the right to raise local taxation to pay for local services, although this right may be exercised by agreement among levels of government about the overall tax rates. In the extreme case, such as Switzerland, the principle of subsidiarity is put into practice: that no level of government should carry on an activity that could be done at the level below. In the United Kingdom local government can only provide services or carry out activities which are legislated for by Parliament, there being no powers of general competence. In addition, as we shall see, there is a collection of controls which central government has over local authorities.

Simon Jenkins[11] argued that the Conservative governments' changes to the public sector were all part of a process of 'nationalization' or a reduction of local autonomy. In Chapter 4 we shall see in more detail how control has grown more centralized under the Labour governments. Detailed administration and management of individual units, such as schools, hospitals and colleges, has been decentralized within a centralized policy and financial framework. In those services still under the control of local authorities, the management task for officials and politicians alike is constrained by the controls and influence from government departments and their various monitoring units and inspectorates, supported by guidelines and procedures written by central government. In the NHS, control is exercised through the targets and directives and funding rules issued by the Department of Health, while detailed administration, within the market framework, remains with the Trusts and Strategic Health Authorities. For those services delivered through executive agencies, ministerial and departmental control is exercised through framework documents, key performance indicators and budgets agreed annually along with business and corporate plans. Of European countries, probably France is the only one that is so centrally controlled and France has been attempting to decentralize in recent years.

Conclusions

Despite changes in the boundary between the public and private sectors, the public sector is still a significant part of the UK economy. However, the job of management is not only about running departments providing services. Many services are now managed through contracts with companies, and many are privately owned and are not managed but regulated. Even when services are provided by directly employed public servants, there are periodic competitions in many areas which mean that public sector managers have both to manage within an environment of rationing and other special public sector characteristics and also be competitive. The other aspect of the managerial environment is that while there is decentralization of budgets and operational management, central government operates strong central control over major policies, how money is spent, performance systems and management arrangements and processes.

Notes

For weblinks relevant to the issues discussed in this chapter see www.sagepub.co.uk/flynn.

1   The survey was conducted in 1994 and not published.
2   Stuart Wilks-Heeg and Steve Claydon, *Whose Town is it Anyway?* (Joseph Rowntree Charitable Trust, York, 2006).
3   Ibid., p. 103.
4   Compendium of Health Statistics, 12th edn (Office of Health Economics, London, 2001), Figure 4.17.
5   Since transfer payments such as pensions and benefits are not included in the calculation of GDP, it is not strictly correct to say that public spending amounts to 40% of GDP, but governments do use this measure.
6   See Hugh Atkinson and Stuart Wilks-Heeg *Local Government from Thatcher to Blair: the politics of creative autonomy,* (Polity, Cambridge, 2002) for a discussion of the degree to which local authorities retained their autonomy.
7   DETR, *Modern Local Government; in Touch with the People* (HMSO, London, 1998).
8   Office of the Deputy Prime Minister, The Future of Local Government: Developing a 10-year Vision. (ODPM, London, 2004b).
9   Tony Travers, 'Local and Central Government', in Anthony Selden and Dennis Kavanagh (eds) *The Blair Effect: 2001-5* (Cambridge University Press, Cambridge, 2005), p. 77.
10 Cabinet Office Agencies and Public Bodies Team, *Public Bodies 2005* (HMSO, Norwich, 2005) p. vi.
11 Simon Jenkins, *Accountable to None: The Tory Nationalisation of Britain,* (Hamish Hamilton, London, 1995).

2

Politics and the public sector

Introduction

In the previous chapter we saw the scale and scope of the public sector. Here, we begin by asking how the current public sector developed. Many of the elements of social security, health and education have been in place since before the Second World War, if in somewhat different form, and subsequently the institutions of the state were strengthened as part of the post-war reconstruction during a period of state involvement in most parts of the economy, including basic industries and manufacturing. While there may have been a majority opinion in favour of the broad shape of what became known as the 'welfare state', there was not a consensus in the sense that all politicians agreed even on the proper scale and scope of the public sector. Indeed as early as the first Conservative government after the war, there were cuts in the size of the Civil Service and attempts to cut spending. Since then there were other attempts to cut public spending, notably during the Labour administration of 1974–79.

What happened when Margaret Thatcher became Prime Minister in 1979 was not, therefore, a sudden ending of a consensus. It was more that those who favoured a smaller state and lower public spending had gained a majority. This majority was more keen to carry out these policies than the previous, Labour, government although it also had tried. Implementing a radical policy of making the state smaller was not to prove easy, except in the cases of the sale of nationalized industries and council houses. Both policies were achieved by giving the people who bought them a chance of making a quick, usually large, financial gain or discount on the market value. The Thatcher administrations also started a process of controlling the public sector, where they could not reduce its size. Efforts were made to control local government and to change the way in which the health service and the Civil Service were managed.

When John Major became Prime Minister in 1990, many administrative arrangements were already there for him to use in pursuit of his policies. He also found the public finances in a better state than they had been when Margaret Thatcher became Prime Minister, with no public sector borrowing requirement. He used the centralized controls to implement his version of conservatism, which was concerned to reduce the role of the state because he felt that state intervention, especially at local level, was the cause of lack of social cohesion, crime and other social problems. His, and his colleagues', solution was 'civic conservatism', which means voluntary action and voluntary associations, rather than the state, preventing and correcting social problems. In practice this meant stopping local authorities from doing things, especially building housing.

The politics of managing the state which the Major governments pursued were based on the idea that state employees are poorly motivated, unless they are on performance-related pay, that their activities need to be measured and controlled and that managers should be given the right to manage, that is to tell people what to do and expect them to do it. This approach was to be followed only if the function could not be privatized. There was a belief, which had been there during the Thatcher period, that the private sector was inherently better than the public. This was not a theoretical position about markets, rather a preference for business people over public servants.

Political alternatives to this approach come from two sources: the left and the management theorists. For a period some Labour-controlled local authorities pursued management policies which flattened hierarchies, trusted workers, developed teams, promoted public service values. Meanwhile the 'New Human Resource Management',[1] as some people called it, recommended a similar set of features: it was argued and implemented in progressive companies that organizations are likely to be more able to change if the workers are committed to their employer, are willing to be flexible because their job is safe, and are likely to be more motivated if they can participate in decision-making.

The Labour government showed some signs of being a more sympathetic employer, taking some categories of staff off short-term contracts and allowing pay rises, especially for occupations where there was a shortage of staff, such as nursing and teaching. On the other hand, it showed itself quite keen on performance pay and very critical of some public sector workers such as doctors and teachers whom it saw as unwilling to change.

Foundations of the public sector 1945–79

The 'welfare state'

There was not a social revolution between 1939 and 1945, although the war did change the relationship between the state and civil society: government ran industries during the war and led the reconstruction after the war. During the immediate post-war period there was rationing of industrial and building materials and planning in the economy, in land use and in public services. Industries such as coal, steel and the railways were taken into state ownership to ensure their survival. It has sometimes been argued that the 'welfare state' was invented during the war and implemented after it in a spirit of consensus and social harmony. The National Assistance Act, Education Act, the establishment of the NHS during and just after the war have been seen by some as the creation from nothing of a new type of state. While institutions were created and legislation passed, many of the elements of the welfare state were in place for working-class people before the war, including a state social security system, means tested access to secondary education and a national health insurance scheme. What happened in the period from the mid-1940s was that these benefits and services became universal. This meant that contributions were no longer voluntary and that the middle classes gained access to services now provided by the state, which they had previously funded from savings or insurance. To ensure universality, services were largely controlled by the central government rather than left to local institutions and organizations.

There may have been general agreement that the welfare state was a good idea, especially from those who benefited from it, which included most of the population. There is no doubt that the returning soldiers and others who had lived through the war were keen for a form of state and welfare provision which would prevent a return to the deprivation of the Depression. However, the welfare state was not without its opponents. Glennerster[2] has shown that there has always been a right-wing group in the Conservative Party opposed to universal benefits and tax-funded services. This right has had periods of influence ever since 1950 and did not emerge without precedent during the first Thatcher government of 1979. The Conservative administration elected in 1951 reduced income tax, cut education spending, introduced prescription charges in the NHS and reduced NHS staffing levels. Differences of opinion about the right scale and scope of the state have persisted both between and within parties ever since.

One interpretation of the immediate post-war period is that there was a settlement between the trade unions, government and employers. Unions would moderate wage demands in exchange for job security and social benefits, employers would respond by offering stable employment and union recognition, while the government would be responsible for managing the services and benefits as well as steering the economy towards full employment. While the post-war government had full employment as an objective, it was achieved as much through foreign aid, reconstruction and the growth of world trade as it was by economic management. If there was an agreement, it was never as explicit as it was in, for example, Sweden, where there were talks among the three parties – employers, government and trade unions – and an explicit agreement was reached and signed at Saltsjøbaden in 1936.[3] An alternative explanation is that the employers found themselves in a very weak position at the end of the war: factories were destroyed or had been converted to arms production, the workers were returning from the armed forces with ideas about collective bargaining and rights, and materials were scarce. The Marshall Plan was making funds from the United States available for investment through the government, which was also organizing the reconstruction. In such a weak position, the employers had to agree to a process of national wage bargaining and a tax and national insurance régime to finance benefits and public services.

The Civil Service

The Civil Service has not been the subject of a consensus among politicians; rather it has had much scrutiny since the war. The Conservative manifesto for the 1951 election promised to cut waste and extravagance in the service,[4] and the non-industrial Civil Service was cut from 425,000 to 386,000 by 1955, mainly as a result of the end of rationing and relaxation of controls. After then there were many efforts to increase efficiency and modernize the management of the service, culminating in the Fulton Report of 1968 which called for improved accountability, a unified system of grading and recruitment on merit. However, growth in numbers and spending soon restarted and the number of civil servants (including industrial civil servants) reached a peak of 747,000 in 1975. Prior to the Thatcher administration of 1979 there had been efforts to improve accountability and efficiency, but no government had much enthusiasm for the task until the Thatcher administrations and their attempts to introduce 'business' methods, or at least business language, initially through Mr Heseltine's attempt to find out who did what in the Department of the Environment (the Management Information System for Ministers), and later, from 1982, through the Financial Management Initiative.

At each change of party control there have been suspicions about the neutrality of the Civil Service, although few ministers, with exceptions such as Tony Benn, sustained their complaints. One aspect of this suspicion was that the Treasury ran economic policy and the Civil Service, if not the government. Two short-lived attempts were made to rectify this: the establishment of the Department of Economic Affairs in 1964, to manage economic policy, and the Civil Service Department in 1968 to manage the Civil Service.

Generally, the Civil Service, and especially the senior ranks, survived the first 30 years after the war well. Despite criticisms, reports and attempts to reorganize, the size, scope and influence of the service remained fairly stable and immune from outside control.

The National Health Service

The NHS was established in 1948, based on the principles of universal access and freedom from charges, which were established during the war. The institutional arrangements were a compromise designed to satisfy a variety of interests, especially the medical professions, and have been adjusted many times. As Klein[5] points out, the dilemmas faced by the original scheme for the NHS have been the sources of political controversy ever since. These included the problem of national responsibility for the service and local management of the facilities, the need to integrate hospital and family health services while preserving the independence of family doctors, how to make comprehensive plans for a service which excluded independent (voluntary) hospitals, how to achieve public accountability while involving professionals in decision-making, how to keep general practitioners independent and promote best medical practice. A further dilemma was between creating and running a national service and having local democratic control and accountability: the debate between localism and nationalism. Klein argues that: 'The history of the NHS since 1948 can largely be seen as the working out of these contradictions: a continuing and never-ending attempt to reconcile what may well turn out to be irreconcilable aims of policy' (p. 26).

In 1974 the NHS was organized into a hierarchical arrangement of Regional, Area and District Health Authorities for budgeting, planning and control purposes, with Community Health Councils to represent consumers. Each tier was served by full-time administrators and advised by an array of advisory boards representing the professions. As with the Civil Service, the idea of management as distinct from administration, using consultation and consensus, was not a feature of the NHS until the introduction of general management in 1983. This was the attempt to control the actions of medical professionals using management techniques. Many more were to follow.

Local government

Many services that are now directly controlled by central government or privatized were previously local authority services. Water, gas, electricity supply, public transport, were all originally started by private companies and then became local government services, together with health services, public health and 'poor relief'. The process of transferring powers from local to central government began during the first Labour government after the war and has continued since. These transfers were not necessarily the result of central government hostility. In some cases it made economic sense to have a national level of provision. In others the nationalization was the result of a desire for equal and universal provision. When municipal services were originally developed, local business people were involved in their own municipality and its development of gas and electricity, water and sewerage. When the ownership of industry became national and then international, such a local focus was less relevant. While local businesses still have an influence on local authorities, there is no longer a strong connection between either the owners of local industry or their trade unions and the membership of local authorities.

Despite losing control of local hospitals in 1946, local authorities were the implementing institutions for two areas of social policy which were to grow in importance in the post-war years – housing and education – as well as having powerful planning and development functions allowing them to shape much of the post-war reconstruction of the cities. As with the NHS, local government was reorganized in 1974 (1975 in Scotland) into a hierarchical structure. In London from 1965 the Greater London Council and in the Metropolitan areas from 1974 the Metropolitan County Councils had 'strategic' functions such as planning and transport, while the main services were performed at London Borough and Metropolitan District level. In Scotland and in the shire areas of England and in Wales, the upper tier had the main functions of social services and education. They had relatively reliable sources of revenue, the domestic and commercial rates, and were seen as the natural providers of local services. The reorganization strengthened the position of local government as a whole, as it provided a reason for allocating extra resources. Indeed, local government spending increases were a large contributory factor to the fiscal problems of 1975/76.

The Labour government attempted in 1975 to introduce controls on local government spending, a process which was continued by successive governments. The attempt by central government to control local authority spending and local authorities' attempts to evade those controls have been continuous since that time and contributed to the distrust which the Thatcher governments had of local authorities, a distrust which eventually led to the abolition of the upper tier in London and the Metropolitan areas of England in 1985, and in Scotland and Wales in 1995.

The Thatcher years 1979–90

When it was elected in 1979 the Conservative government found itself in charge of a large and relatively strong public sector. Public spending was 43% of gross domestic product (GDP), which, although lower than its peak of 49% in 1975, was 3 points higher than it had been when they had last come into office in 1970. The institutions were fairly robust: the Civil Service had mostly resisted attempts to modernize it and the Treasury was still the most powerful department within it. Local government still had a degree of independence, a tax base and a grant system which required the government to pay a grant from taxation to contribute to any spending the local authorities decided to make. The NHS was still strong and the medical professions, especially doctors, well placed to influence it. Only 5% of the population was covered by private health insurance, indicating a high degree of satisfaction with the state service among the middle classes.

New or Old Right?

There was a view during the 1980s that Ronald Reagan and Margaret Thatcher especially, but also other right parties in Europe and the Labour Party in New Zealand, represented a new sort of politics, sometimes called the 'New Right'. The idea was that the mid-1970s recession which followed the oil price rise of 1973 produced a break with the previous consensus about the role of the state, welfare services and individual responsibilities which had lasted since the Second World War. The new circumstances produced a new set of right-wing politicians who would reverse the previous policies towards the economy, the labour market and the welfare state. The emphasis of economic policy would no longer be on managing demand to maintain full employment but rather on stimulating profits by removing regulations and making the labour market more free. Protection of workers, either by law or trade unions, would be reduced to allow wages to find their market level and to allow managers to manage.

Part of the project was to restore to the private sector those industries which had been nationalized in the 1940s. The circumstances that made nationalization desirable were now gone and such businesses should no longer need state support.

While the inclination of this group of politicians may have been similarly to restore the institutions of the welfare state to the private sector, or abolish them, this would be more difficult than selling nationalized industries. In the early years, the policy was confined to trying to control spending, either directly or by finding more efficient ways of managing.

For the public sector, there is an important question about the Thatcher period. Did the Conservative governments of the 1980s and 1990s produce a radical break in the history of the welfare state and public services? We have seen that there was not a universal consensus on the role and size of the welfare state or on the level of public expenditure, but there had been a period of relative stability or growth for most of the post-war period. Government spending on goods and services had been a fairly constant proportion of GDP since the war, apart from the aberration of the mid-1970s, when it grew to more than 25% before settling down to the trend of around 20%. If there was not a consensus, in the sense that politicians of all persuasions agreed with all the attributes of the welfare state, there had been no radical changes in its basic form or the money spent on it.

Of course there were rhetorical speeches about individual responsibility and the dangers of reliance on the 'nanny state', of the tyranny of taxation and the debilitation of dependency. But was there a radical change in policy towards the 'welfare state' at the beginning of the 1980s? There was not a step change in 1979 in the significant areas of policy which the Conservatives claimed they would change. The targets for growth of the money supply were never met and were eventually quietly abandoned. Monetarism as the basis for economic policy was thus forgotten. Public expenditure was not drastically cut; public borrowing was initially reduced as debts were repaid briefly in the late 1980s but then the economic cycle continued and borrowing increased again. Taxation has fluctuated as a proportion of GDP but this has been cyclical rather than a strong downward trend. The only area in which a truly Right agenda was achieved was the privatization of nationalized industries, public utilities and public housing.

There were really only two efforts to implement the 'New Right' policy of state withdrawal from welfare activities: the attempt to privatize pensions and the privatization of council housing. The government offered inducements for people to withdraw from the state earnings-related pension scheme and join company or individual pension schemes. At the same time indexing the state pension to prices rather than earnings reduced its value. Housing privatization was achieved by selling houses and flats to their tenants, at a discount from their market value, and by virtually preventing local authorities from building any new accommodation for renting. However, the state has not withdrawn from housing and is still paying housing benefit to those unable to pay their own rent. Social housing is still available, but new building is almost entirely by housing associations, where building subsidy still exists.

As we shall see in Chapter 3 the distribution of expenditure between departments and programmes has changed over time, but the radical changes have been in the methods used to manage the institutions. The Thatcher governments hired advisers from business, especially retailing companies, to help them to think about how public services should be managed. The solutions included internal markets, competition with the private sector, performance measurement and management, decentralized operational management and revised payment systems. They do represent a change in attitude and practice, although not of the type spoken in the New-Right rhetoric: the institutions were reformed rather than abolished.

The Major years 1990–1997

During the Thatcher administrations the manner of government was forceful and based on some overwhelming convictions about what was right. Consultation was reduced, consultative processes of decision-making were not used, opposing views were ignored or punished. In part, it was the style of government which finally produced opposition within the party: if the Prime Minister had listened to advice she might have made fewer policy disasters such as the Poll Tax. John Major reversed some of these tendencies during his period of office, adopting a more open, consultative style and more collegial cabinet.[6]

However, did the content of policies towards public services change with the change of Prime Minister? In a speech made at the Carlton Club in 1993, John Major reasserted some Conservative beliefs, invoking Disraeli and Burke, which underlay his policies. One of these was the danger of over-government:

> We know the State can destroy, as surely as it can preserve – and more conclusively than it can create ... we utterly reject the idea that the State can manage economic and personal relations between people better than businesses and better than families.[7]

While in the same speech he spoke of quality public services and the need for good management, there was one passage where he revealed a deep belief in the evils of state intervention and the creation of crime: the council estates of the inner cities are the cause of problems, not the solution:

> Look at our suburbs and small towns and villages – where people, by and large, own their own homes. Here you will find networks of the voluntary associations which tie people into their neighbourhood, from Rotary Clubs to the active PTA to fund-raising and to Meals on Wheels. The big problem lies elsewhere. It is from the inner cities, where the State is dominant, that businesses have fled. It is in the inner cities that vandalism is rife and property uncared-for. It is there that fear of violent crime makes a misery of old people's lives. Now that comes as no surprise for Conservatives ... it is where, over many years, the State has intervened most heavily, that local communities have been most effectively destroyed.[8]

David Willetts, Minister of State for Public Services, saw the state as destroying genuinely local and voluntary organizations. While the government was deciding to close St Bartholomew's Hospital, for example, he blamed the fact that it was a state institution for its closure: '… it is no exaggeration to say that Bart's fate was sealed when it was nationalised in 1948 and lost control of its destiny, becoming a tool of health planners.'[9] In this version of 'Civic Conservatism', any institution is preferable to one owned by the state, whether at local or national level. Willetts even argued that market reforms were designed to strengthen local institutions: 'The market – contracts, choice, competition – is being introduced within the public sector to achieve the authentically Tory objective of strengthening local institutions'. This belief in the benefits of competition survived the change of government in 1997, although the antagonism (or 'visceral antipathy' as Prime Minister Blair defined it)[10] abated.

One result of this deep-seated belief was that institutions of the state and especially local authorities could not be trusted with any major programmes. So, for example, the creation of Grant Maintained Schools (Chapter 4) was seen as 'the emancipation of governing bodies and head teachers, taking the local authority straitjacket off their back'.[11] Another consequence of lack of confidence in the state is that even in those areas where the Prime Minister recognized need for state intervention, if that could be carried out by the private sector on behalf of the state, then such an approach would be preferred.

Other members of John Major's government expressed views about the state which illuminated their approach to the management of the institutions. Michael Portillo, when Chief Secretary to the Treasury, made a speech in which he echoed Mr Major's attitude to people who live in the inner city, when he asserted the difference between the deserving and the undeserving poor:

> To talk today of the deserving and undeserving poor is guaranteed to make people wince: a mark of the triumph of political correctness ... So our system tends to treat alike the unfortunate and the feckless, the thrifty and the profligate. Consequently it undermines the provident and demoralises the industrious.[12]

The solution was to shrink the scope of the state and make people take more responsibility for themselves:

> Citizens grow to respect themselves and so come to accept that there are clear limits to what the State should do for them. Then support increases for a smaller State and for the necessary measures to put and keep the public finances on a sound footing. As the State shrinks and the public finances are kept under control there is scope for permanent reduction in taxes, increasing international competitiveness and the rewards for individual effort.[13]

The implications of this for people working in public services were twofold. The principle of universality was challenged: service providers had to distinguish between the deserving and the undeserving, between scroungers and the unfortunate victims of circumstances. For those working in services which are accepted as universal, such as child benefit or state pension distribution, there is no question of selectivity or rationing. However, when people working in community care are allocating services and budgets, the rationing process is very explicit. Applying eligibility criteria and allocating help to those who need it most has always been a feature of the daily work of people in public services. Applying criteria of deserving and undeserving is a different matter and relies on a moral judgement, rather than an assessment of need. At the same time, people have been encouraged to make their own arrangements for insurance or care or help, without relying on the state.

The second implication was that management effort was dominated by the need to make cuts in spending. The overriding priority was to shrink the state and reduce taxes. While the fiscal balance has cyclical variations, both with regard to the periods of growth and stagnation and decline in the economy and with regard to the electoral cycle, deficits increasing in the approach to elections, there were enough supporters of the 'small state, low taxes good' position for there to be a consistent presumption against public expenditure as a solution to economic and social problems.

Michael Howard, who served in the Departments of Employment and Environment before becoming Home Secretary in 1993, extolled the virtues of voluntary collective action and decried the efforts of local authorities:

> Communities' built on collectivism are characterised by town hall socialism and housing and social security dependency. Their predominant features are

alienation, atomism, lack of confidence and crime. The strongest communities exist where voluntary collective action is most apparent. These communities are characterised by neighbourliness and a strong sense of identity.[14]

He proposed that the government should, when confronted with a problem, think first about the voluntary sector and volunteers, before considering state intervention. When it has found ways of involving this sector, it should distribute funds in a such a way as to create 'leverage' from the private sector. This is a conception of the state as pump-primer and fund-raiser, rather than as a tax-raiser and service-provider. Not all members of the Major governments held these views but they had a sufficient majority to press for such policies.

The first Blair government 1997–2001

In 1998 Prime Minister Tony Blair published a Fabian pamphlet called *The Third Way: New Politics for the New Century*. Social Democrats in Europe and the then Democratic President of the USA proclaimed that they represented a new type of politics, leaving behind old definitions of Left and Right. This was not the old Third Way between capitalism and communism but a new Third Way. As Blair explained: 'The Third Way is not an attempt to split the difference between right and left. It is about traditional values in a changed world. And it draws vitality from uniting the two great streams of left-of-centre thought – democratic socialism and liberalism.'

What this meant in practice is that policies could be picked from a fairly narrow menu without the prejudice of principles. If a market solution looks acceptable, then it is based on the good parts of liberal individualism. If public spending is required, for example to reduce child poverty, then the decision is based on the socially responsible parts of social democracy.

The attitude towards the relationship between public services, voluntary organizations and individual volunteering and charitable giving was a development of aspects of the Major government's themes. Compare the quotation from Michael Howard, above, with this one from Blair's 1998 pamphlet:

My politics are rooted in a belief that we can only realise ourselves as individuals in a thriving civil society, comprising strong families and civic institutions buttressed by intelligent government ... In recent decades, responsibility and duty were the preserve of the right. They are no longer, and it was a mistake for them ever to become so.

The idea that public services and benefits, as supported by the old Left, were responsible for a decline in individual responsibility and duty is broadly similar to Howard's and Major's beliefs that council estates create unemployment and crime. It certainly has the same results in practice in the social security system and the attitude to the management and ownership of public housing.

To win power the Labour Party had 'modernized' itself and re-branded itself as New Labour. It had changed the party constitution to give less power to organized and especially trade union interests. Internal processes of discussion and decisions through branches to the annual conference were changed so that the leadership could more easily control the policies adopted by the party. Symbolically Clause IV of the constitution, calling for public ownership, was scrapped. Elections were from now on to be fought in the media and campaigns to be managed by the party's public relations machine. Policies presented at the election were more defined by what they were not: the party did not stand for higher tax (or at least for a higher rate of income tax); it was not in favour of re-nationalizing the public utilities and the railway; it did not align itself with the unions. Five specific pledges were made in 1997 for its term of office: class sizes for 5–7 year olds to be cut to 30; fast-track trial and punishment for young offenders; 100,000 fewer people on waiting lists; 250,000 young people to go from benefit to work; no rise in income tax rates and a cut in VAT on heating to 5%. The first four required the government to be able to influence departments and local service delivery in the school system, the courts, the NHS and Social Security and Education and Employment departments.

'Modernization' meant many different things. Detailed diagnoses of problems in local government, the Civil Service and the NHS varied. The solutions, as we shall see in the rest of the book, followed a pattern of trying to assert control over organizations that were seen variously as too bureaucratic, too professionally dominated and in some case self-interested and self-serving. The methods used were chosen eclectically. 'Modernization' of government was closely connected to the modernization of the Party and especially the abandonment of the commitment to public ownership. It was also about methods of service delivery and service design, especially getting access to services through the internet and call-centres. A quotation from the 'Vision' chapter of the White Paper gives an idea of the interpretations of modernization:

- We live in an age when most of the old dogmas that haunted governments in the past have been swept away. We know now that better government is about much more than whether public spending should go up or down, or whether organisations should be nationalised or privatised. Now that we are not hidebound by the old ways of government we can find new and better ones.
- Information technology is revolutionising our lives, including the way we work, the way we communicate and the way we learn. The information age offers huge scope for organising government activities in new, innovative and better ways and for making life easier for the public by providing public services in integrated, imaginative and more convenient forms like single gateways, the Internet and digital TV.
- We must unleash the potential within the public service to drive our modernising agenda right across government. There is great enthusiasm and

determination within the public service to tackle the problems which face society, to do the job better.

- Distinctions between services delivered by the public and the private sector are breaking down in many areas, opening the way to new ideas, partnerships and opportunities for devising and delivering what the public wants.[15]

While asserting that the new was now able to sweep away the old, as we will see, many of the actions taken were a continuation of the old ideas of the preceding governments. Even so, the Prime Minister was often frustrated by the progress of the 'modernization' programme. He said in a speech to a group of venture capitalists: 'People in the public sector are more rooted in the concept that if it's always been done this way it must always be done this way than any group of people I've ever come across … It's not that there aren't wonderful people now with a tremendous commitment to public service, but you try getting change in the public sector and public services – I bear the scars on my back after two years of government.'[16]

Previous Conservative governments had felt the need to break down resistance to change, whether it came from professional groups, trade unions or departmental interests. They had used market mechanisms, managerial authority and the undermining of public support for particular groups. The incoming government in 1997 obviously felt that the struggle had to continue. Perhaps there was less overt antagonism between politicians and these organizations than in previous governments that were openly hostile to the public sector, but the tension and frustration brought forward some strong measures to try to deliver the election pledges and more generally to make services more efficient, effective and popular.

We will also see in the next chapter that the overwhelming emphasis on cost reduction for public sector managers during the Conservative era was slowly relaxed towards the end of the first Blair government. It had become the only priority, with successive rounds either of simple budget cuts or 'efficiency savings' included in budgets. While such savings were still called for, they were within an expanding overall total, with quite large increases in some sectors.

The second and third Blair governments 2001–2005, 2005–2007

The spending plans for the second term were set out in the Comprehensive Spending Review of 2000. In real terms (1999–2000 prices) expenditure limits were to be raised from £191 billions in 2000–2001 to £223 billions in 2003–2004, an increase of nearly 17%. The NHS was to get an increase of £8 billions and education £5 billions. With these increases in spending, unlike anything the public services had seen for 30 years, came increased scrutiny and measurement and a series of initiatives. The Government and especially the Chancellor and Treasury had made a bold effort at increasing the resources available and wanted to make sure that they produced results. In practice this meant elaborating the controls exercised in local government through the Best Value régime and in central government through the Public Service Agreements.

The efforts to reduce poverty, especially among children and more especially among children of working families, continued. The main tax, tax credit and benefits mechanisms had been put in place in the first Labour government and were continued in the second. Overall efforts at altering income distribution also continued but the results from the first term were offset by the underlying tendency for income distribution to become more unequal.[17]

The reduction of unemployment was also an important objective of the second Labour government. One element of policy was changes to the benefit system to reduce the 'poverty trap' by which it was not worthwhile for people to take low-paid jobs in preference to staying on benefits. This was combined with 'active labour market policies', especially through the New Deal, that both encouraged people to seek training and jobs and stopped their benefit if they did not. In addition the labour laws under which people could be hired and fired maintained their previous freedoms for employers. As a result of these policies the UK government to a large extent avoided the growth in unemployment suffered in the rest of Europe. One consequence was a large number of people in low paid insecure jobs at the bottom end of the labour market whose employment had to be subsidised by social security payments such as the Working Families Tax Credit. The combination of a liberal labour market and targeted benefits for working families constituted a distinctive New Labour approach to welfare. The approach may be summed up in the subtitle to the 2005 Budget: 'Fairness and opportunity for Britain's hard-working families'.

The politics of management

While the Major governments still did not achieve a big cut in the role of the state, ministers' attitudes such as those expressed above had an impact on the way services were managed and funded. The managerial agenda of the Thatcher period continued with even more vigour. It was rooted in a general set of ideas about how people behave.

The first element is that people always act rationally and in their own self-interest, whether they work in business or public services.[18] They respond to incentives, such as the incentive to expand their budget and the number of staff in their unit. They cannot therefore be trusted to act in any interests other than their own. Producers 'capture' services and the users of those services are disempowered. The consequence of this belief is that the power of producers has to be reduced and that incentives have to be found to make the producers act in the interests either of the government or of the consumers.

The second is that competition is the main incentive to improve performance: the fear of going out of business, or losing a job, is the main motivator for individuals.

Monopoly in any form is a bad thing and public monopolies allow costs to stay high and quality to stay low. Without competition, managers will have no incentive to make improvements either in cost or quality and therefore will not do so.

The third is that managers should have the right to manage. Any force that reduces this right, such as trade union rights or professional organization, should be removed. Managers with incentives and authority are essential to good organizational performance. The right to manage is seen as the right to tell people what to do and expect them to do it. It is not about the right to develop staff, encourage commitment, form teams or instil loyalty. It is an instrumental view of management, implying hierarchy, authority and fear. The Labour government shared some of these attitudes with its predecessors, although from the beginning it emphasized the possibility that motivations other than selfishness can be present in people working in the public sector. It also initially played down the beneficial effects of competition and emphasized the need for co-operation in many areas of public sector work, especially where policies had to be pursued by more than one agency. In the second term competition regained importance, through a new internal market in the NHS, and by various competitions for funding.

The belief, through both the Thatcher and Major periods, that the private sector is innately superior to the public sector was replaced by a declared agnostic stance, represented by the Deputy Prime Minister: 'Traditional values in a modern setting should be our guide, not an ideological argument about public or private ownership'.[19] In practice the policies implemented often pushed managers towards deals with the private sector or outsourcing, but this was presented as a pragmatic approach not an ideological one.

There have been other political approaches to management. Some Labour local authorities, especially in the 1970s and early 1980s, promoted an approach to management which reflected their political values. They encouraged collaboration rather than competition. Another belief was that everyone had the right to have good ideas, so that consultation and non-hierarchical relationships were encouraged. Some of these beliefs came from the feminist movement which sought alternatives to hierarchical and authoritarian ways of working. People with such views lost influence during the 1990s, partly as a result of the politics of the Labour Party favouring more male-oriented and hierarchical ways of working. The other reason for the loss of popularity was the need to compete with private companies whose attitudes to workers were more authoritarian and which concentrated on costs rather than quality or innovation.

Strangely, experience of 'Human Resource Management' in successful private companies has shown that flexible and adaptable companies are those that adopt the less hierarchical, more consultative style and operate through developing commitment rather than fear. Companies such as Hewlett–Packard, Google and Microsoft have developed such approaches to managing their workforces. There is little sign of these ideas in the Labour approach to management. In fact one of its innovations is the introduction of call centres, through NHS Direct from 1998 and Jobcentre Plus among others, a method of service delivery that is notorious for its regimentation and mechanistic managerial control over the workforce. There has been talk of greater 'partnership' between managers and trade unions but this has not extended to the agreements under the Private Finance Initiative whereby companies take over basic services along with building construction and financing. 'Modernization' has included implementing Investors in People in all government departments, but this may be more of a ritual than a genuinely participatory style of management.

A new consensus?

From the 1997 election until 2000 the Labour Party's themes about the public sector were similar to those of the Conservatives: the need to control expenditure in order to keep taxation levels down, the importance of a mixed economy of private, individual provision and state services and benefits, the need for efficiency. A new consensus seemed to have emerged, which is at least as strong as, if not stronger than, the supposed post-war one.

The size of the public sector is one element in the consensus. The Labour government's spending plans, as we shall see in the next chapter, were for an increase in public spending as a proportion of GDP. Previous governments had tried, mostly without success, to bring this figure down. In the campaign for the 2001 election the Conservative Party mostly accepted the spending plans as necessary to improve public services, implying a more relaxed attitude to public spending and its impact on the economy than that of the Conservatives in power. The Conservatives under numerous leaders adopted various policy stances after the 2001 election, until the campaign for the 2005 general election saw the Conservatives revert to low taxation and low spending as their main stance. After the third defeat, in 2005, and changes in the leadership, the David Cameron-led party reverted to the consensual position.

The Labour Party's rejection of its constitutional commitment to public ownership represented more than a change in attitude towards nationalized industries; it also represented a shift towards the idea of a mixed economy in general and a tolerance or encouragement of private pensions, schools, hospitals, home helps and refuse collection companies.

What may be emerging is a consensus on management. It was natural for the Conservatives to adopt the approaches which were common in certain businesses in the late 1980s and early 1990s: they had friends and allies in business, recruited business people as advisers and in some cases as civil servants, and were generally more impressed by the style and manner of business than they were by public service. The Labour government shares both the belief and the use of business people as advisors. On some of the fundamentals of management, such as the use of performance control and performance pay, benchmarking and competition, outsourcing, there is little difference between the main parties. Competition among the parties is based to a large extent on which one is more competent to manage, within the prevailing consensus.

Conclusions

Politics has affected the public sector both in policy and in management. If ruling politicians are deeply opposed to the activities and institutions of the state, managers at senior levels may feel the need to protect services as well as manage them. At worst the tensions between managers and hostile politicians can produce stressful and unproductive relationships. If politicians have strongly held views about the motivation and performance of public sector workers which lead them to insist on authoritarian styles of management, managers have little discretion: they will be forced to behave or appear to behave in such a way. If not, they can be replaced by managers who will.

Management is not a neutral, technical activity. Management techniques and styles are themselves political and people with different political views will have different ideas about management. In the United Kingdom this does not mean that each party has an identifiable set of ideas about management: all parties have their share of authoritarians.

There has been a period of what was felt by many people working in the public sector as a political attack which, to date, the institutions have been fairly well able to resist. However, the management style which managers are now encouraged to follow is the result of a political attitude of low trust. Some of the details of how this style or styles were encouraged in the different sectors are in Chapter 4.

In the next chapter we look at public spending and how it has been affected by changes in government. We also look at the processes by which spending choices are made, at central government level and further down the public sector hierarchy.

Notes

For weblinks relevant to the issues discussed in this chapter see www.sagepub.co.uk/flynn.

1   See, for example, Laura Hall, Derek Torrington and Stephen Taylor, *Human Resource Management* (FT Prentice Hall, Hemel Hempstead, 2004).
2   Howard Glennerster, *British Social Policy Since 1945* (Blackwell, Oxford, 1995).
3   S. Wilks, 'Class compromise in the international economy: The rise and fall of Swedish Social Democracy', *Capital and Class*, 58 (1996).
4   K. Theakston, *The Civil Service Since 1945* (Blackwell, Oxford, 1995).
5   Rudolf Klein, *The New Politics of the NHS,* 4th edn (Routledge, London, 2000).
6   D. Kavanagh and A. Seldon (eds) *The Major Effect* (Macmillan, Basingstoke, 1994), pp. 154–66.
7   John Major, 'Conservatism in the 1990s: Our Common Purpose', Fifth Carlton Lecture (Carlton Club Political Committee and Conservative Political Centre, London, 1993).

8   Ibid., pp. 16–17.
9   David Willetts, *Civic Conservatism* (Social Market Foundation, London, 1995), p. 22.
10 In Tony Blair, *The Third Way: New Politics for the New Century* (London; Fabian Society, 1998).
11 Willetts, *Civic Conservation*, p. 29.
12 Michael Portillo, 'The Blue Horizon', speech to Conservative Party Conference 1993 (London, Centre for Policy Studies, 1993).
13 Ibid., p. 13.
14 Michael Howard, 'Conservatives and the Community', the 1994 Disraeli Lecture (Conservative Political Centre, London, 1994).
15 *Modernising Government* (1999), para 1.2.
16 Prime Minister Tony Blair, 7 July 1999.
17 See Tom Clark, Andrew Dilnot, Alissa Goodman et al. 'Taxes and Transfers 1997–2001', *Oxford Review of Economic Policy*, 18, 2 (2002) pp. 187–201.
18 The academic name for this is 'public choice theory'. For an explanation, see P. Dunleavy *Democracy, Bureaucracy and Public Choice* Harvester Wheatsheaf, Hemel Hempstead, There have also been critiques of this theory, for example, H. Stretton, and L. Orchard, *Public Goods, Public Enterprise, Public Choice. Theoretical Foundations of the Contemporary Attack on Government* (Macmillan, Basingstoke), and L. Udehn, *The Limits of Public Choice: A Sociological Critique of the Economic Theory of Politics* (Routledge, London, 1996).
19 Deputy Prime Minister John Prescott, Local Government Association Conference 8 July 1999.

3

Public Spending

Introduction

This chapter looks first at trends in public spending. It shows that aggregate expenditure as a proportion of GDP historically has ranged between 40 and 50%. During recessions and in line with the electoral cycle the proportion varies. In the five years before the 1997 election there was a decline in spending and no real-terms growth in the first two years after 1997.

It then looks at the changes in fiscal policy brought in by the 1997 government. There was a break with previous policy to reduce spending as a proportion of GDP and a new set of rules about how much should be spent and how it should be financed. The growth in public spending brought in by the three Labour governments was a radical break with previous policies, breaking a trend that reached back to the previous Labour government's spending cuts in 1975. The chapter then looks at trends in taxation policy to pay for these increases in spending.

The rest of the chapter shows how budgets are made as an iterative process between the Treasury and the spending departments. It shows that in the short-term budget decisions are quite constrained but over the longer term the cumulative effects of budget decisions can radically change spending.

The chapter concludes with a discussion about financial management of the budgets once they are set.

Trends

Despite the variety of political opinions about public expenditure and the relative weight of the public sector in the economy, the trend in public spending has been fairly stable. Figure 3.1 shows the trend in Total Managed Expenditure as a percentage of Gross Domestic Product from 1967 to 2008. The variance over that period can partly be explained by the economic cycle but also partly by politics.

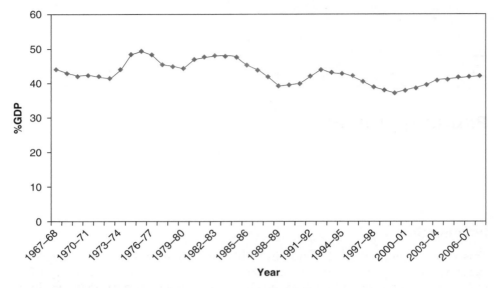

Figure 3.1   Total managed expenditure as % GDP 1967–2008

Sources: HM Treasury, 2000; HM Treasury, 2005, *Budget*

The growth in the first half of the 1970s was in part a response to demands for social spending, and its decline after the IMF visit was a response to creditors' pressure to cut spending. In 1975–6 public spending as a percentage of GDP almost reached 50% and by the time the Thatcher government was elected in 1979 the figure had been cut to under 45%.

Although the first Thatcher government may have been ideologically inclined to cut the public sector, there was a steady rise in the public sector proportion to 48.2% in the financial year of the general election in 1983. Then economic growth and spending restraint brought the proportion down and it went below 40% in 1988–9. After John Major became Prime Minister in 1990 the proportion went up again prior to the 1992 general election and then fell again in the period up to the next election in 1997.

In the medium term of a couple of years, or half a Parliament, spending levels are fairly committed: to reduce spending requires cancellation of employment or supply contracts; to increase spending on, say, education or health requires training and recruitment of professional staff. This inertia in spending is played out through the expenditure planning process through which departments negotiate for their budgets with the Treasury. A Treasury determined to cut

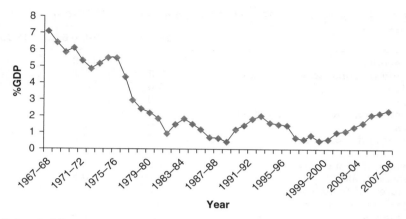

Figure 3.2   Public sector net investment as % GDP 1967–2008

Sources: HM Treasury, 2000; HM Treasury, 2005, *Budget*

spending is likely to be offered the easy short-term option for cutting spending, which is to cancel or not start capital projects.

Figure 3.2 shows the trend in public sector net investment, or purchase of assets less disposals, as a percentage of GDP from 1967–68 to 2007–08. It shows that the response to the IMF visit was to cut the building and investment programme from 1976 onwards. Investment was boosted prior to the 1983 and 1992 general elections and was then increased again in the spending plans of the Labour government but, as with current spending, not until three years into the administration. Capital investment never recovered to its mid–1970s level.

One consequence of the depression of capital spending was the accumulation of a backlog in building and repair programmes in all public services including the railway, hospitals, schools and public housing. The incoming Labour government of 1997 first contributed to correcting this long-term deficit by changing the accounting arrangements for investment, making it a distinct category of central government spending for the first time. The idea was that people responsible for public services would think of capital spending as investment and that it would be acceptable to borrow for investment but not to cover current account deficits.

They also used alternative methods of financing an investment programme, the Private Finance Initiative and Public Private Partnerships that had been developed by the previous government. Chapter 11 gives more details of these arrangements. Spending plans announced in 1999 included an increase in capital spending eventually to restore it to its 1992 level.

Table 3.1 shows the main trends in spending by service as a percentage of GDP in 1981–2, 1995–6 and 1999–2000, the year before the first growth budget of the Labour government. It shows that while the total of spending has remained a

Table 3.1   *Spending as % GDP, United Kingdom 1981–2, 1995–6 and 1999–2000*

	1981–2	**1995–6**	**1999–2000**
Social security	11.5	12.8	11.5
Health and personal social services	6.2	6.7	6.8
Education	5.4	4.9	4.6
Defence	5.0	3.0	2.6
Trade, industry, energy and employment	2.5	1.3	1.1
Transport	1.9	1.6	1.0
Law, order and protection	1.8	2.2	2.1
Housing	1.6	0.7	0.4
Other environmental services	1.5	1.2	1.0
Overseas, inc. aid	0.6	0.5	0.4
Agriculture and fisheries	0.6	0.6	0.6
Heritage (culture, media, sport)	0.5	0.5	0.6
Miscellaneous	1.3	1.4	1.1

Sources: 1981–2, HM Treasury (1996) *Public Expenditure: Statistical Analyses 1996–7*, Cm 3201. London: HM Treasury, 1995–6 and 1999–2000, HM Treasury (2000) *Public Expenditure: Statistical Analyses 2000–2001*, Cm 4601. London: HM Treasury

fairly constant proportion of GDP, its distribution among services changed somewhat over 20 years. Education spending had been especially squeezed by 15% as a proportion of GDP, defence by 48%, trade, industry etc. by 56%, transport by 47%, overseas (especially aid) by 33%. The housing reduction represents a switch in housing subsidy from a building subsidy to a rent subsidy, counted under social security. Health and personal social services grew slightly but stayed at levels well below those of other European countries such as France and Germany who were spending about 8% of GDP on health services.

About one fifth of social security spending goes to unemployed people and to those who are economically inactive who might otherwise be in work if there were jobs available. The only ways in which governments could avoid this effect are either to reduce eligibility to benefits or to cut their level. Both are difficult in the short term.

Labour's fiscal policy 1997–2006

Gordon Brown, the Chancellor in all the Labour governments, made 'prudent' his favourite word in his early years, using it in the title of the 2000 budget statement.[1] Prudence was represented by the 'golden rule' of fiscal policy, that the public sector current budget should be in balance or at least not in deficit on average over the economic cycle. Borrowings should be made only to finance capital spending, rather than to finance current account deficits.

The 'sustainable investment rule' was that investment as a proportion of GDP should be brought up and then maintained as a proportion over the economic cycle.

A target proportion was not set. In any case the level of outstanding debt should be reduced to less than 40% of GDP. This fiscal stance produced by these two principles was presented and largely accepted by the media as being a necessary prelude to joining the Euro.[2] While the government decided not to join the Euro, they signed the 'Growth and Stability Pact', as part of the Maastricht agreement to bring Eurozone fiscal policies in line with each other. In practice they were slightly more fiscally conservative than the required criteria: deficits of up to 3% of GDP were permitted and outstanding debt was required not to exceed 60% of GDP.

The buoyancy of the economy allowed the Chancellor to meet the prudent targets earlier than originally planned. By 2000 the budget surplus had grown to £17 billion, much higher than the 1999 estimate. This was mainly because the continuing growth in the economy brought extra tax revenues. The 2000 budget planned to increase public spending in line with economic growth, estimated to be 2½% for the subsequent three years. In addition an extra £3 billion of current spending and £1 billion of capital was allocated to 2000–01. This reflected a view of the public finances that was in contrast with previous governments' positions, which had been based on a desire continuously to reduce spending as a proportion of GDP. In the March 2001 budget the Chancellor announced that the budget surplus projected for the 2000–01 financial year was £23.1 billion. This allowed some repayment of debt and by the end of 2002 net debt was reduced to 30.3% of GDP. The plan was to keep debt at or below 30%, a plan that was not to work out in practice. Reducing the outstanding debt allowed the government to reduce its debt servicing payments and allowed for an expansion of spending in future years without having to proportionately increase revenue. While the golden rule put an upper limit on spending it also indicated that the consumption of public services and income transfers could grow at the same rate as the economy.

These increases had been set out in the 1999 Comprehensive Spending Review, the first expansionary spending plan under Gordon Brown's Chancellorship. Table 3.2 shows the aggregate expenditure plans announced in the 1999 Comprehensive Spending Review. It shows the cuts in spending that had been inherited, a 3.7% and 3.6% cut in spending as a percentage of GDP in 1996–7 and 1997–8 respectively. From 1998 onwards the plan was to build up the figure to around 40% again, much of the extra money going into Social Security benefits, health and education, all of which were given planned real-terms increases.

The growth was continued in a way that reversed the previous history of spending, of slight variations around the trend and mainly incremental changes in the aggregate and in particular programmes. The ambition was to renew the priority public services both by improvements to the physical infrastructure and by hiring more staff and increasing capacity. Spending plans were summarized in the 2005 Public Expenditure Statistical Analysis (PESA) and show the spending pattern for the three Labour governments. There is a summary in Table 3.3.

Table 3.3 shows Departmental Expenditure Limits (DEL) which are the running costs budgets for departments, and Annual Managed Expenditure (AME) which

Table 3.2 *Public expenditure 1995–96 to 2001–02,   £billions and % change*

	Real terms departmental expenditure	Real terms Education	Real terms Health	Cash SS benefits	Aggregate as % GDP
1995–96	167.8	37.6	34.8	86.1	42.7
% change	–1.0	–0.8	–0.3	4.3	–3.7
1996–97	166.2	37.3	34.7	89.8	41.1
% change	–2.1	–2.9	1.7	1.4	–3.6
1997–98	162.7	36.2	35.3	91.1	39.6
% change	0.8	2.5	2.3	4.8	0.8
1998–99	164	37.1	36.1	95.5	39.9
% change	3.5	5.1	5.5	5.2	0.3
1999–00	169.7	39	38.1	100.5	40
% change	3.5	5.9	4.7	2.5	1.0
2000–01	175.6	41.3	39.9	103	40.4
% change	2.8	4.4	4.0	5.7	0.5
2001–02	180.5	43.1	41.5	108.9	40.6

Source: Calculated from HM Treasury (1999) *Comprehensive Spending Review*

Table 3.3 Resource budgets in real terms 1999–00 to 2007–8

	1999–00 outturn			2007–08 plans			1999–2007 % change
	DEL	AME	Total resource budget	DEL	AME	Total resource budget	Total resource budget
Education and Skills	14250	6925	21175	26827	8509	35336	67%
Health	45591	3887	49478	81019	9507	90526	83%
of which: NHS	44996		44996	79180		79180	76%
Transport	4446	1995	6441	8945	2581	11526	79%
Office of the Deputy Prime Minister	2612	521	3133	6544	131	6675	113%
Local Government	37452	221	37673	46400	340	46740	24%
Home Office	8221	344	8565	12729	1	12730	49%
Constitutional Affairs	2560	96	2656	3491	87	3578	35%
Law Officers' Departments	399		399	650		650	63%
Defence	34589	4586	39175	29955	5045	35000	−11%
Foreign and Commonwealth Office	1256		1256	1561		1561	24%
International Development	3028	64	3092	4797	129	4926	59%
Trade and Industry	4402	760	5162	5837	311	6148	19%
Environment, Food and Rural Affairs	2443	2421	4864	3093	2160	5253	8%
Culture, Media and Sport	1147	1291	2438	1514	1018	2532	4%
Work and Pensions	6401	96086	102487	7445	111518	118963	16%
Scotland	14595	1912	16507	21822	2441	24263	47%
Wales	7493	104	7597	11578	491	12069	59%
Northern Ireland Executive	5319	4120	9439	7279	6267	13546	44%
Northern Ireland Office	1253		1253	1033	229	1262	1%
Chancellor's Departments	3881	10642	14523	4710	22746	27456	89%
Cabinet Office	1589	4630	6219	1913	5448	7361	18%
Invest to Save budget				22			
DEL reserve				1600			
Unallocated special reserve							
Allowance for shortfall							
Total Resource DEL/AME	202929	140566	343495	290700	178958	469658	37%

Real terms are the cash figures adjusted to 2003–4 price levels, using GDP deflators

Source: Calculated from HM Treasury (2005) *Public Expenditure Statistical Analysis*, Table 1.6

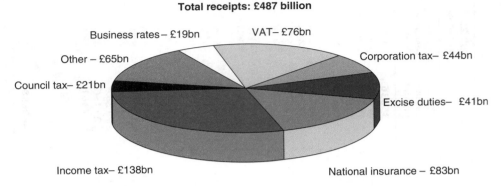

Total receipts: £487 billion

Business rates – £19bn

VAT – £76bn

Other – £65bn

Corporation tax – £44bn

Council tax – £21bn

Excise duties – £41bn

Income tax – £138bn

National insurance – £83bn

Figure 3.3   Government receipts 2005–6.

Source: HM Treasury, 2005–6 projections. Other receipts include capital taxes, stamp dutes, vehicle excise duties and some other tax and non-tax receipts – for example, interest and dividends. Figures may not sum to total due to rounding.

are the transfer payments handled by departments. Together they make up the Total Resource Budget for each department. The table is adjusted for inflation and so shows real-terms changes. The total growth between the start of the spending growth in 1999 and 2007–8 is 37%. The biggest percentage growth was in the Office of the Deputy Prime Minister, explained by an accretion of functions over the period. The biggest absolute growth was in health and education, the government's main priorities. Scotland and Wales also received big increases to be spent by the devolved arrangements and there is growth everywhere except in defence.

Where does the money come from?

The incoming government of 1997 pledged not to increase spending in real terms in the first two years and not to increase the income tax rates for the whole of the parliament. Taxation was increased (Table 3.4), partly to transform the overall budget balance from a deficit of £24 billion to a surplus of £17 billion or about 4% of spending.

Within this adjustment there was also an increase in the proportion of tax gathered by the then Inland Revenue, generally progressive taxes, and a decrease in the proportion of the direct taxes that were collected by the then Customs and Excise. While there was never an explicit commitment to shift the burden of taxation from indirect to direct taxes, this was the effect of the budgets. One of the more striking changes was in the category 'petroleum revenue tax, capital gains tax, inheritance tax and stamp duties' that increased by 250%. The main progressive tax, Income Tax, increased by 3 percentage points of the total receipts, while VAT declined slightly.

Table 3.4   General government receipts 1996–7, 2001–2 and 2004–5

	1996–97 £ billion	%	2001–02 £ billion	%	2004–5 £ billion	%
Inland Revenue and Customs and Excise	**186.76**	**66**	**264**	**66**	**291.3**	**65**
Income tax	70.2	25	109.6	27	127.2	28
Corporation tax	26.6	9	38.7	10	34.1	8
Petroleum revenue tax, capital gains tax, inheritance tax, stamp duties	5.9	2	15.2	4	15.5	3
Tax credits			–7	–2	–4.3	–1
Value-added tax	47.9	17	61.5	15	73	16
Fuel duties	17.4	6	23.6	6	23.3	5
Tobacco duties	7.7	3	7.6	2	8.1	2
Others	11.4	4	14.7	4	14.4	3
Other taxes and social security contributions	**82**	**29**	**108.8**	**27**	**133.7**	**30**
Social security contributions	46.9	16	62.3	16	78.1	17
Business rates	14.7	5	17.7	4	18.7	4
Council tax	9.9	3	14.7	4	20.1	4
Oil royalties, vehicle excise duties, others	10.5	4	14.7	4	16.8	4
Interest, dividends, rents, etc.	**16.1**	**6**	**31**	**8**	**57**	**13**
Current receipts	284.8	100	399.4	100	448.4	100

Sources: HM Treasury 1995 Pre-budget Report, Table 4A.1; 2000 Pre-budget Report, table B11; 2005 Pre-budget Report, Table B14

Why is the level of public spending important?

Taxation is an important political issue. Voting behaviour is influenced by expectations about the level of tax a party will charge. While public opinion polls consistently report people's preferences for improved public services, even at the expense of higher taxes, politicians of all parties are nervous about testing that proposition in a general election. Some taxes are less visible to voters than others and it is easier to raise taxes on businesses than individuals without generating adverse reactions from voters.

Some taxes are redistributive. If parties gain their support from people who are mostly net losers from progressive taxation, they will either make sure that most taxes are regressive or neutral or will try to keep tax levels down, or both. The Conservative governments before 1997 gradually shifted the balance of taxation from income tax to other sources, a trend that was reversed after 1997.

At local authority level, the link between politics and local taxation has been effectively broken. Council tax accounts for an average of only 20% of local government spending; spending is actually or potentially 'capped' and the distribution of grant and the business rate is subject to manipulation. It is virtually impossible for politicians at local level to offer a programme of improved services, financed by a proportionate increase in local taxation. Bristol City council held a referendum in 2001 offering a better education service in exchange for a higher council tax rate. The proposition was rejected. In any case, although the Labour government removed the cap on local spending the powers are still there and authorities know that they are subject to central government control as a last resort and were used in 2006.

Part of the 'New Right' philosophy was that public expenditure and investment 'crowd out' private sector investment. Government borrowing puts up interest rates and deters investors, hence reductions in borrowing (and, by implication, spending) will encourage investment and growth. The government was successful in pursuing spending and borrowing targets between 1985 and 1988, when there was a negative public sector borrowing requirement (PSBR) and spending was below 40% of GDP. However, such targets are subject to cyclical pressures and borrowing was required again by 1992 and was necessary until 1998–9.

There have also been arguments about the public sector starving the private sector of physical resources, including people. Some have argued that the public sector used to expand in times of recession, as governments spent money to encourage an up-swing and that such expenditure could never be reduced during periods of growth because of the vested interests of those benefiting from the expenditure, either as users of services or employees. Over time, therefore, there would be a cumulative growth of the public sector at the expense of the private.

A variant on the argument about the scale of the public sector has been that the 'social wage' is itself a determinant of economic success. This argument has two parts:

1   Inward investment to the United Kingdom (or anywhere else) is attracted not just by low wages and the fact of UK membership of the European Union, but also by the low taxes and other social costs payable there. Low taxes are seen as a national competitive advantage. As tariffs are reduced and capital becomes more mobile as part of the process of globalization, such pressures on national competitiveness get stronger.

2   For those companies already operating in the United Kingdom, low taxes are themselves an important element in a competitive strategy based on achieving low unit costs.

The strength of these arguments depends on the actual impact of taxation levels on competitiveness with the other European economies. It is unlikely that unit costs would be made comparable with very low wage economies, such as China, the Philippines or North Africa, where salaries are about £50 per month, just by reducing taxes. If production workers' wages are at a small fraction of European levels, tax reductions are unlikely to attract manufacturers back to Europe. The important issue is attracting investment from companies wanting to operate within the European Union. The policy has been successful to a certain extent, in that the United Kingdom spends slightly less than the EU average on social expenditure as a proportion of GDP. It spends somewhat less than Germany, Denmark and France and much more than Portugal, Ireland and Greece.

Other public expenditures, such as those on education, training and infrastructure, could be seen as contributing to competitiveness rather than detracting from it. A well-educated workforce, using modern transport and communications, is an important element of an economy which is competing on quality and value rather than low labour costs. The post-1997 government tried to distinguish between expenditures that contribute to growth and competitiveness and those which create a burden.

Managing public spending

The national budget process

The budget process is an iterative one between a Treasury trying to keep spending under control and Departments and Ministers pushing their departments' case for more spending. Over the years there have been attempts to design a system under which this bargaining can be harnessed to pull in the ruling party's preferred political direction and to make it more comprehensive. Comprehensiveness was required if the individual budget decisions were to add up to the government's priorities. Piecemeal negotiations would produce results that were random with respect to political decisions.

The budget process provides both a planning and a control mechanism. When the emphasis is on reducing or controlling spending, for economic or ideological reasons, the process is more confrontational and consists of finding items of spending that can be cancelled or postponed. At various times governments have wanted to make the process more scientific or rational. From 1961 the mechanism used to bring some order to the process was the Public Expenditure Survey Committee (PESC), a committee of ministers whose job was to align spending with the government's priorities, take a longer than one-year view of spending and think about the affordability of the spending plans. At times of financial stringency the process has been harsh, often involving confrontations between the Chancellor and ministers who were told individually what their next year's spending limits would be.

While the incoming government of 1997 did away with the PESC it adopted its own version of an oversight and review process, the Comprehensive Spending Review (CSR), a process under which all spending was looked at simultaneously before resources were allocated for the next year, with firm projections for some parts over a three-year period. It had many similarities to its predecessor the Fundamental Expenditure Review in that it asked basic questions of spending areas, such as whether they were necessary and whether their results could not be achieved in some other way. Doing nothing was not an option in the process. The least that could be done to a service was 'internal restructuring', if alternative forms of provision were not available. This use of the financial planning process as a challenge not just to spending levels but to the fundamentals of services was an innovation introduced during the Conservative governments. The CSR covered the whole budget quite as radically in 'thinking the unthinkable' as previous reviews under PESC.

While the CSR was in part an exercise designed to hold back ministerial and departmental ambitions, it also formed the base for the budgets in subsequent years. Since 1993 decisions about spending and taxation have been taken together. The mechanism chosen to bring them together is the pre-budget report that appears about four months in advance of the budget, contains plans about both spending and revenue and is based on the previous Spending Review.

In practice, financial planning is mainly incremental. The great bulk of spending in any one year represents commitments from the year before. In both central and local government, the aim of the CSR and the Best Value process respectively is to question the degree of commitment to continuing the same expenditure on the same services year after year. Under Best Value, each service has to be radically reviewed on a five-year cycle. The challenge to the commitment could be to the need for the service to be provided, or the way in which it is delivered and the choice of service provider. The solution to the problem of committed expenditure in the NHS is slightly different in that the people commissioning services are not in principle committed to buying next year everything they bought last year. In practice of course the bulk of what was done in the previous year will be required again this year and next.

Budgeting is sometimes presented as a linear process of building up the required level of expenditures either by forecasting totals with marginal changes or by building up from estimates of the requirements to spend on individual services. On the income side, decisions have to be made on taxes, duties and charges to cover the required level of spending. The process may be more or less comprehensive and more or less 'rational' in the sense of trying to fit the money to the needs or demands for services or the outcomes required.

However it is organized, the process is a political one in which interests and power are articulated through formal and informal iterative discussions. The interests represented range from poor children to oil companies and the power sources include electoral support, party funds contributions, bureaucratic authority and closeness to the centre of government. Both interests and power sources are fluid and the processes through which they are articulated vary over time. To understand the budget process at any level of government requires knowledge of both elements, beyond the official descriptions of the formal procedures.[3]

Some parts of the budget are easier to control than others. At one end of a scale there are demographic factors that determine expenditures: the numbers of school children or pensioners have a big influence on the level of spending on schools and pensions and while in the long term adjustments can be made to entitlements to education and pensions, in the short term demographic change triggers a change in the demand for spending. At the other end of the scale there are discretionary expenses. Military and cultural spending are largely a matter of taste and can be varied according to political preferences, subject of course to interests and power. One of the reasons that some items are easier to change is that they are more invisible than others. This is especially so when cuts in spending are made: some services have more direct contact with the public than others.

On the income side the same is true: the rates of income tax and Value Added Tax are very visible and sensitive. Adjustments in items such as exemptions in corporation tax payments affect fewer people and are therefore less sensitive for electors. One main determinant of government revenue is the level of activity in the economy and while this may be affected by policy, the actual amount collected in any year has to be a forecast range in any budget.

Figure 3.4 shows the main components of the central government budgeting process. The first Labour government's plan was that income should match expenditure over one phase of the economic cycle. However the budget is made, the process has to be an iterative one between finding an acceptable level of forecast income, with the tax and duty rates implied, and an acceptable level of expenditure. Arriving at a balance involves central management of the process to ensure that spending decisions and taxation decisions are co-ordinated.

In central government Total Managed Expenditure is divided into that part that is used to run government and deliver services and collect taxes, and that part that consists of grants and benefits. The running costs are labelled 'Departmental

Expenditure	Income
Departmental Expenditure Limits (3-year budget) =	Taxes and duties
	less tax allowances
Previous year's budget adjuste for estimated actuals	+ National insurance contributions
+ inflation in prices and pay	+ Business rates, council tax, oil royalties etc.
+ changes in volume of activities	+ 'Treasury' earnings
+ new outcomes	± debt repayments or borrowings
− productivity improvements	
− activities abandoned	
− price and pay reductions	
Annually managed expenditure (one-year budget)	
Forecast eligible populations Rates of benefits and grants	
= **Total Managed Expenditure**	= **Forecast income**

Figure 3.4   Central government budget making

Expenditure Limits' and are planned on a three-year cycle. Spending on benefits, grants and other transfers is called Annually Managed Expenditure and because it is subject to changes in the levels of unemployment and other cyclical factors, is planned annually.

The starting point for next year's Departmental Expenditure Limits is last year's budget, with adjustments for whatever spending has already been done in the current year. This is then adjusted for the next year by forecasting changes in things such as pay and prices and by making decisions about the volume of activities and what services should be added to or dropped from last year's list. Additions to activities should be defined by the expected outcomes or results of those activities.

Forecast changes in productivity and in pay and prices are a mixture of prediction and ambition. There might be an aspiration to reduce costs by better procurement or higher productivity. Forecasts of changes in pay may be used in the process of bargaining pay changes. In these cases the financial planning process is used as one way of influencing management and of managers increasing their control over staff. If a pay rise can be financed only through productivity improvements, this is a bargaining point for managers trying to get people to produce more.

Budgeting for Annual Managed Expenditure involves forecasting the numbers of people eligible for benefits or grants and the levels at which they will be paid. Some of these are fixed by statute, while others, such as overseas aid or financial support for people with disabilities, are more discretionary.

Meanwhile the Treasury forecasts the government's likely income. Some of this is subject to a decision for the budget period, such as the tax levels or the decision to take on new debt or to repay some of the outstanding debt. Other parts involve making a forecast, such as for the price of oil and its impact on oil royalties or the level of transactions generating Value Added Tax.

It is unlikely that independent processes for predicting and planning income and spending would produce a balanced budget. Departments are concerned to secure enough revenue to run their services, while the Treasury looks for acceptable tax levels. Guidelines are issued for spending plans so that departments have targets for their DELs. Political guidelines are given for acceptable tax and duty rates. During years when spending is being cut back there is a downward pressure on all the elements of spending.

Local government budgeting

In local government, budget making is similar but generally less subject to discretion. Figure 3.5 shows the main elements in a local authority budget process. As in central government, the starting point for the expenditure side is last year's budget together with what is known so far about the current year's spending. Changes to last year's budget will come from a mixture of changes in activities and changes in costs, whether up or down. Some changes will be the result of new legislation bringing new commitments. Examples would include things such as a new Mental Health Act, a requirement to look after refugees or provide new service for children at risk. Also as in central government there may be discretion to cancel or cut back on some services. During times of spending cuts those services that are not prescribed in detail by statute will be cut first. Libraries have been a favourite in recent years, as have youth services, arts and recreation subsidies and other discretionary services. Savings may be found in productivity improvements, in getting lower prices for goods and services bought as well as in cuts in the volume of services.

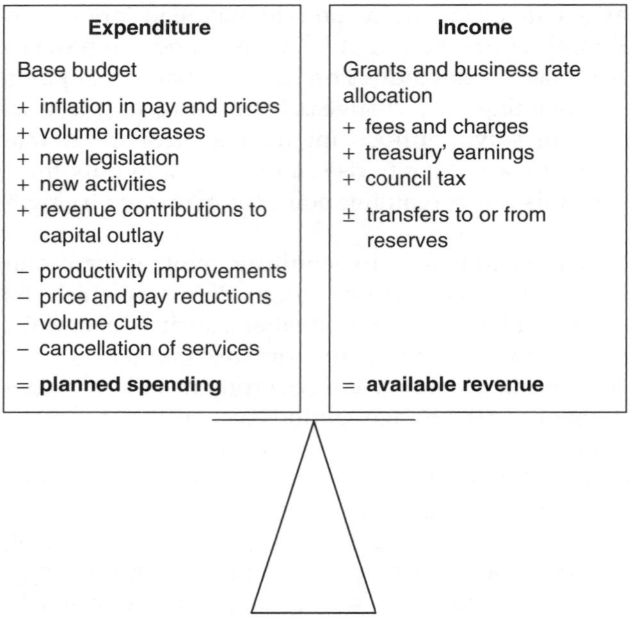

Expenditure	Income
Base budget	Grants and business rate allocation
+ inflation in pay and prices	+ fees and charges
+ volume increases	+ treasury' earnings
+ new legislation	+ council tax
+ new activities	
+ revenue contributions to capital outlay	± transfers to or from reserves
− productivity improvements	
− price and pay reductions	
− volume cuts	
− cancellation of services	
= **planned spending**	= **available revenue**

Figure 3.5   Budget making in local government

Sources of income are subject to central government controls. Each service is allocated a level of spending required to provide a 'standard' level of services, known as the Standard Spending Assessment. Each authority is then allocated a grant (the Revenue Support Grant or RSG) and a share of the business rate that would allow it to provide a standard level of service if it raised a standard level of council tax. While it can raise more or less than the standard council tax, there are reserve 'capping' powers to stop any authority spending what the government defines as excessive amounts.

A local authority's ability to determine its income level is limited to changes in the council tax and its level of fees and charges. These include rents on houses and commercial premises, car parking, commercial waste collection, museum charges and so on. Together council tax and sales, fees and charges add up to only one third of local authority revenues. Because of this relatively low discretion to vary the revenues raised at local level, the task of balancing the budget at local level is more difficult than at national level. Consider the options if the level of the SSA for all services together is lower than the level of spending the authority thinks it needs to make or than the level it is currently spending. If it decides to spend at that level, it has to find the money from fees and charges and the council tax, since the level of RSG and share of business rates are fixed.

At times of budget cuts, some councils have simply found it impossible to get spending down to the level implied by the grant settlement. The combination of the 'negative' elements of the expenditure side of the equation in Figure 3.5, productivity improvements, pay and price cuts, volume cuts and service cancellations are always hard. In extreme they can prove to be impossible for managers and politicians.

Meanwhile the government is encouraging local authorities to follow two aspects of its own financial management. Best Value, a process of challenge to current practices of service delivery and financing, emulates the CSR at local level and is backed by an inspection process. Local authorities have financial incentives to meet their outcome targets in their Public Service Agreements (PSAs). The PSAs are the mechanism through which the Treasury exercises influence on performance, of departments and local authorities, as part of the budget process. They are dealt with in more detail in Chapter 5.

Budgeting in the NHS

There are two main budget decisions in the NHS: resources are allocated to geographical areas according to a weighted per head formula that has been developed over the history of the NHS. The purpose of this calculation has always been to try to ensure that the resources available for treatments are spread evenly so that individuals' probability of receiving treatment is unaffected by where they happen to live. Throughout the history of the service this aim has been affected by the fact that facilities and personnel are not evenly distributed and that the maintenance of existing facilities requires an uneven distribution of resources.

The second choice is that of which services should be funded, a choice that is carried out according to a process of programme budgeting, whereby funds are allocated to a list of treatments and procedures. During the allocation process, funds are allocated to the Primary Care Trusts, who can then choose to spend some of their allocations with secondary providers of their choice; to various joint funds and arrangements among health and social care providers, and to other NHS services and functions. About 75% of the budget is allocated to the Primary Care Trusts. Before the introduction of 'payment by results', a system of fixed price contracting, PCTs made annual contracts with providers, at agreed prices. The contracts ensured that capacity was paid for and services provided at close to marginal cost. The system produced stable financing for providers but did not exert consistent competitive pressure on costs. A priority for budget making throughout the system since 1997 was the government's priority: to reduce waiting lists.

In the 'Payments by Results' system, payments are based on standard prices for procedures and unpredictable volumes of work. For the secondary care providers, especially the NHS Trusts, incomes, and therefore their budgets, depend on how much activity they carry out. Their financial health depends not on keeping their spending within a fixed revenue budget as much as keeping their income up to the level of their expenditure.

Financial control: cash and resources

Since the 2000 Spending Review financial planning in central government has been done on what is called a 'resource basis' or accruals accounting. This means that instead of each department having a cash budget for the coming periods of one and three years, they have a budget to cover the resources used up in providing services, divided into current and capital costs. Capital costs are budgeted through an allowance for depreciation and a capital charge to reflect the costs of using the assets. Together the revenue and capital used to provide services make up the Departmental Expenditure Limit.

This form of accounting and control was assumed to have some real impacts on management. First, the fact that departments have a budget that covers more than one year and that expenditures can to some extent be postponed or brought forward means that the traditional rush to spend or make arbitrary savings by the end of the financial year, to make the cash budget balance exactly, is consigned to history. It was widely believed that such practices were wasteful.

Second, the process implies that decisions about whether to spend on capital or current expenditure can be made more objectively than in a system where only annual cash outlays are considered. Since capital spending is accounted for over the life of the project rather than according to the cash consumed each year, real comparisons can now be made of the relative efficiency of current and capital spending. In practice this decision is made less clear by the need to finance capital spending through a separate investment budget or PFI credit.

Third, the separation of running costs (Annual Managed Expenditure) from programme budgets (Departmental Expenditure Limits) enables financial planning to focus on the two issues separately. While it has always been possible to identify the two, in practice they have been mixed up. When the Social Security programme budget was growing under the Major administration, for example, the Department was expected to make saving in running costs because of a sense of panic about the overall budget. A more calm approach might have suggested that if more cash were being handed out it would cost more to do it.

Decentralized financial management

During the 1980s a belief developed that if financial management were devolved to the operational level resources would be better used. 'Frontline' managers would be in a better position to make decisions about the fine detail of resource allocation and would be less likely to waste money than remote financial controllers. The idea spread. Area teams in social services, clinical teams in hospitals, individual schools and many other local units were allocated budgets and told to manage them. An early example was the Financial Management Initiative in the civil service, followed by the Local Management of Schools. The principle of allocating a budget to a unit had important consequences. First there was an accounting task to be able to break down the budgets. If teachers' pay is to be allocated to the school rather than the education authority, how much cash should be transferred? The average salary multiplied by the number of teachers? What happens if all the teachers move up the pay scale in one year and nobody leaves? Should the school get a bigger allocation to cover the extra cost, or should they have to manage within a fixed budget? If they simply get reimbursed for all the teachers they happen to have, what advantage is there in devolving the budget?

The accounting got more complicated when budgets began to be allocated for the cost of outputs rather than the expenses incurred on the inputs. To re-cast accounts to include such unit costs is a big job and subject to a different set of errors from a budget based on the cost of inputs.

As well as these technical matters that took up a lot of management time, there were some real effects of the devolved budgets at local level. Managers who became budget holders for the first time needed to think about finance in a different way. A school Head, for example, before the budgets were devolved, would have a real budget only for books, equipment and materials, possibly school cleaning, ancillary staff and other relatively small items. Once devolved, the budget covers everything. Responsibility for under-spending or over-spending then becomes part of someone's job at school level, whether the Head or the governors. This is mainly a positive effect, because the Head no longer has to defer to the decisions of a remote bureaucrat and can be more sensitive to her own local situation. On the other hand it is an extra responsibility and in most cases incurred extra cost as schools hired bursars to look after the money. Schools also lose the benefits of central purchasing.

Another effect was to create larger contingency funds. A central contingency fund in a department or authority is effectively an insurance against unexpected events or natural disasters. The amount that managers need to hold to cover the same degree of risk increases as smaller units have to provide for their own contingencies. NHS Trusts with unpredictable incomes have to keep contingency reserves to cover revenue shortfalls.

A third effect of budgets being allocated to small units is that uneven incidence of demand can lead to unequal access to services. A good example is the Community Care budget, money for individuals requiring support services. Since the call on the funds depends on the needs arising at any time, the allocation of the funds to geographical areas is necessarily based on some prediction of those needs. The smaller the areas into which the funds are allocated, the less accurate will be the predictions. To cope with demand that follows a pattern different from that predicted, some financial manager above the area level will either have to claw back some money from 'underspending' units to give to those under pressure, or will have to hold some funds back for allocation later in the year, partly negating the idea of devolved budgeting.

Conclusions

During the 1980s and early 1990s there was a presumption against public expenditure. Conservative philosophy was that tax rates should be lower and that people should make their own, individual decisions about what to spend their money on. There was a belief in the Labour Party that it lost the 1992 general election partly because its policies implied higher taxes. In practice, although cuts were made it was difficult for a succession of governments to make big inroads into the proportion of national production that went into public spending. Government practice has normally been to increase spending before elections, not necessarily with a concomitant increase in taxation.

The 1997 government promised to keep for two years to the previous government's spending plans and its fiscal stance, which was for a balanced budget over the economic cycle and for an increase in public sector investment. This implied that once spending was set as a proportion of GDP, it would increase with growth in the national product. In 1999 it revealed its plans for the following three years and the growth was slightly ahead of growth in the national product. In the campaign for the 2001 election, the Conservative opposition did not promise to reverse the trend in spending, although it said that it could reduce taxation. The other parties, including the Liberal Democrats, Plaid Cymru and the Scottish Nationalists, accepted a relaxed attitude to public spending and rejected previous policies of trying to cut back the scale of state activity. There seemed to emerge a new consensus, that the level of public spending should settle at about 40% of GDP.

For managers this means that the long-standing pressure on spending is slightly eased. Certainly the restoration of capital spending has led to an easier task in keeping the infrastructure going, although funding through Public–Private Partnerships means that different skills are required to manage the projects much more indirectly than is the case with directly funded schemes. Certainly the growth in spending led to increases in the numbers of people employed, especially in the NHS and in education, which reversed the sense of decline and despair from the long period of spending cuts.

The three-year planning horizon for budgets allows managers the opportunity to think more strategically than annual budgeting. Especially in circumstances of spending growth, it is possible to make changes in the ways money is spent and how priorities are pursued. On the other hand, a budget process that has built-in contractual arrangements between the Treasury and the rest of the public sector inhibits autonomy. Budgeting by managers is essentially a process of balancing these two tendencies.

Notes

For weblinks relevant to the issues discussed in this chapter see www.sagepub.co.uk/flynn.

1   HM Treasury, *Prudent for a Purpose: Working for a Stronger and Fairer Britain* (HM Treasury, London, 2000).
2   e.g. '... arguably the best kept secret in British politics: the extent to which our public spending is now dictated by our obligations under Article 104 (c) of the Maastricht Treaty to get the British economy into shape to join the single currency.' *Sunday Telegraph*, 14 May 2000, p. 16.
3   David Lipsey, *The Secret Treasury* (London, Viking, 2000) gives detailed descriptions of the process in central government.

4

Social policies and management

Introduction

In this chapter we look at the changes that governments have made in recent years in some of the main areas of social policy. It is not intended that this should be a complete review of all aspects of social policy, rather to examine the changes that affect the way in which managers in the different sectors have to work. In some cases the trends we look at are directly about management itself, rather than what is normally known as social policy. Management and social policy have become closer as governments have pursued different aims of policy through a series of managerial measures.

Six themes have dominated the development of policy over the thirty years since the last public spending boom ended. We saw in Chapter 2 that a convergence has emerged between the main parties in England about the nature of the welfare state and how it should be managed. There is a consensus about what the public services should *not* be: a monopolistic, monolithic, uniform and universal set of services based on a set of state owned and managed institutions employing public servants. In the event, the institutions have proved remarkably resilient to change, with over a million people employed in both the NHS and local authorities, half a million civil servants in post, over nine out of ten children being educated in state schools, the distribution of pensions and benefits still done by public servants. We will see that there were some successes in breaking up the monolith, council houses sold either to tenants or to special organizations set up to own and run them, the switch of elderly people's homes to the private sector, some increase in private sector provision in health care.

The first theme was a move from equality of treatment to the promotion of responses tailored to individual need. The most obvious example of this was the change in the school system from a comprehensive system towards selection by schools, providing some degree of choice by parents and children and differences between types of school. Of course the education system never was completely comprehensive: the private schools survived and remained the preserve of people who could afford the fees and a few scholarship winners. Direct grant schools, such as the King Edward schools in Birmingham, retained selection under Labour governments and Labour education authorities. But the changes brought about by the Thatcher and Major governments were designed to increase inequality (or 'diversity', as it was called). While the first Blair government did away with the institutional form ('Grant Maintained Schools') that the Conservatives designed, they were eventually, during the third government, restored under a different name.

Another example was the move away from a universal entitlement to unemployment benefit for unemployed people. First, the increased use of means testing meant that people with savings were excluded. Second, the introduction of the 'jobseekers' allowance' meant that entitlement was not universal but dependent on persuading a civil servant of the applicant's diligence in seeking work. This continued through the New Deal, under which claimants are also offered more help with finding work or training. Another example is the change in policy towards older people and elderly people's homes. Until the NHS and Community Care Act people could refer themselves, if they chose, to a home and the state would pay the rent and care costs, subject to a means test. Now, they can only receive such care if they are judged to be in need by a social services department. In all these cases, the management of the services has changed from being focused on making sure that everyone received the same service towards allocating individually tailored services to different people following some form of assessment or selection.

At the extreme, this change involves the second theme, which is the change from universal eligibility to rationing against strict eligibility criteria. For example, when housing subsidy was payable to all local authority housing construction, it was relatively easy for working-class people to obtain a council house. Points systems were in operation, according to size of family and current housing circumstances, but most people, especially if their parents lived in a council house, would eventually be housed. Now a majority of people who are being offered social housing are previously homeless and mostly not working.

Housing policy is one example of a third theme that represented a belief strongly held by Conservative and Labour governments, the presumption that public services should not be provided directly by public bodies but through private or mixed private and public provision. Public housing was privatized by selling houses and flats to tenants, by diverting money from local authorities to housing associations and by privatizing housing management. The Prison Service introduced private companies into the management of prisons and the provision of new ones. Elderly people's homes and home care services are predominantly privately owned in England and Wales. The Labour governments have declared themselves agnostic on the question of ownership. Ministers have said that they wanted only to promote 'what works' and if the private sector is better then that is where services should be provided. An example is the abolition of compulsory competitive tendering for local authority services, under which most services had to be periodically tested against private competitors. However, for example, under the Best Value[1] régime local authorities have to demonstrate that cost and quality are the best available, and that means competitive with the private sector. There is also in practice a marked presumption, at least for larger scale building projects, that they will be financed through the Private Finance Initiative or Public – Private Partnerships through which private sector participation in service provision is required. So, although there is no longer a declared ideological presumption in favour of the independent sector (private and voluntary), in practice private or mixed public/private provision is becoming the norm.

A fourth theme, which has been more slowly implemented, is the move from a position of no choice for the service user to some choice or the illusion of it. One example is the abolition of school catchment areas so that parents and pupils could choose their schools. There is some choice of service and service provider in the community care régime, once people have passed the need and eligibility tests. 'Direct payments', under which people assessed as being eligible for care can receive cash to buy their own care, has grown slowly to around 10% of the social care budget.[2] Choice of health care providers was introduced slowly, 'choose and book' finally coming into force for secondary health care treatment in December 2005. Under this scheme patients are offered a choice of hospital, rather than being allocated one by their family doctor. This direction is further emphasised by 'practice-based commissioning' through which an increasing volume of health care will be commissioned locally by general medical practitioners, ostensibly with and on behalf of 'their' patients.

The fifth theme is the move from local policy autonomy to central control, combined with a contrary tendency towards more local managerial and financial accountability. This shift in public policy is becoming most marked through the delivery of criminal justice services.

An example is the Probation Service, for which the Home Office imposed a set of national standards for how probation work should be done, took more central control over the cash limits for the service but made Probation Committees more managerial. The Labour government went a stage further and established a single, national Probation Service accountable to the Home Office. It then merged the Probation and Prison services in a single organization, the 'National Offender Management Service' (NOMS), with a single hierarchy stretching down from the Home Secretary. In addition, there is to be introduced a deliberate policy of 'contestability' through which independent sector organizations will be invited to compete to take on responsibility for delivering firstly probation services and then prison services through a process comparable to 'Best Value' described above.

Similarly in schools, budgets are now handled locally and governors and headteachers have more freedom in daily management, but there is a strengthened system of national curriculum, national testing and national inspection, and publication of test and examination results. Labour's policies are mostly centralist. Institutions defined as 'failing', whether education authorities, schools, NHS Trusts, are subject to intervention from government. Local authority management is subject to continuous instructions and directives from the centre and requires a steady flow of monitoring and control information to central government.

A sixth theme involved the use of funding arrangements to influence behaviours. Increasingly, funding is based on some measure of performance or volume of work. Schools are funded according to pupil numbers, universities according to student numbers and an assessment of teaching and research quality. Local authority capital budgets are allocated according to a competition, in which money is dispensed according to official judgement of the proposals' merits. The change from 2005 in the NHS funding arrangements, called 'payment by results', is an extreme example of payment being based on the volume of work done, rather than some assessment of needs or projection of actual costs.

The policy directions that were labelled a 'third way' by the first Labour governments were mainly a continuation of the older, Conservative policies. Were there themes that distinguish the Labour governments from their Conservative predecessors? Michael Freeden[3] analysed the ideology underneath the government's first two years of policies and showed how its eclecticism allowed it to operate a variety of practices from liberalism, conservatism and social democracy. In social policy the mix contains elements from all three. From conservatism comes an emphasis on 'family values' and a desire to exercise strict control over individual institutions, from liberalism a belief in a mixed economy and a contractarian relationship among the state, civil society and the individual, and from social democracy a belief in progressive taxation and a concern for the very poor. In addition to these broad beliefs, Freeden identified the desire for 'modernisation' which he sees as itself essentially conservative, quoting Prime Minister Blair: '"modernisation" is in reality … an application of enduring, lasting principles to a new generation'.

The early eclecticism in government policies gave way to an increasing reliance on market-based, selective and pluralist policies and mechanisms. For example, the scrapping of the internal market in the NHS represented a break from previous governments' belief in the superiority of market forces, but the internal market was later re-introduced in a more extreme form, with centrally imposed pricing. The main break with previous ideology, especially after 2000, was the willingness to increase spending, raising the level of public spending as a proportion of GDP, especially in the priority areas of health and education.

Income maintenance

Governments concerned to contain the total of public expenditure have sought to limit the growth of social security spending, by dissuading people from claiming benefits, changing eligibility criteria, changing the levels of benefits, preventing fraudulent claims and encouraging private insurance for some elements of social security. At the same time, the agencies responsible for distributing income maintenance payments have been trying to improve customer service by making benefits more accessible and understandable and by paying more promptly.

Unemployment Benefit, Income Support, Jobseeker's Allowance and the New Deal

Successive governments have pursued an employment policy based on the fear that the benefits system could produce disincentives to work, especially at the bottom end of the labour market where wages are close to benefit levels. The solution to this was that the benefit system should 'work with the grain of policies to help unemployed people to compete effectively for jobs and find employment as quickly as possible, by creating and supporting incentives to work'.[4] This policy was continued by the Labour government, which tried to create a benefits system that contained incentives to work and penalties for staying on benefits without trying to find work or training.

Up to October 1996 unemployed people were entitled to Unemployment Benefit (UB) for 12 months if they had paid the right amount of National Insurance contributions, or means-tested Income Support if they had not. The replacement benefit régime, Jobseeker's Allowance (JSA) has a non-means-tested element if National Insurance contributions have been paid and is a means-tested benefit for those who have not. The main difference between JSA and the previous system was that automatic entitlement was reduced from 12 to six months, people aged 18 to 24 have a lower rate of benefit than others, and the previous allowance for an adult dependant has been removed. The effect was to reduce the amount of benefit paid to unemployed people. As well as this increased incentive to work, unemployed people had to sign and keep to a Jobseeker's Agreement, setting out what they would do to look for work. Failure to keep the agreement results in loss of benefit. The Labour government introduced what it called the New Deal, a continuation of the Jobseeker's Agreement, initially for young unemployed people and then for all unemployed people under 50 years old, except single parents and people with disabilities. Under the New Deal unemployed people have to pursue one option, whether employment, education or training, as a condition of receiving benefit. If no job is available the options are a subsidised job, work for the voluntary sector or a job with the Environment Task Force. Refusal to follow an option results in the withdrawal of benefits for 26 weeks. Social Security Secretary Angela Eagle emphasised the responsibility of unemployed young people to find work: 'We promise the New Deal will provide every reasonable chance for young people. But in return we will not tolerate those few who shirk the system. Our plans draw the line in the right place.'[5] In January 2001 the government re-introduced home visits to claimants, a measure to reduce fraudulent claims that was cancelled in a previous round of cost savings.

In 2006 the government produced a White Paper[6] on benefits. The proposals were based on a target of increasing the employment rate[7] from around 75% to 80%. The groups the government were concerned about were people on incapacity benefits, lone parents and people aged between 50 and 60, all of whom were to be given incentives and support to get back to work. The 2.7 million on incapacity benefit were a major concern, as they seemed to be stuck on benefits for ever once they started claiming. The new proposals included reassessment of people's capabilities and various efforts to get them into work.

Working Families Tax Credit and the Social Fund

One of the policy problems in social security is that people who can command only small incomes may have no incentive to get off benefits and take a job. The net change in income may be so small that it is not worth the individual's while to take a job, especially as this involves stopping being registered for benefits and having to re-register if the job does not last. Also, there are other benefits, such as free school meals, free prescriptions for medicine, free dental treatment, which are available for people who are on benefit. If these benefits are also lost, the disincentive effects are even greater.

There are three potential solutions to this problem: reduce benefits so that staying on benefit becomes less attractive; introduce a minimum wage so that work becomes more attractive; extend the chances of being able to work and claim benefit at the same time so that people have a reason to take a job. An early effort to tackle the problem of the benefits trap was the introduction of Family Credit, a benefit for families with children. To reduce the benefits trap, people were allowed to claim Family Credit if they worked part time and were allowed to offset childcare costs against earnings (up to £40 per week). Family Credit was part of the policy designed to remove the disincentives to work, especially in low-paid work, provided by the removal of benefits when people started earning.

The Labour government's main effort to eliminate the benefits trap was the introduction of the Working Families Tax Credit to provide a minimum income for families with children. This benefit is designed to maintain the incentive to work even at low levels of pay by topping up the earnings. It replaced the Family Credit system at the beginning of 1998 and is administered by the Inland Revenue department. Alongside this benefit is a new Child Care Credit to pay for child care and a National Minimum Wage to try to stop very low wages being paid.

The Social Fund is a cash-limited fund held at local level for loans to help people in emergencies, repayable from future benefits. It was an innovation in social security in that whether a person receives a loan or not now depends not only on whether they meet the eligibility criteria but whether the fund has any money left in it when they apply. This required discretion and responsibility of Social Fund managers and workers which did not apply to other benefits: the rest of the system consists of applying a set of rules and criteria to applicants for benefit, whereas the Social Fund also implies rationing, in the same way that cash-limited funds for community care have to be allocated according to eligibility rules and available budget. However, the Fund is a very small proportion of the social security budget and the principle of cash limiting has not been applied elsewhere.

Pensions

The Conservative governments claimed that publicly-funded pensions, providing a reasonable standard of living for pensioners, are unsustainable in the long term. Other parties have also said that there must be ways of funding pensions other than the National Insurance scheme and taxation: personal and occupational pensions have to substitute for the state pension or at least enhance it up to a level which will provide a decent living standard. Pensioners' relative living standards have been cut by indexing them to inflation, rather than to the growth of earnings. In practice, those pensioners without personal or occupational pensions have had their earning enhanced by Income Support and in some cases by Housing Benefit. The other way in which the Conservative governments tried to contain spending on state pensions was to encourage people to withdraw from the State Earnings-Related Pensions Scheme, by offering them money to withdraw and start personal pension plans.

For the social security system, these changes have meant that the state pension is becoming a small residual amount, rather then the main source of income, for people over retirement age. An increasing number of pensioners have been eligible for means-tested benefits, putting more demands on the means-tested parts of the social security system. The Labour government came under public pressure to improve the basic state pension, and while the government did not introduce earnings indexation for pensions it did put up the rates by more than price inflation. At the same time the government tried to make private pensions easier to arrange and more portable, with a new 'stakeholder pension' to be available along with personal and occupational schemes. A pensions crisis emerged, caused partly by the failure of several company pension schemes and partly by stock market volatility. While the government commissioned studies on alternatives, the third Labour government found no permanent solution to the pensions problem, and instead started to make changes to elements of it, such as delaying the retirement age for public sector workers.

Housing Benefit

Housing Benefit, a rent subsidy, is financed by central government but administered by local authorities. It is the main means by which government subsidizes housing costs. About 3 million council tenants have their rent subsidized in this way in Great Britain, 1.5 million private tenants and 412,000 housing association tenants. The régime of spending controls and rent levels imposed on local authorities and housing associations means that most 'social housing' is allocated to people on benefits. This is for two reasons: the volume of housing is so limited that it is allocated only to those most in need; rent levels which cover the cost of providing housing are comparable to the cost of renting in the private sector or buying accommodation with a mortgage. This has resulted in geographical polarization, with economically inactive and unemployed people concentrated in social housing while those in work live in private rented or owner-occupied property. As the Rowntree Inquiry into Income and Wealth said:

> The concentration of social housing resources on those in greatest need has led to concentration of disadvantaged households, leading to communities where there are few adults who have jobs. Nearly half of non-pensioner council tenant households have no earner.[8]

This demographic distortion has been further reinforced by the introduction of the 'Supporting People' policy through which a range of individual statutory and local benefits for disadvantaged people were pooled to form a single budget controlled by local authorities. This fund is allocated following assessment to provide support services for individual tenants with special needs who are usually, although not exclusively, resident in public housing. This can further 'ghettoize' some of our most vulnerable fellow citizens, depriving them of the informal support systems which are usually available in more balanced communities.

The policy of council house sales has also had a polarizing effect. The most attractive council houses were individual houses with gardens and these sold in greatest numbers. The stock available for rent as social housing is therefore limited to less attractive properties. Not only are social housing tenants most likely to be unemployed or economically inactive; they are also likely to be living in the least attractive housing.

The changes to the tax and benefits systems after 1997 were designed to benefit the poorest working households with children. An assessment of the impact of the changes from 1997–2002 concluded that the effects of taxation and benefits changes on the income distribution were progressive but were offset by changes in income distribution caused by changes in the labour market:

> The reforms announced to the tax and transfer system between 1997 and 2001 were large, and highly progressive. The changes to the personal tax

system tended to favour those on lower incomes, and the increases in benefits were targeted on those with the lowest incomes among the benefit recipient population. The structure of the benefit system has therefore shifted even further towards means-testing, and subsequent announcements have continued this direction of change. Despite the progressive nature of these changes, inequality has remained at broadly the same level as in 1996/7. Changes to the underlying distribution of income, which is less directly under government control, have offset the changes made to transfer payments.[9] (p. 200)

Implications for managers

The social security system is both a safety net for people in temporary difficulties and a system devised to encourage or force people to go to work. For managers and workers in the system, this expresses itself as a dilemma: good customer service demands that people are helped to receive their entitlements while unemployed claimants are encouraged to look for work. When UB was paid through a separate system the distinction was easier to make, whereas the JSA is designed to encourage the search for work, whatever the probability of finding it.

There are conflicting expectations from the benefits system. Ministers expect certain things: an efficient delivery of service, especially to those people considered 'deserving', such as genuinely disabled people, widows and pensioners, while making benefits difficult to obtain by the 'undeserving' who might have different definitions by different ministers: single and never married parents, fit unemployed people, new age travellers. Service management is difficult if such distinctions have to be made at the point of service delivery. In practice, staff have commonly dealt differently with different classes of claimant, although managers have encouraged them to deal equally with everyone.

Senior management, especially in the Benefits Agency and the Employment Service, encouraged good customer service, through middle management initiative, the development of innovative solutions, the establishment of telephone help-lines and better designed forms. The Labour government decided that better service would be provided by a merged organization, initially called ONE, then Jobcentre Plus, containing the benefit elements of the Benefits Agency and the Employment Service, reverting to an arrangement that had existed before the Agencies were founded.

Health services

Since it was founded in 1948 the National Health Service has been subject to many reviews and reorganizations. From the beginning, there have been debates about how local the management of the service should be, how politically accountable, whether it is a national service and how reasonably equitable national standards might be achieved. The role of doctors in the service has similarly always been controversial, as has the nature of the contractual relationship between the NHS and the various medical professions and factions. Structural changes have been frequent, including the creation and destruction of a wide variety of organizations at subnational levels, sometimes for small areas, sometimes for large areas, sometimes with two tiers of administration between the Department of Health and the service providers, sometimes with indirectly elected boards and sometimes with appointed boards. The only option which has not been tried is the transfer of health responsibilities to local authorities, which was rejected from the beginning, although some joint working and joint budgets are being implemented between health bodies and local authority social service departments.

The Conservative governments of the 1980s and 1990s made two main changes. They divided the service into a set of 'purchasers' and a set of 'providers' of health services and started a set of controls to give the Secretary of State for Health and the National Health Service Executive considerable control over what happens in most parts of the NHS. Previous reorganizations and interventions failed either to equalize access to health facilities or to bring doctors under political control. The second main change was to introduce explicit objectives about the incidence of ill health, rather than the volume of treatment to be provided for people who are ill.

Working for patients: markets and competition

The White Paper *Working for Patients*, 1989 (whose title implied that before then the NHS was working for someone else), established a different form of financial management in the service. The idea was that budgets would not be allocated to people providing services, rather to another set of people who would specify what they wanted the providers to do. These people would, initially, be the district health authorities and the larger GP practices. The new arrangement meant that service providers, such as hospitals, would not have a plan for the year and a budget, but rather a set of contracts for the year with agreed prices. Where there was only one large contract with the local health district, the arrangement was very much like a budget and a plan. Where there was a variety of purchasers and many providers in competition, the new arrangement had some characteristics of a market and a set of contracts.

In these latter cases managers and medical professionals were put into competition with each other. In the previous system the volume of work which a hospital did was determined by how much budget it received, how many patients were referred to it and how efficient it was. The budget was based mainly on historical patterns with some adjustment from 'over-provided' areas. Referral patterns were mainly historical, based on where people lived and which general practitioners knew which hospital doctors. Efficiency was set by how well managers were managing, how good the facilities were and how hard the medical staff worked. In the new system, the idea was that hospitals would compete on price and/or the quality of work. Most contracts were large 'block' contracts which contained not only an allocation of funds but also a specification of what the providers were expected to do for the money. Efficiency was slightly more easy to measure, because procedures would have their unit costs defined. At the same time, purchasers would ask for an efficiency improvement each year, expressed as a reduction in the unit prices, achieved by individuals doing more work, by speeding up the throughput of patients (sending them home sooner) or by paying people less.

Another big change was to transfer a proportion of the health budget to GP fundholders, who could purchase services for their patients from hospitals or other providers of their choice. As the amount spent by GP fundholders grew, their influence on hospitals increased. While there is evidence that costs were not reduced as a result of this, the change did alter the relationship between general practitioners and their traditionally more senior hospital colleagues.

The Health of the Nation

In 1992, the government published a White Paper, *The Health of the Nation*, which set out targets for improvements in health in five 'key areas': coronary heart disease and stroke, cancers, mental illness, HIV/AIDS and sexual health and accidents. Twenty-seven specific targets were also declared. Some referred to incidence of diseases, such as the proportion of people with coronary heart disease or lung cancer. Some were causes (proportion of people smoking or obese) and some were outcomes (accidents and suicides). The paper recognized that the targets were achievable through a variety of preventive measures and that their achievement required the collaboration of a range of organizations.

The idea was that regional health authorities should adopt their own targets to contribute towards the achievement of the national ones. Each year, progress towards the targets is monitored and published. While the achievement of the targets was not within the competence of any single body within the NHS, it did provide a focus for efforts to prevent the main avoidable causes of death and disease. It especially provided a way of making primary health care more important than hospitals in improving health standards, as well as helping with collaborative efforts.

What is radical about these targets is that they are not concerned with the activities of any organization, but rather the effect of organizations working together to achieve a particular result. As we shall see in Chapter 5, it is only when results are measured or assessed that management can be fully turned towards achieving what people need.

The NHS Plan

The Labour government's policy towards the NHS contained some continuities with the past and some changes. What did not change was the struggle to maintain some central control through a system of target setting and managerial mechanisms and incentives. The old power battles between professionals, managers and politicians continued, in an atmosphere of crisis and problems. Reducing the size of waiting lists and the time spent waiting for treatment were specific manifesto commitments by the Labour party, and the government was not satisfied that the inherited arrangements were adequate to allow it to fulfil its promises. The internal market was dismantled and new institutional arrangements established. As the NHS Plan (2000) said:

> Competition between hospitals was a weak lever for improvement, because most areas were only served by one or two local general hospitals. Other methods of raising standards were ignored. The market ethos undermined teamwork between professionals and organisations vital to patient-centred care. And it hampered planning across the NHS as a whole, leading to cuts in nurse training and a stalled hospital building programme.[10]

The new arrangements replaced the market with an attempt at centralization in which the 'centre' would 'set standards, monitor performance, put in place a proper system of inspection, provide back up to assist the modernisation of the service and, where necessary, correct failure.' (para 6.6) Underneath the NHS Executive and its regional offices were the Health Authorities which, together with the local authorities, were responsible for setting the health targets for their area. NHS Trusts, including Primary Care Trusts, ran services, whether in hospitals or in the community. Services were commissioned by Primary Care Groups which made 'commissioning plans' but did not organize competitions or market mechanisms as they commissioned care from the Trusts and, in certain cases, from the private and voluntary sectors. This replaced the system of GP fundholding. The other organizational innovation was the establishment of the National Institute for Clinical Excellence whose job is to set national guidelines for prescribing and treatment. Its principle is 'evidence-based treatment', which is interpreted as treatment based on nationally collected evidence about 'what works'. These changes were introduced early, following a White Paper called *The New NHS*.[11] While the internal market and competition were abandoned, the changes did not reverse the decision to separate the functions of commissioning and providing services, with budgets allocated to the commissioners. This was one of the most significant of the previous changes as it aimed to change the balance of power away from the service providers. The power shift was not as great as it might seem because the service commissioners are dependent on the providers for the services they fund, unless there is spare capacity and competitors within reasonable distance.

The changes were not enough to solve the political problem that the NHS was causing the government, expressed in the size of waiting lists and time spent on them and in a general feeling of crisis and under-investment. The main new solution was to commit more money and aim to increase the amount spent on health care to a proportion of the national product closer to the European average. The problem of the backlog of hospital and clinic building and maintenance was to be solved through extensive use of the Private Finance Initiative. Neither of these measures could produce immediate results. Health care professionals have long training periods, and instant staff increases can be achieved only by importing qualified staff, a solution that was tried. A lasting solution to a shortage of staff could only come from growing the medical schools and other training and paying staff enough to keep them in the service and in the United Kingdom. The building programme got underway but not without controversy, as we shall see in Chapter 11, because of the additional costs involved in providing a profit for the PFI partners.

Apart from the financial solutions, the institutional arrangements replaced the market but continued with a series of targets, national standards, service frameworks and a system of inspection and monitoring with attached incentives. The Commission for Health Improvement was expanded and all parts of the NHS were classified as green, yellow, or red, with organizations that achieve green status having easier access to cash for investment and a light touch inspection. While this was initially a very centralized system, the ambition was eventually to devolve performance management to Health Authorities, provided that they achieved 'green' status.

The new arrangements, as with so many other changes, were announced as 'modernization' and indeed one of the new bodies was called the Modernisation Agency whose job is to help service providers to redesign their service access arrangements. The 2000 White Paper, *Modernising the NHS*, claimed that the organizational form and management methods were rooted in their 1946 origins, despite the extensive reorganizations and system changes that were put in place during the previous twenty years, with planning, targets, general management, the internal market, the switch of budgets from providers to commissioners. It was as if 'modernization' was an absolute term in the sense that organizations and services are either modern or not. For practitioners, it was just another set of institutional arrangements in a long series of attempts at change.

The King's Fund believed that the NHS Plan marked a fundamental change in the nature of the NHS:

> The NHS Plan signalled significant reform. The Government has set out a new vision of the NHS where instead of being a monolithic structure that both commissions and provides care, is to be a set of rights to treatment, at specified and assured standards, from a widening base of diverse suppliers, public and private ... This is an NHS that Aneurin Bevan, its Labour founder, would struggle to recognise.[12]

Shifting the Balance of Power

Shifting the Balance of Power was the title of the 2001 White Paper that created the Primary Care Trusts that took on the function of the health authorities as the conduit for about 80% of the NHS budget. Above them, 28 Strategic Health

Authorities[13] act as the agents of the Department of Health in controlling the PCTs. After these structural changes were made, in 2004 the process of giving patients choice of health care provider was started. By the beginning of 2006 the NHS had introduced 'Choose and Book', a system under which patients, with their general practitioners, get to choose among four or more providers for their secondary health care. Meanwhile a new funding régime was introduced, called 'Payment by Results'. This was not an accurate title, since the new system introduced payment not by results, but by the volume of activity at a nationally agreed tariff. The tariff is based on average costs, modified slightly to take account of local circumstances. The idea behind the change in the payment system is that since service providers get paid according to their level of activity, they have incentive to do more work. Purchasers faced with choices at fixed prices can choose where to get treatment on the criteria of convenience and quality, subject to adequate information about these.

Patricia Hewitt, Secretary of State for Health, said that the new arrangements were not a market, especially because they did not involve price competition:

> We are often accused of introducing a 'market' into the NHS. But although I have described, very fully and I am afraid at some length, the changes we are making, I have not once used the word 'market'.
>
> I do not believe that we are turning the NHS into a market, and nor do I think that we should. Indeed, it would be a pretty odd kind of market where the user cannot pay and the providers cannot compete on price.
>
> Yes, we are giving patients and users more choice. Yes, we are giving providers more freedom to innovate and, where it is appropriate, to compete against each other. And where we mean 'competition', we should say so, instead of pretending that 'contestability' is something different. Yes, money will follow the patient. But why should choice, innovation, competition and financial discipline be confined to private markets? Why should the use of the private sector, when it gives us new hospitals, when it benefits patients and the public, have to mean 'privatisation'?
>
> What we are creating – not only in health and social care, but in education and many other public goods – are not markets, but modern public services. And I believe we do ourselves a disservice when we use the jargon of markets, instead of coming back to our values, the values of public service, and the goals we seek to achieve on behalf of all those we represent.[14]

Whether the system should be called a market or not, the combined results of these changes caused some stress to the funding system. Under the previous régime spending by purchasers was more predictable: they had block contracts with hospitals and other providers at a predictable volume and cost. The new arrangements fixed prices but made volumes unpredictable, thus increasing the risk to the PCTs of running out of budget and the risk to Trusts of failing to collect enough revenues to cover their costs. The Audit Commission reported:

As commissioners, PCTs face major risks, since they are committed to pay for work at a nationally set price, but have limited influence over volumes. Providers face greater financial exposure as a result of changes in demand and activity levels. They need to be much more aware of their costs in relation to the national price. Those that are relatively high cost face a rigorous cost improvement agenda in order to be financially viable in the new environment.[15]

Trusts operating at or below the average costs implied by the tariffs, and getting sufficient volumes of work, could operate at a surplus. All these changes took place while the level of spending was increasing quickly.

At the same time as the new funding arrangements were introduced, there were two other major changes to the NHS in England. There was yet another White Paper (*Our Health, Our Care, Our Say*) that paved the way for more contracting out for PCTs and encouraged private and 'social enterprise' bodies to take the provision of health care away from the PCTs. At the same time, yet another reorganization was proposed, reducing the number of Strategic Health Authorities and PCTs and making them co-terminous with the local authority tier responsible for adult care services. These changes were introduced just as the levels of pay in the NHS were restructured and increased under another initiative, 'Agenda for Change'. This was a job evaluation solution to the problem of equal pay for equivalent work in the NHS, especially the disparity between men's and women's pay for equivalent work. It also allowed a general increase in pay for most staff in occupations that were to expand in numbers.

During fiscal year 2005–6 the financial system became unstable, as some Trusts overspent their budgets, up to a total of about £1 billion[16], while others underspent, to a total of about £300 million. The net effect of the two was a deficit in the NHS budget as a whole of just less than 1%. The old problem of hospitals stopping work to save costs towards the end of the financial year was back: the 'payment by results' régime made it necessary for the 'failures' to stop work, or reduce costs. Early evaluation of the scheme suggested that there was not much impact on the volume of work that could be attributed to the new arrangements.[17] In fact 'Non-elective activity increased at a significantly higher rate for NHS trusts that were not operating under payment by results ... than for foundation trusts [that were].'[18]

The quest for greater autonomy for managers resulted in the establishment of 'NHS Foundation Trusts', a scheme under which NHS Trusts could opt to become 'public benefit corporations', with locally selected Boards and a more independent management régime. A Pamphlet about the scheme claimed that the trusts were central to its management strategy:

NHS Foundation Trusts will be at the cutting edge of the Government's commitment to devolution and decentralisation in the public services. They will not be subject to direction from Whitehall. Local managers and staff working with local people – rather than remote civil servants – will have the freedom to innovate and develop services tailored to the particular needs of their local communities.[19]

The freedom includes a less tight financial control from the Treasury, and governance arrangements that emphasize local appointments. They would still, of course, be subject to national standards and the national prices set through Payment by Results.

Private health care

There are two sets of providers of private health care: private and charity hospitals and private wards and wings in the NHS hospitals. People pay for private care either through individual or employee insurance policies or with cash. In 1996, about 6 million people were covered by private health insurance, or 11% of the population. By 2000 the proportion had grown slightly to 12.3%. Of these, about one third were individually insured and the rest were covered by company schemes. Not all those insured were covered for all possible health treatments, but 20% of elective surgery was done privately.

While the proportion of the population covered by private health insurance has grown slightly, the capacity of the private sector, as measured by available beds, is shrinking. The other private provision is in NHS hospitals, where the number of beds in dedicated private units is 1400.[20] Spending on private health care is just under £15 billion, compared with NHS spending of around £70 billion. In certain sectors the private provision is important. For example, there are 70 independent mental health hospitals, providing half the national capacity of medium-secure accommodation for the mentally ill.

The doctors who work in the private sector also mainly have jobs in the NHS. They are paid by the operation in their private capacity and may earn two or three times their NHS salaries by doing so. For managers, this sort of competition produces different problems from simply managing the service: they have to attract insurers by offering high quality at a competitive price; they have to attract insured patients by a level of 'hotel' facilities and speed which matches those of the private hospitals. They also have to offer consultants and other specialists enough money to persuade them to do the extra, private work.

One of the ways in which the Labour government tried to control the consultants who work in the private sector as well as the NHS was to specify the number of hours that NHS consultants must work for the NHS before going off to their private practices. New arrangements for clinical governance were designed to hold managers responsible for the doctors they hire, rather than being protected by doctors' clinical independence. Together these are the main means to solve the problem that has indeed been apparent since the establishment of the NHS, that of how to control the clinicians, especially the doctors.

The Labour governments have been willing to use the private sector, either contracting out items such as psychiatric services and termination of pregnancy or using private provision for waiting-list initiatives and encouraging the development of private treatment centres.[21] The government came increasingly to the view that the mixed economy is appropriate in health care and agreed a 'concordat' with the private sector in 2000. Private diagnostic and treatment centres were set up in an attempt to increase capacity, along with encouragement of the use of the private sector by PCTs. By the third Labour government, a mixed economy of health care, based on competition, was at the heart of health policy.

Implications for managers

There are three main implications for managers of these changes. Competitive behaviour is dealt with as a special topic in Chapter 9, but clearly managers have to analyse the nature of their competitive environment, assess how the competition is being organized and behave accordingly. With the internal market resurrected, managers need to sharpen up their cost control and their management of capacity, in order to avoid deficits.

One result is that the relationship between managers and professionals changes. All previous attempts at imposing management on the NHS since 1983 were diluted by the power of doctors, especially their power to commit beds and therefore other resources. The contractual régime meant that their interest was in performing the sort of work and in the volumes that would generate revenue for their hospital. Doctors became more involved in managing this process, through mechanisms such as clinical directorates and in co-operating with general managers and finance directors for whom the business side of the NHS is important and who previously had been considered inferior and irrelevant to the real task of treating individual patients.

A third result of the allocation of budgets to commissioners is the concentration on volume and unit costs. Information systems have been improved to comply with the need to count activity to claim payment, and have allowed managers and medical professionals to be clearer about how much work they do and what it costs. This process itself was not cheap, doubling the number of administrative and clerical staff. The abandonment of the internal market removes some of the need for clerical effort in writing contracts, administering transactions and measuring all the services being bought and sold. The inspection and monitoring system put in its place, however, also requires a good deal of administrative and clerical effort.

Community care

'Community care' is a term normally used to describe a range of personalized services, for example social work, home help, occupational therapy, residential care and day care support, provided to people in their own homes in order to sustain their independence with a reasonable quality of life. These services are usually the responsibility of local authorities working in partnership with family doctors and other community health services.

Older people

Over 75% of community care funds are deployed to meeting the needs of older people, who form the largest client group in this category. Before April 1993, elderly people who wanted to live in an elderly persons' home could do so and have their rent and other costs funded by the Department of Social Security. This right had been established in 1980 in the Supplementary Benefit Regulations and was exercised by a large number of people. Private and voluntary-sector residential homes expanded to accommodate the demand and to replace the local authority homes that were either closed or transferred out of local authority ownership. This policy was an expensive open-ended commitment: once someone decided to enter an elderly persons' home, the state was committed to pay for them for the whole of their stay there. The NHS and Community Care Act of 1990, among other things, closed the commitment and made access to services by older people subject to an assessment of need and a means test. From April 1993, the budget for old people's care was transferred from the Department of Social Security to local authority social services departments, who were then responsible for deciding whether individuals were entitled to help as a result of some dependency. If they were entitled, an individual care plan was drawn up following a 'needs assessment', which might enable the person to stay at home or might allocate them to a residential or nursing home. Figure 4.1 shows the impact of this policy on the number of local authority beds in homes for elderly people and the slowing of the growth of private residential beds in the independent sector.

The funds for these services were absorbed into local authority social services budgets, where they had to compete with demands from other services such as education or road building. The Audit Commission[22] (1994) reported that while some authorities faced budget problems, most were managing to stay within their budget. Those authorities which later faced difficulties suffered from an accumulation of commitments: as people were allocated places in residential care or care at home, the authority was committed to that expenditure for as long as that person remained in need:

> Authorities face hard choices. It is also particularly worrying that some authorities audited were unable to assemble the sort of information needed to check the financial implications of placements already made ... rates are actually rising through a combination of rising demand from within the community and increasing pressure from hospitals. (p. 19)

The combination of accumulated commitments, increasing expectations from older people themselves, and from hospitals wishing to reduce both their long-term care

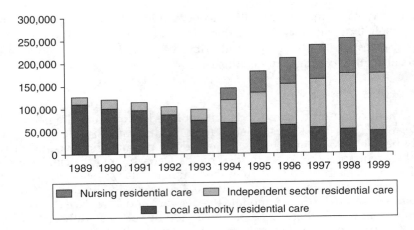

Figure 4.1   Adults in local authority care

Source: Chief Inspector, Social Services Inspectorate (1999–2000), Figure 2.5.

liabilities and the time periods required by people needing in-patient treatment, put serious pressure on community care budgets. Authorities had constantly to constrain their eligibility criteria, offering help only to those in greatest need.

The purposes of the rationing process were to target the care available on those in greatest need and to try to help people to stay in their own homes as long as possible. Table 4.1 shows a reduction in the numbers of people receiving home care since 1993, despite an increase in the proportion of people getting 'intensive' home care, the people in greatest need of help. This indicates that the home care service is being targeted at the most needy group. However, Table 4.1 also shows the rapid growth in the numbers of people supported in residential and nursing homes in the first five years of the new policy.

The White Paper *Modernising Social Services* drew attention to these trends, criticized the way in which care services are allocated and recognized that many people are excluded from services:

> Eligibility criteria are getting ever tighter and are excluding more and more people who would benefit from help but who do not come into the most dependent categories. (para 2.3)

Of course, that is what targeting intended, to allocate services to those in greatest need. The White Paper re-stated what councillors had been saying since 1993, that it is unpopular to withdraw services from a large number of people to make more intensive services available to a smaller number.

The solutions proposed in the White Paper were better reviews of individual cases, more joint working between health and social services and greater use of

Table 4.1   *Adults receiving personal social services, England*

	1993–94	1994–95	1995–96	1996–97	1997–98	1998–99
Households receiving home care	514,600	538,900	512,400	491,100	479,100	447,200
Of whom, % receiving intensive home care	12%	15%	21%	25%	28%	31%
People aged 65 or over in residential care	89,827	103,120	116,117	129,358	135,271	137,779
People aged 65 or over in nursing care	23,113	39,874	52,845	60,787	67,451	67,548

Source: Chief Inspector, Social Services Inspectorate (1999–2000)
Appendix A, p.101

direct payments to help people look after themselves. The newly merged inspectorate for social services, the Commission for Social Care Inspection (CSCI), made an assessment of the impact of these arrangements in 2005.[23] Its judgement was that services had improved but that the strict rationing and assessment dominated the system: 'People wait too long to be assessed, and often they receive services that do not entirely fit their needs ... Many people, both adults and children, just do not qualify for services because of the high thresholds which give access to them.' (p. 1) Of course, wherever a rationing threshold is set, some people will fall below it, but the increase in spending (13.4% in real terms between 2001–2 and 2003–4) was not enough to make professionals feel comfortable with the decisions that they have to make. The CSCI reported 'continuing chronic difficulties in recruitment and retention, endemic throughout the whole social care sector.' (p. 3)

Statistics from 2005 show that home care provision peaked at 497,000 people aged 65+ in England in 2002–3, falling to 483,000 in 2004–5. Similar falls in numbers occurred in residential care, both private and local authority.[24] Table 4.2 shows the mix of care packages offered in 2004–05. It shows that a large majority of people receiving care get community-based services and half of those get some level of home care. In residential care, there are now five times as many people in private residential care as in local authority-staffed care homes. Of the 1.2 million people receiving care, only 24,000 were receiving direct payments to organize their own care provision.

Table 4.2 *Community Care Services. Estimated number of clients receiving services during the year by service type and age, 2004–2005.*

	2004–5, thousands, England		
	All ages	18–64	65+
Total number of clients	1720	492	1228
Community-based service	1470	445	1025
Day care	242	107	135
Meals	176	11	165
Home care	583	100	483
Overnight respite, not client's home	71	21	50
Short term residential, not respite	68	13	55
Direct payments	24	17	7
Professional support	420	204	216
Transport	63	24	39
Equipment and adaptations	478	102	376
Other	94	36	58
Residential care			
Independent sector	206	49	157
LA staffed residential	39	6	33
Nursing care	112	11	101

Source: Office for National Statistics, 2006, Table 5

Mental health

Since the late 1950s mental health policy has been designed to transfer mentally ill people from large mental institutions of about 1,000 beds into 'care in the community', which may include domestic-like 'group homes' for three or four people supervised by visiting social workers and community psychiatric nurses or therapeutic residential care units for between 12 and 15 people with professional staff on-site.

It has been argued by some that the policy has not been supported by sufficient resources for the care required in the community. The Health Select Committee (1994) expressed concern about the uneven success of the policy, especially the fact that minimum levels of provision had not been established and the low priority given to mental health services by health purchasers. One source of concern was the publicized growth of attacks, murders and suicides by people with mental illness who were not in secure accommodation, either prison or a special hospital.[25] In September 1994 the Royal College of Psychiatrists reported that Inner London mental health units were operating over their capacity and turning patients away.

It became clear that the policy of transferring people from mental hospitals to the community was not without problems generated by lack of resources and the difficulty of achieving co-ordination between different mental health professionals and their employing agencies. Part of the problem was caused by a large increase in the number of people suffering from mental illness transferred from prison to hospital, from 227 in 1984 to 1018 in 1994.[26] One solution was to introduce supervised discharge of certain categories of people with mental illness, whereby a worker would be assigned to each patient discharged. Even so, many such 'key workers' claimed to have too many people to oversee properly.

There was some good collaborative work among the various agencies involved in the process of discharging people with mental health problems from hospital to the community, but there remains a problem of resources and a clear idea about which agency is responsible for the people discharged and the services they need to survive.

A series of scandals occurred involving people with mental illness, whose supervision was inadequate, committing violent crimes. The various reports repeated the analysis of poor co-ordination and lack of accountability. During 1999 the government proposed a change in the 1983 Mental Health Act, especially the introduction of compulsory treatment. The changes involve small changes in the process of compelling people with mental disorders to accept a compulsory assessment, in exchange for an undertaking that appropriate treatment will be made available whether in hospital or at home. The changes included a new definition of one type of mentally ill person, 'Dangerous Person with Severe Personality Disorder'. Once defined as such, people with this 'condition' could be detained before committing any offence.

Implications for managers

There were two main implications for managers in community care. Those running statutory services increasingly had to compete with the private and voluntary sectors, as purchasers looked for value for money for their budget allocations. Purchasers of services had to learn how to contract with other agencies and companies and to stimulate the provision of services, while working within a strict rationing régime. For some the new activities contradicted their professional values, which made them feel uneasy about having to be gatekeepers for services. These values, combined sometimes with poor management information systems, allowed many local authority community care budgets to be overspent.

The new arrangements caused many social services departments to reorganize. Because services had to be commissioned partly from the independent sector and because in-house services were in effect in competition with the independent sector, many social services departments divided themselves into two parts. One part was responsible for assessing needs and commissioning services. The other was responsible for running services, such as a dwindling number of residential homes, home care services and day centres. The rationale behind this was that the former group would 'purchase' services from the latter, thus establishing an internal market. While we will see the implications of this sort of arrangement in more detail in Chapter 9, this change was similar to those in other parts of the public sector: central government direction combined with devolved accountability for services and the establishment of market-type relationships. However, underlying the community care changes was a desire to cash-limit an apparently open-ended commitment to spending on older people and to reduce the number of people in mental institutions.

Children

One side-effect of the Community Care changes was the reversal of the trend towards 'generic' social work through which integrated teams carried out social work functions for all the people in an area. Specialization returned, along with the separation of assessment of people's needs and rationing the resources from the provision of care services. One specialism that re-emerged was children's services, on which many social services departments had originally been founded.

Improving the quality of life for children was part of the Labour government's policy towards social exclusion. Over one in five children live in poverty, according to the government's definition, and 333,000 are in care[27] under the Children Act; a further 1.5 million get some social care services each year. Some of the income support measures we saw above were designed specifically to help poor children, as was a programme for pre-school children called 'Sure Start'.

Children's services were subject to periodic scandals and evidence of poor services, resulting in efforts to improve the quality of services culminating, in England, in a programme of efforts under the heading 'Quality Protects' from 1998. The programme aimed to improve the procedures by which children's services were delivered. An easier and clearer choice was to be offered among fostering, adoption and residential services. Processes of assessment, care planning and record keeping were to be improved, not only to improve service standards but also to avoid the mistakes reported in repeated child care disasters. Management Information Systems and Quality Assurance procedures were also to be improved or put in place. Special attention was to be paid to listening to the children being looked after and to providing support to children after they left care. Authorities were also asked to improve the education and health provision to children in care. To help all this, a Special Grant was established, of £885 million over five years.

A programme of inspections by the Social Services Inspectorate was set up to monitor progress on Quality Protects. After two years, progress on process improvements was said to be encouraging but it was not yet possible to demonstrate that the outcomes for children were any better: 'many of the achievements this year are still concerned with *process*, and are hard to translate directly into better lives for children. Few councils have yet reached the point of *both* being able to identify, implement and monitor a strategy for change, *and* then demonstrate the effect of that change in terms of outcomes.'[28] For managers, Quality Protects brought a tightening of procedures and an increase in record keeping. As CSCI reported,[29] 'Much of the improvement in council performance is in infrastructure, processes and managerial systems. Many of the improvements which people want to see in the quality of service they receive are proving slow to achieve.' (p. 1)

Child support

The Child Support Agency was separated from the rest of the social security system in April 1993. Its purpose was to assess the liability of 'non-resident' parents for maintenance, collect money from them and distribute it to the 'resident' parents. The Agency was one of the least successful elements of social policy, service delivery and, incidentally, of the application of information technology. The assessment of non-resident parents' finances and calculation of what they should pay their children always proved too difficult. By July 1994 only £15 million had been collected from an estimated 900,000 absent parents and in September came the first Chief Executive's resignation. The second resigned in 1996 when the backlog of unpaid maintenance topped £1 billion. In 1998 the Labour government pledged to simplify the system and buy new technology to make it all work smoothly. The new systems were finally delivered, two years late, in 2003. The backlog of 1.2 million cases could not be transferred to the new system. By November, only 4% of new applicants for child support had received any cash.

Targets were set for the number of assessments and their accuracy, and were consistently missed. The annual accounts were qualified every year. The 2004–5 accounts[30] showed that running costs for the year had been £325 million and that £603 million had been received from non-resident parents. The computer system had cost £456 million. After the resignation of yet another Chief Executive, the government announced, in February 2006, that the Agency and its system of child support would be replaced.

The CSA had many of the features of other aspects of the welfare system: targeted benefits, based on means-testing of the non-resident parent; an agency dedicated to a single task; outsourced computer system design and delivery; a system of annual performance targets and performance reporting; a single individual, the agency Chief Executive, responsible for delivery.

Education

Education was subject to all the sorts of reform which the Conservative governments promoted: competition among schools and colleges; centralization of control by ministers and ministries; decentralization of financial management; publication of performance standards and results; bringing professionals under control by national curriculum and national tests and through an inspection process; the introduction of appointed people to sit not just on boards of governors of schools and colleges but on a set of central institutions created by the Secretary of State for Education.

Although Margaret Thatcher had been Secretary of State for Education, education was apparently not a high priority of the early Thatcher governments. The main changes did not occur until 1988, nine years into the Thatcher period. The pace of change increased during the Major administrations, completing a transformation of the governance and management of education.

Labour made an election issue of educational standards. Its Secretary of State for Education and Employment, David Blunkett, had been the leader of Sheffield City Council and therefore had direct experience of local education authorities. With few exceptions they followed the lead of the Conservatives in their mistrust of local authorities to run an effective education service and their belief that teachers needed to be subjected to more control, inspection and incentives if they were to teach well.

Schools

School education in Britain is a centralized affair. Over 90% of pupils attend a state-run school and follow a national curriculum. Standards are set and monitored nationally and there are national standard attainment tests and public examinations. All teachers in state schools have to have Qualified Teacher Status. There are some schools that vary from the standard Comprehensive School system. Some secondary schools are allowed to select their pupils on educational merit and an interview with their parents, despite being state funded. There are over 500 'specialist' schools, comprehensives that follow the national curriculum while offering extra teaching in technology, languages, sports or arts. In addition, at the end of 2000, City Academies were announced, replacements mainly for inner city schools, whose buildings and equipment are funded partly through sponsorship by companies and voluntary organizations such as the Church of England. Specialist schools and city academies are all in inner city areas. The types of school that pupils attend in the United Kingdom are shown in Table 4.3.

Schools have boards of governors made up of parents, teachers and members of the local community. The governors are supposed to set the direction for the school, select the head teacher and make decisions on staffing and the use of the school's budget. Local Education Authorities have education departments that are responsible for a limited range of support functions, many of which are provided to schools in competition with other service providers. The LEAs are in principle responsible for the educational standards in their area and for the provision of school places but their powers and budgets were curtailed during the Conservative governments.

The 1980 Education Act stopped education authorities from restricting pupils to the secondary schools in their area. While apparently minor, in practice this change started the process of allowing parents and pupils to choose their school and, perhaps more significantly, of allowing schools to choose their pupils. Comprehensive education was not favoured by a government which believed in

Table 4.3   School pupils by type of school, United Kingdom, Thousands

	1970/71	1980/81	1990/91	2000/01	2003/04	2004/05
Public sector schools						
Nursery	50	89	105	152	150	142
Primary	5,902	5,171	4,955	5,298	5,107	5,045
Secondary						
Comprehensive	1,313	3,730	2,925	3,340	3,456	3,457
Grammar	673	149	156	205	216	217
Modern	1,164	233	94	112	107	107
Other	403	434	298	260	235	220
All public sector schools	9,507	9,806	8,533	9,367	9,271	9,189
Non-maintained schools	621	619	613	626	654	652
Special schools	103	148	114	113	109	107
Pupil referral units	–	–	–	10	13	15
All schools	10,230	10,572	9,250	10,116	10,048	9,963

Source: Social Trends 36 2006 Table 3.2

individualism and the attainment of privilege through ability. The establishment of compulsory boards of governors for schools was a prelude to the process of handing control over state institutions to appointed bodies and taking them away from both the professionals and the elected local authorities. This process was completed by the Education Reform Act 1988, which made the management of schools more independent of the local authorities, both by transferring financial management to schools and by allowing them to opt out completely from local authority control. Both these measures appeared to give the schools more autonomy, at least from their local authority.

While the introduction of this legislation was accompanied by rhetoric about autonomy and self-management, the Act increased central government control. A national curriculum was introduced, to be overseen by a new body, the National Curriculum Council (NCC). National testing was also introduced, again overseen by a national body, the Schools Examination and Assessment Council (SEAC).

Some of these measures were further strengthened in the 1993 Education Act, which took more steps to encourage schools to opt out of their education authorities. Of course, those schools which decided to leave the control of their education authorities had to have their budgets allocated centrally so a national funding body, the Funding Agency for Schools, was established. At the same time the NCC and the SEAC were combined into a new central body, the School Curriculum and Assessment Authority (SCAA) later replaced by the Qualifications and Curriculum Authority.

These changes had a big impact on the management of the education system. The local education authorities previously had a great deal of influence and direct control over what happened in schools. They planned the distribution of schools in their areas, appointed headteachers and had a large say in curriculum and teaching methods. After the 1992 changes their powers were greatly reduced. Governing bodies appointed heads, schools ran their own budgets and those schools which opted for grant-maintained status were completely independent. Those functions through which the education authorities exercised influence, such as in-service training for teachers, inspection, curriculum development, were subject to the market. Local authorities had to allocate a small fixed proportion of their budgets for education authority functions, the rest being allocated to the schools. If the authorities wanted to provide services for schools whose costs exceeded the fixed proportion of the budget, they had to be paid for out of school budgets. Schools were free to choose from whom to buy support services and the educational professionals changed from being powerful superiors to competitive service providers.

In many cases the education authorities had to reduce their staffing levels to match the amount of budget they were allowed to retain and their success in competing to supply services to schools. The changes also increased the power and responsibility of headteachers. While governing bodies were nominally more powerful, in practice the headteachers gained power through their expertise and knowledge and the fact that they were full-time.

Heads had to use their new authority, in part, to ensure the survival of their schools. Competition for resources meant competition for pupils. In areas where there is spare capacity in the number of places, there is competition for numbers. In areas in which schools are close to each other, there is competition to attract those pupils who will achieve the best examination results. The publication of the proportion of pupils who achieve five GCSE grades C and above makes some schools look better than others. Competition is based on a variety of factors: school discipline, uniforms, the fact that a school is single-sex as well as its examination result scores.

As in all markets, the market for pupils produces winners and losers. Schools with good results are able to attract pupils who will achieve good results. The reverse is true for the rest: bad results deter parents. In practice, much of the differentiation between schools is based on the class background of their pupils. There is a high correlation between examination results and social class. Attracting successful pupils means, in effect, attracting middle-class parents. Although schools are allowed to select only 10% of their pupils, priority can be given to siblings of existing pupils. In any case, although catchment areas are no longer in force, there are practical limits to the distances pupils can travel. While comprehensive schools were segregated according to geography, the current system exaggerates the differences.

The 1992 White Paper *Choice and Diversity: A New Framework for Schools* promoted such diversity. It advocated the creation of different schools for different sorts of pupils: academic schools for those of more academic ability and practical schools for the rest. There was an experiment with a new sort of school, the City Technology College, which would be technically well equipped and sponsored by industry. While a few of these were established, industry was, in general, reluctant to fund education.

There was not a complete victory for the government in these changes. While mechanisms were established to run the whole of the secondary school system from the Department for Education and the quangos it established, the people who staff the educational system were not prepared simply to submit to central government changes. Despite the financial inducements for schools to opt out of local authority control and become grant maintained, fewer than 1000 schools voted to do so, about a quarter of the secondary schools in England and Wales. The rest decided to maintain their links with their education authority, albeit within a new régime which gave them more financial and managerial autonomy. One reason for this is that many headteachers see themselves as part of a local education system, rather than a small enterprise in the education business. They respect the support they receive from the education authority and the stability provided by a system which manages through planning, to the limited extent that the education authorities can in the current system. Another reason may be the difficulty which schools found in finding members of governing bodies who were willing to volunteer enough time to run their schools. Just as business largely refused to fund schools through the City Technology College initiative, individual people showed unwillingness to manage their local schools.

The innovations introduced by the Labour government from 1997 were based on many of the same principles as the previous government's. Selectivity rather than universality and uniformity; a belief in the mixed economy; a mixture of central control and individual accountability; an element of competition for funds. They also included the newer principles identified at the beginning of this chapter: a desire to exercise central control over individual organizations, in this case schools; an eclectic attitude to ownership; a belief in 'modernization'.

The system established by Conservative governments was largely preserved by the Labour administration. Selection was upheld, although selective schools could hold a ballot among their pupils' parents about whether to continue selection. A variety of schools was maintained, whether specialist schools or the old state-funded grammar schools, and more schools were encouraged to become specialized. Grant Maintained Schools lost their privileges in 1999 on the grounds that their status gave an unfair advantage to their pupils. This decision was in effect reversed by the 2006 Education and Inspections Act.

The Labour governments introduced some managerial innovations to the school system. Some were concerned with the general level of standards while others were about what to do about schools that were doing very badly. On general standards the national scheme of testing pupils and publishing the results school by school was extended down the age range. A new pay and performance régime was introduced from September 2000, after much opposition from the teachers' unions, under which teachers assessed as reaching a threshold of competence would get extra pay and the chance to get on a pay scale with a higher top end.

By January 2001, 650 schools had been declared as 'failing' by the Office for Standards in Education. Failing is defined as 'failing to give its pupils an acceptable standard of education'. The 'Special Measures' that result include an Action Plan to be approved and monitored by the Secretary of State for Education, through the inspectorate. Of schools classed as failing, 546 were declared successfully saved from failure within two years by a variety of management interventions and staff changes; 84 were closed. Twenty were given a 'fresh start' under new leadership and a lot of publicity for the newly appointed 'superheads', but without much success.

A similar scheme applied to LEAs. If they were declared as 'failing' they could be prescribed a rescue package or could be handed over to private managers to run. Some authorities decided to contract out the management of their LEA services before being forced to by the government.

As well as these measures for individual schools and LEAs, groups of schools in deprived areas could be declared an Education Action Zone, of which 99 were established between 1998 and 2001. Schools in the zones would get extra funding and special help and were supposed to attract sponsorship from the private sector, amounting to about 10% of the government funding.

Funding for all schools was also increased, as we saw in Chapter 3. Some of the capital funding was given a special label, such as the New Deal for Schools in 1997, or Building for the Future, but the funding was a necessary response to the long backlog of repairs and renewals and to the need for the provision of new school places.

As for other parts of the public sector, Prime Minister Blair called for changes in the education system. A typical remark came in a speech at Cranfield School of Management in September 2000:

> We want first-rate secondary education for all, with the excellence and flexi-
> bility within every school to make the most of every pupil. Let's be clear what
> this means. It means big change from the old comprehensive model. Modern
> comprehensives should be as dedicated as any private school or old gram-
> mar school to high achievement for the most able.

After over two years in government, after an election in which 'education, educa-tion, education' had been declared as the three main priorities, this showed a degree of frustration with the public education system and the changes the gov-ernment had so far made. One of the solutions was to make, eventually, all schools into 'specialist schools', emphasizing some aspect of the curriculum.

'Academy' schools started to be opened in 2002 and the government planned to open 200 by 2010. Academies were located in deprived areas, often on the site of schools that had previously performed badly. Sponsors were sought who, in exchange for a £2 million contribution to the capital costs, could nominate the board and the senior staff and have an influence on the curriculum and 'ethos' of the schools. All other capital costs and running costs were to be contributed by the normal school funding mechanism. The start-up costs of the schools ranged from £18 million to £37 million. Of the 27 Academies that had opened by 2006, seven were sponsored by Churches (the Church Schools Company or Roman Catholic Dioceses), the Corporation of London and two Livery Companies, the Haberdashers and the Mercers, Amey plc,[31] Bristol City Football Club and a col-lection of rich individuals. One such individual, Peter Vardy, sponsored three Academies through his Emmanuel Schools Foundation with fundamentalist Christian beliefs.

There was more reform to come. In 2006 the government enacted the Education and Inspections Bill through which 'trust schools' were established, based on sim-ilar principles to the Academies, but without the sponsorship. These were designed to 'give schools access to the freedoms enjoyed by other foundation schools – owning their own assets, employing their own staff … and setting their own admission arrangements.'[32] These were Grant Maintained Schools by another name – the policy had taken 18 years to circle back to the 1988 Education Act. The 2006 Act was passed in the House of Commons only because of the support of the Conservative party.

Post-school education

Administrative changes were made to all those parts of education in the post-school years. In part these changes were a response, common in most European countries, to changes in the labour market. While employers were demanding better qualified workers, unemployment rates among school leavers increased from the early 1980s and accelerated during recessions. Increased participation rates in higher education were one answer to both of these problems. At the same time, the UK government was unwilling to continue to pay the same unit cost for the extra students as they were paying for the existing ones. The expansion was to take place without a proportionate increase in funding, resulting in a sharp drop in the amount of funding per student in further and higher education.

As well as these underlying considerations, the changes followed the familiar pattern. Local authority control, first of Polytechnics and then of Further Education and Teacher Training colleges, was to be replaced by rule by board. Both sets of institutions became corporate bodies (in 1989 and 1992 respectively). Funding arrangements were adjusted, to make student numbers a more important determinant of income, and the institutions then competed for students. The number of full-time students in further and higher education grew by 47% between 1990/91 and 1993/94 and a further 44% by 1998/99, and the number of part-time students by 8% and then by 70% by 1998/99. The rate of growth then slowed. The growth in higher education student numbers had been remarkable: undergraduate numbers grew by 260% and postgraduate by 500% in 25 years.

The competition process in the higher education sector increased when the polytechnics were allowed to become universities with degree-awarding status from 1992. The creation of corporate status took some institutions from the status of technical college to university in three years. Sometimes the development of the facilities did not match the change in status and activity, but that was not the purpose of the exercise: the changes successfully increased the proportion of the post-school population at university, a growth that continued into the new century.

As well as the competitive environment, changes in the post-school sector included the establishment of instruments of control: the funding arrangements imposed a planned system of student numbers and subjects, while inspection mechanisms for teaching and research give central leverage through direct intervention and financial inducements.

Outside the educational institutions, other changes have taken place. Training and Enterprise Councils (TECs), another set of quangos, were funded by government (through the departments of Education and Employment, Environment and Trade and Industry) to commission a variety of training, work experience and

Table 4.4 *Enrolments in further and higher education, United Kingdom, thousands*

	1980/81	1990/91	1993/94	1998/99	2003/4
Further education					
Full-time	350	480	738	1065	1080
Part-time	1321	1759	1756	2978	3770
Higher education					
Undergraduate					
Full-time	473	665	948	1127	1207
Part-time	247	342	471	535	706
Postgraduate					
Full-time	62	84	116	117	221
Part-time	45	86	129	254	308

Sources: Social Trends 26, HMSO, 1996, Table 3.21, Social Trends 31, HMSO 2001, Table 3.15, Social Trends 35, 2005, Table 3.8

other activities aimed at creating an employable workforce and, to some extent, jobs for that workforce. They operated through an operating agreement and a funding agreement with the government, which set out in detail what they would do during the year. In turn the TECs entered contracts with service providers, including the state further education sector. This mode of control, from Ministry to TEC (itself a quango) to private and incorporated providers, was an ideal type of how the Conservative governments preferred to operate: appoint people you can trust (preferably from business) who are accountable to you, and establish funding and control mechanisms which enable you to determine what they do. Eventually the Labour government replaced the training functions of the TECs with a new arrangement, the Learning Skills Councils, that were set up under the Learning and Skills Act 2000. From April 2001 these new bodies also took over the functions of the Further Education Funding Council in allocating money to sixth forms and further education colleges, with a budget of £6 billion.

Early in its period of office, the Labour government commissioned Sir Ron Dearing to look into funding and other issues for higher education. It accepted his recommendation that fees be charged for all higher education and that the systems of quality and other controls be further strengthened. The Scottish Parliament did not accept that fees should be charged for higher education, and abolished fees in Scotland.

Implications for managers

Managers of educational institutions are in an increasingly competitive environment, for students and pupils and for resources. More financial independence means that managers have the responsibility for keeping costs down, by whatever means are available. Local discretion leads to local bargaining and decisions about staff recruitment and retention. For example, half of further education colleges now negotiate their staff terms and conditions of employment.

Competition tends to reduce collaboration. In the secondary education sector, for example, headteachers are unwilling to share good practice developments and to share in-service training for fear of giving their neighbouring schools a competitive advantage. In higher education, the competition for research funding led to a 'market' for researchers. Each institution is graded according to the quantity and quality of its research output. A transfer market for researchers developed so that research output looked better on the day on which the research assessment exercise was carried out. As well as the impact of competition and relative independence, there was a simultaneous decrease in local discretion, as more influence was wielded by the new bodies attached to the Department for Education and Employment, including resource allocation, curriculum content and inspection of standards. The Office for Standards in Education has claimed that the inspection régime has improved standards in schools. This has been at the cost of some stress to teachers in schools, called by one group of researchers 'pre-inspection panic and post-inspection blues'.[33] Snap inspections, with three days' notice, were partly designed to reduce the stress.

The main result for managers of the expansion in further and higher education is that they have to achieve two things: attract enough students to generate revenue and to increase productivity (measured in cost per student) of the staff in order to cope with the reduction in unit funding. Few people living in the United Kingdom can have missed the efforts made to achieve the first of these: universities even advertise with posters on buses and on television. The second objective has been achieved less visibly, with larger classes, more use of part-time and casual staff, and an increased workload for existing teachers. Local bargaining in further education has created a new set of negotiations on pay and hours of work. Fortunately for the managers, the over-supply of graduates has contained the pressure for pay rises from teachers and lecturers, although the National Association of Teachers in Further and Higher Education retained a national agreement in many colleges.

Housing

One of the main objectives of Conservative housing policy was to promote home ownership by allowing Council and Housing Association tenants the right to buy their house or flat, at a subsidized price: 1.5 million units were bought in this way, bringing owner occupation up to 69% of the housing stock in 1999. The other tenures were Social Housing, including Housing Associations and local authority and other public sector with 22%, and private rented 9%. The sale to tenants of municipal housing was the biggest of the privatizations and changed for ever the policy towards publicly owned housing. Whereas local authority housing was a

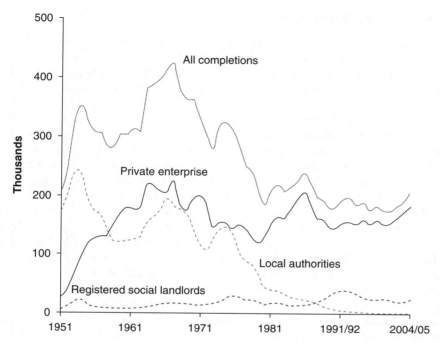

Figure 4.2   Housebuilding, completions by sector, United Kingdom, 1951–2004/5

Source: *Social Trends* 36, 2006, Figure 10.3

normal tenure for working people in the post-war period, the policy of privatization and reduction of the volume of construction made Council and Housing Association housing into 'social housing' available only for those with no alternative: new lettings by the 1990s were predominantly for poor people, either economically inactive or unemployed. In some areas, especially in the north of England, there are surpluses of social housing and estates have become 'difficult to let'.

Local authorities and Housing Associations

The policies have virtually stopped the construction of local authority homes for general use, almost all 'social housing' now being provided by the Registered Social Landlord (RSL) sector, as is shown in Figure 4.2, which also illustrates the dominance of private sector housebuilding in the last two decades.

Other forms of privatization

Another objective of government policy has been to transfer the management of the residual housing stock which local authorities own. Various schemes have been tried. Housing management was included in the compulsory competitive tendering régime. Local authority housing managers had to compete for the management contract of the authorities' houses if companies are prepared to bid for the work. As an alternative, the 'large scale voluntary transfer' was a way of councils transferring the management to private companies or housing associations, sometimes formed by existing managers. In many authorities, tenants now control the management of their estates, including maintenance and security.

Meanwhile, Housing Associations have become more reliant on private finance. The Housing Corporation, which provides funds to Housing Associations, used to provide 100% capital funding through the Housing Association Grant for house building or purchase, but now provides funding of 58 %, the rest made up by private borrowing, in line with other initiatives to introduce private finance into public spending. The flow of funds in these schemes is interesting: lettings are mainly to people in receipt of housing benefit, so the private investor or lender's risk is underwritten by the Department of Social Security's rent guarantee. The scheme does not transfer much risk to the private sector, but it does reduce the figure for public sector capital spending. The main foreseeable problem (apart from the difference in rates of interest) is that the right to buy for Housing Association tenants potentially removes a revenue stream to the private investor, as homes are removed from the rental stock. This is an example of the contradiction between individual choice and offering the private sector guaranteed return on its investment. In practice the private sector does not want to take the risk of investing in property which the tenants have the right to buy at a discount.

The Labour government maintained the overall policy of encouraging home ownership and trying to divest local authorities of their direct housing provision function. As in other sectors, the government recognized the huge backlog of housing repairs and maintenance in the residual public sector housing stock, which it put in the Green Paper at £19 billion. This was to be remedied, eventually, by an injection of cash and permissions to enter PFI schemes. It also increased the allocation of funds to the Housing Corporation to increase the scale of RSL building. In the event, PFI was not much used for housing renewal and repair. The stock transfers were funded by borrowings from financial institutions. As Peter Malpass said:

> At one level stock transfer can be understood as a massive re-mortgaging exercise. The organisation acquiring the stock has to arrange a loan both to buy the houses and fund the promised investment. The total amount raised for stock transfer in England between 1988/89 and 2002/3 was £11.8 billion, of which £5.5 billion was for purchase.[34]

As far as the management of public sector housing was concerned, the main policy was either to transfer management to RSLs or to persuade local authorities to set up 'arm's-length' companies through which to manage the housing stock. The White Paper said that the government would support the transfer of up to 200,000 homes each year from local authorities to RSLs.

Remaining housing problems

Replacement rates

Housing policy is not producing a balance between supply and demand, especially for social housing. In 1994 Ford and Wilcox[35] estimated that England required 120,000 new social rented houses per year. The 1995 White Paper showed that the government planned 70,000 new lettings in the social housing sector for England and Wales together, including letting made available by inducing people to move to the owner-occupied sector. The 2000 White Paper announced a doubling of the funds available to the Housing Corporation and extended their remit to include 'key worker housing' for public employees who could no longer afford to live in the areas in which they worked.

The Office of the Deputy Prime Minister commissioned another review of housing from Kate Barker, who reported in 2004.[36] The review found that house price inflation was caused by the lag between supply of houses and new household formation. New households are formed at about 179,000 per annum, while around 130,000 houses are built.[37] As prices rose, the supply of housing stayed constant. The government responded to the review by making a commitment to increase the rate of house building to 200,000 per year by 2016, increasing the provision of shared ownership housing and making more land and infrastructure available in areas of housing shortage, notably the south east of England.

'Ghettos'

The cumulative effect of the policy of increasing rents to cover costs, and the housing benefit régime being the main source of subsidy, results in fewer tenancies in the local authority and Housing Association sector being for working people. Social housing is increasingly available only to those for whom the state pays the rent. Prescott-Clarke et al. estimated[38] in 1994 that there are 240,000 new local authority lettings per year, or about 11% of the stock. They found that 66% of new tenants were not in work, including 64% of the under 35s and 51% of those aged 35–54. Half of new tenants had incomes of £75 per week or less and 60% of new tenants were in receipt of housing benefit.

Owner occupation is not a universal solution

Owner occupation makes owner occupiers vulnerable to changes in interest rates and entrants to the housing market vulnerable to the level of house prices. House price booms in the mid 1980s and again in the mid 1990s led to big, temporary increases in the proportion of incomes devoted to mortgage repayments. Recessions have led to repossessions of homes by lenders as people made unemployed are unable to meet their repayments. In areas of housing surpluses because of scarce job opportunities, previous council houses bought under the right to buy remain unsaleable.

One of the problems caused by the dependence on owner occupation as the main form of tenure and the overwhelming tenure of newly built housing is that there is a class of workers who cannot find anywhere affordable to live in prosperous areas. Many of these are public sector workers such as nurses, teachers, ambulance drivers and other essential staff. The problem was made worse by policies of selling off nurses' housing and replacing police housing with housing allowances. It remains to be seen whether 'key worker' housing will solve this problem.

Implications for managers

Some estates have become more difficult to manage. The implications for people working in housing is that the tenants are increasingly concentrated among poor people. Housing estates which are populated by people with low incomes have the problems associated with poverty, such as families breaking up and poor health. Once public housing becomes a residual function for people with nowhere else to go, its management becomes less of a housing management job and more of a social welfare and crisis intervention one.

Criminal justice

The Conservative governments frequently claimed that 'law and order' was a major priority. However, the volume of recorded crime increased during the period of Conservative rule. Figure 4.3 shows the increase in the number of offences recorded by the crime survey between 1981 and 1993, and its decline after 1995. Table 4.5 shows the trends in activity in the criminal justice system and the people employed to carry it out.

There have been many attempts to reform the main institutions of the criminal justice system: the police, courts, prisons and probation services. In each case there have been similar themes: a desire to increase central control and direction, especially by the Home Office; a desire to improve performance and increase efficiency. The approach has been similar to that used in other parts of the public sector. Management methods have included the establishment of performance targets and indicators, attempts to link pay to performance, standardization of work processes, removal of both local and professional autonomy and the introduction of competition. Although the organizations of the criminal justice system were relatively late in receiving the attention of the reformers, when it happened they were by no means immune from it. However, the target in this case was

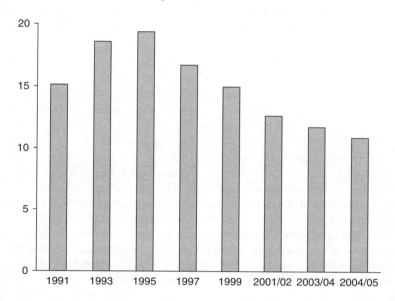

England & Wales Millions

Figure 4.3   Crimes identified in the British Crime Survey, England and Wales, 1991–2004/5

Source: Social Trends 36, 2006, Figure 9.1

Table 4.5   *Criminal justice, England and Wales: sentencing and staffing, thousands*

	1981	**1991**	**1999**
Probation orders	36	45	56
Community Service	28	42	51
Combination orders			21
Probation service employees	13	18	15
Prison service employees	24	33	43
Prison population	44	46	65
Police	120	127	124
Civilian staff in police service	28	46	53
Recorded crimes	2964	5276	5301

Source: *Social Trends* 31, 2001, Tables 9.3, 9.19 and 9.23

rather stronger and more able to resist change than some other groups. When magistrates and chief constables are asked to change, they can call on their connections with powerful interests.

There was one specific manifesto commitment about criminal justice: to reduce the time taken to bring prosecutions against young people. This involved speeding up court and reporting processes, rather than any change in policy about prosecutions.

Police

The Major government introduced fundamental changes to the management of the police service. There was frustration with the increasing level of crime, which increased spending on the police forces failed to stop. A review of the way in which police officers are managed and paid was called for in May 1992. The report[39] had many recommendations, including the abolition of certain management grades and the introduction of short-term contracts, reduction in salaries for new recruits and performance-related pay. The various organizations representing police personnel and police authorities organized protests and lobbies and managed to make the reforms less radical than proposed by Sheehy.[40]

However, changes were introduced, including changes in pay and grading. A pay system was introduced which linked pay to the appraisal scheme. Short-term contracts were introduced for chief constables. The idea was to avoid the 'job for life' attitude which was believed to detach police officers from any need to do well. Meanwhile the structure was flattened, with greater accountability for operational units, which became known as Basic Command Units.[41]

The Police and Magistrates' Courts Act 1994 changed the relationship between the Home Office and the police authorities and made the police authorities more independent of local authorities from April 1995. Announcing the proposed changes, the Home Secretary, Kenneth Clarke, said:

> Given that I provide 90% of the money on behalf of central government and that nine out of 10 people think that I run their local service, it is time that I held police authorities to account for performance and was then held to account by this House.[42]

The funding of the new authorities was subject to central cash limits, unlike the previous arrangement in which the government paid its share of the locally determined budget. While the original proposals were to fill the police authorities with nominees of the government, amendments to the legislation ensured the presence of local authority elected members on the authorities. The composition of the authorities is nine local councillors, three magistrates and five appointed members.

However, the new arrangements allowed the Home Secretary to set targets, implemented through a Local Policing Plan. As with other public sector changes, these contained a combination of increased local accountability, through plans, performance measures and reporting arrangements, and increased central control through target and priority setting and direct control over finance. The targets related to the Home Secretary's priorities were set out in the form of key objectives and performance indicators. They included: detection rates for violent crime and domestic burglaries; prevention of crimes which were a special local problem (performance indicators for this proved too difficult); visibility of the force to the public; response times to emergency calls.

The government pursued a model that was similar to its plans for the NHS. There would be national targets and indicators set centrally and monitored on behalf of the Home Secretary. Police authorities were to act as if they were purchasers of police services, specifying what should be achieved, rather than managing the operations. Basic Command Units would be the equivalent of Trusts, operating within guidelines but with some managerial freedom.

When the government proposed to reorganize the police service in England and Wales again, in 2006 after thirty years with the same 43 forces, the Basic Command Units were seen to be one of the successes and not liable to reorganization. The perceived problem was the need for 'a more efficient, integrated operating platform above BCU level.'[43] The solution was a proposal to create bigger forces by amalgamating the existing ones into units containing at least 4,000 police officers. Many of the existing forces, according to Her Majesty's Inspector of Constabulary, had poor capability in relation to terrorism, domestic extremism, serious and organised crime and public disorder. Reorganization was not the only answer to the problem of capability; processes needed to be redesigned as well, including intelligence and the performance framework in the priority areas of work.

Prisons

The prison population has grown rapidly over the past two decades and especially the last ten years. Figure 4.4 shows the total numbers of prisoners in Great Britain from 1980 to 2004.

The prison population slightly exceeds the official capacity. The Home Office 'Prison Population Brief' in June 2000 said that the England and Wales prison population exceeded the Certified Normal Accommodation level by 2%. This figure disguises the overcrowding that occurs in some prisons.

A report[44] published in 2000 on the management of prisons found much to be improved: standards needed to be established, accountabilities clarified, the volume of instructions from headquarters to prison governors reduced, financial management improved, personnel policies brought up to date. In fact there was hardly any area of prison management for which improvement was not recommended. This was despite at least ten years of efforts to reorganize and improve the management of prisons. The two mechanisms used were market testing, an attempt to test the Prison Service against the cost and quality of private

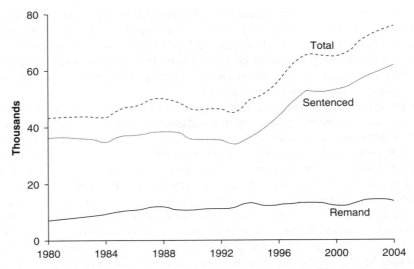

Figure 4.4   Average prison population, England and Wales, 1980–2004
Source: Social Trends 36, 2006, Table 9.21

organizations, and the establishment of the prison service as an 'Executive Agency', the managerial solution of preference of the Conservative governments.

'Market testing' of prisons was introduced to promote changes in management. The first to be market tested was Manchester Prison.[45] In 1990 there had been a riot in this prison, the consequence of which was a repair bill of £70 million and a damaged reputation for the establishment and the Prison Service in general. In 1992, following a report by the Inspector of Prisons identifying the cause of the riot, the management of the prison was put out to tender. The causes identified were many and complicated and included a problem of inadequate staffing. However, many of the problems were due to poor management, especially by middle managers.

Putting the prison out to tender produced quick changes in management and in the régime in the prison. The managers realized that it was not going to be credible to promise an improved régime in the bid document if such a régime could not be demonstrated in practice. The governor of Manchester Prison has argued that the process of redesigning the régime and the management arrangements was evolutionary rather than revolutionary.[46] He may have displayed undue modesty because the change in the relationship with the Prison Officers' Association was significant. The threat of losing the prison to the private sector provided an incentive to produce a better service. The success of the process led some to believe that market testing was just a mechanism to reduce the power of the Prison Officers' Association to resist operational changes. This was not to be the case, and the programme of competition continued. Private companies were invited to run new prisons without a counter bid from existing employees of the Prison Service. The first contract to manage a prison was awarded to Group 4 Remand Services Ltd for the management of the newly built Wolds Remand Prison which opened in April 1992 for 320 adult prisoners. The stated aim of this process was not to save money, rather to improve the régime. In the event the winning tender was not the lowest bid and the actual running costs exceeded the accepted tender because of mistakes and omissions in the tendering process.[47]

By 1996 there were six private and 140 public prisons in Great Britain; by 2003 the number of privately operated prisons had risen to ten. The plan was clearly to have a parallel private system alongside the public one, but expansion of the private sector has been slow: since the 1997 election the prison service has had some success in tendering, for example retaining Manchester prison and winning Blakenhurst, a prison that had been an exemplar of the successful private sector. The private operators could be used as a standard for the public prisons and a useful item in negotiation with prison officers and managers.

In addition to the privatization programme for the management of prisons, other elements of the service, such as the prison education service, drug and alcohol services, transport from court to prison, were subjected to competition from private companies and voluntary organizations.

HM Prison Service and the Scottish Prison Service were launched as Executive Agencies in April 1993. The new agencies were given the task of improving the way prisons were run. They produced corporate plans setting out their targets and proposals for meeting them, including ideas about devolving operational responsibilities to individual establishments, changing the pay and grading system and introducing competition for certain services.

As well as the structural changes and the introduction of companies into the management of prisons, the 1995 budget brought a budget cut to the Prison Service, at a time of increased prisoner numbers. Ironically, the private prisons were protected against both these changes, as their legally binding contracts guaranteed their income and prisoner numbers. Such pressures have shaken up the management of the Prison Service, but have not solved its problems. Recent inspectors' reports have indicated that some of the problems identified by Woolf persist, such as long hours in-cell, insufficient rehabilitation, work, counselling and education. The main response by the Labour government was to announce the biggest ever building programme, £660 millions for 16 new prisons over three years, through the Private Finance Initiative method.

Probation

The Probation Service has also been subject to policy and managerial changes. Since the Probation Rules of 1907 the ethos of the service was that it was to 'advise, assist and befriend' offenders. Probation work was based on social work ideas about intervening in the lives of offenders to help them to avoid crime. The qualification for those working in the service was a social work one and officers worked in a relatively autonomous way, with a professional relationship with the courts. While there was 'supervision' by senior officers, this was conducted as a conversation between professionals rather than between a boss and a subordinate. Practice was based on legislation and learned practice rather than predefined routines of behaviour.

The Home Office made various attempts to assert control over the service. In 1984 it published a statement of objectives specifying that the purposes of the service were to prevent re-offending, reintegrate offenders and divert them from custody. While these were uncontroversial they were a prelude to a series of attempts to bring the service under national control. This became a more important matter when the government decided to change the role of the Probation Service. Probation was to become 'punishment in the community', rather than a social work-based process applied to offenders. The 1988 Green Paper *Punishment, Custody and the Community* and the Criminal Justice Act 1991 made it clear that the government wanted non-custodial sentences to be punitive and to be a sentence and punishment in their own right, rather than an inferior alternative to custody. This was part of a wider concern that the Conservative government had to be 'tough' on crime. This was essentially a political stance, that harsh sentences on those who were convicted of crime were likely either to prevent crime, to satisfy a need for retribution or at least to assure the electorate that the government was concerned about the rapidly increasing level of crime. This approach was strengthened after the 1992 election. As David Faulkner said:

> the Government ... approach ... relied on law enforcement, and especially the disabling effect of imprisonment and the supposed deterrent effect of conviction and punishment more generally, as the principal means of tackling crime. This approach paid little attention to prevention, to the social and economic circumstances in which crime becomes prevalent, or to the influences which affect a person's behaviour or pattern of life.[48]

In 1992, the Home Office issued a set of national standards for the Probation Service. These were partly a description of the activities carried out by the service and partly an attempt to enforce routines of behaviour.[49] Many probation officers were concerned that such precise prescriptions changed the nature of the activity from that of an autonomous professional making judgements within a legal framework to a service which consisted of following routine. In practice the framework still allows professional judgement within a framework of timetables and reporting régimes.

The national standards were a prelude to an attempt to detach the Probation Service from its social work origins. The Dews Report[50] questioned the relevance of a social work qualification as a prerequisite to becoming a probation officer. In particular, it questioned the relevance of social work values: 'We ... heard much of the importance of "social work values" but nothing to suggest these were different from the values of many professions and we noted that this was not a concept embraced by the Home Office' (p. 26).

One solution to the problem of social work values was to change the qualification of probation officers. Dews recommended a diploma in probation studies which would be 'skills-based and the assessment would focus entirely on whether the trainee was competent to begin practising core probation work' (p. 35). The Home Secretary was keen to replace social work attitudes with attitudes more appropriate to punishment in the community by recruiting and qualifying a different sort of probation officer, including people with police or military experience. The Dews report was met with hostility by the Association of Chief Probation Officers and the National Association of Probation Officers. The hostility was partly motivated by protection and partly by the challenge to the underlying values of the service. There were those who argued that the social work qualification was not adequately geared towards probation practice but there were few within the profession who agreed with the proposal for a competencies-based qualification without educational content.

The Labour government completed the process of transforming the Probation Service into a national service for punishment in the community. From April 2001 the Probation Service in England and Wales was reorganized as the National Probation Service[51] with a National Director accountable to the Home Secretary in charge of 42 Areas, co-terminous with police authority boundaries.

A review[52] of the prison and probation services published in 1998 said:

> Successive Governments have neglected the organisational framework which supports the work of probation officers. A series of Acts of Parliament have merely served to consolidate an outdated reflection of a service that has been engaged in change and modernisation for many years. Legislation still directs probation officers to "advise, assist and befriend" offenders. This is completely out of line not just with the expectations of the courts but also with the reality of the work which probation staff undertake day in and day out.

The optimism with which the Home Office pursued the centralization of the service does not reflect the concerns of the report on the Prison Service quoted above, in which poor centralized management and unclear accountabilities for performance were seen as the major contributory factors to the creation of bad prisons.

National Offender Management Service

The trend towards amalgamation and bigger organizations was continued with the merger of the probation and prison services into the National Offender Management Service, with a unified command structure and budget. The role and organization of the new service was set out in the Carter report:[53]

> National Offender Management Service
>
> The delivery of rigorous sentences will need a clear focus on managing offenders, the targeted use of resources and greater contestability.
>
> - A National Offender Management Service (NOMS) should be established, accountable to Ministers for punishing offenders and reducing re-offending.
> - This would restructure the current activities of prison and probation to provide the end-to-end management of offenders, regardless of whether they are given a custodial or community sentence.
>
> There should be a single Chief Executive to lead the service.
>
> - He or she would be accountable to Ministers for the delivery of offender outcomes and the efficient operation of the public sector providers.
> - He or she would have overall responsibility for the strategic development of the sector. This would include developing policy and standards, the provision of a shared offender database, strategic finance and HR.
> - He or she would agree operating targets and annual plans with the operational heads.
> - He or she would have responsibility for ensuring contestability in the provision of prison and probation by attracting new providers into the market, through a planned programme of market testing.

A centrally managed budget, 'contestability' by bringing in new providers, and a single hierarchy were a model that has been tried in many areas of policy.

Implications for managers

The management of professionals, who have their own ways of working derived from training and professional ethics, is appropriate only where such conditions apply. Prison officers receive training in the routines of the prisons and in counselling and talking to prisoners, but never established a profession in this sense. The Police Service is in an ambiguous position: individual police officers, including constables, have always had a great deal of discretion about how they behave when they are in contact with the public and with criminals, because direct supervision is not possible.

What managers have had to do has been to reduce the autonomy and independence of action of the practitioners and make them conform more to a set of expectations and rules of behaviour. In the cases of the Police Service, the managers have always themselves had experience as workers in the service and have learned directly how practice operates. In the Prison Service, the head of the service has normally been a career civil servant and in one case someone with no public service experience. Very senior probation officers were traditionally selected from career probation people but there have recently been appointments from other backgrounds.

This distinction is important: the application of a set of rules and procedures is possible only when individual discretion is reduced to a set of decision rules. When the top managers are former practitioners, it is harder for them to argue for a reduction of discretion: outsiders are better placed to tell workers and middle managers to follow rules rather than use their experience to inform their discretion.

Relationships among policy areas

One of the problems for managers operating in these policy areas was that the policy process itself was fragmented from the highest level. Ministries and policy divisions within them are concerned with small areas of policy. For example, policy on housing and housing subsidy was set in the (then) Department of the Environment, while income support was a matter for the Department of Social Security. Mental health was the concern of part of the Department of Health, while prison policy and practice is thought about in the Home Office.

These divisions produced both inconsistencies and contradictions. For example, managers concerned with the welfare of people with mental health problems have to cope with a range of policies. The policy to close the mental hospitals and let people who previously lived there live in 'the community' was mainly developed by the Department of Health. Local authorities were involved in the process of finding accommodation and support for the people who moved. Housing, when it was provided, was the concern of housing associations and the local authority. The police became involved when people committed offences. Such fragmentation inevitably led to failures to provide adequate services for people at whom the policy was aimed. A series of reports on the disasters which occurred (many resulting in murders) emphasized the fragmentation of policy and service delivery.

Another example was the treatment of children with behavioural and emotional difficulties. The Children Act 1989 says that such children's interests should be central to what happens to them and that they are entitled to help. The Education Reform Act set schools in competition with each other and allows schools to exclude and eventually to expel children with behavioural problems. Schools excluded the children because they disrupt the activities of the school and threaten its results in the competitive examination result league tables. Such children were therefore excluded from the help, socialization and integration which they would receive in schools. Meanwhile, the special schools to which they could have gone were being closed because they are too expensive to run within the constraints of overall budgets.

The Labour government saw fragmentation of policy making and service delivery as one of the main problems facing it. It had two solutions: organizational changes, such as giving magistrates' courts, police and probation services the same boundaries; co-ordination and collaboration mechanisms to help policy makers and service deliverers work better together. At the heart of government it set up a large range of new task-forces, committees and units to pursue its declared aim of 'joined-up government'. The most publicized was the Social Exclusion Unit and its eighteen Policy Action Teams, attached to the Cabinet Office. Task forces brought outsiders (mainly business people) into government to give advice on issues that mainly crossed over departmental boundaries. A review by Cranfield School of Management carried out nine months after the 1997 election found more than 75 task forces and 200 policy reviews and counted 350 business people involved in the process. The reviews covered a very wide range of issues, including 'Music Industry and New Creative Industries', 'Better Regulation', Education, Youth Justice, Tax and Benefits, Drugs, Banking, Construction, Contraception, Rebranding Britain (appropriately called 'Panel 2000'), Human Rights, Cleaner Vehicles, Literacy and Coalfields. After 100 days of the new government, Sir Robin Butler, Head of the Home Civil Service, called a moratorium on policy reviews.

Actions to encourage organizations to work together included area initiatives for health, education, urban renewal, crime prevention, mental health. Often funding was linked to resource allocation. The implications of collaborative working are explored in Chapter 8.

Conclusions

In the introduction to this chapter we saw that there were six themes which we could identify in the governments' policies towards public services. The move from equal treatment of everyone to difference has been reasonably successful in some sectors. Universal access to state services has been reduced; even state pensioners only receive an income on which they can live reasonably if they apply for means-tested benefits. Child benefit and retirement pension are the only remaining universal state benefits. The changes should not be overemphasized. There is still universal access to education and health care.

The private sector, together with voluntary and community agencies, is involved in public services in a way which seemed unlikely when the Welfare State was established. The involvement of the private sector in the Prison Service was a great surprise to people in the Prison Service, as well as to many outside it. Ironically, this shift has accelerated since Labour came to power. Whether through the provision of direct services, such as prisons, residential care for older people, secure mental health hospitals, fostering services for children or home care, or management consultancy support, the private sector are major players. In addition, the voluntary and community sector has seen its role expanded. Through significant resource investment, for example £125m through 'Futurebuilders', government is increasing the capacity of what is now termed the 'third sector' to deliver effective public services commissioned by the state.

Central policy control has been a very clear success. The autonomy of local authorities and the professions has been greatly curtailed. Social workers are engaged in rationing services, probation officers are offering punishment in the community, teachers have been controlled and even doctors are acting under instruction from managers. The success of output-based funding of capital schemes has yet to be seen. When the intention was mainly one of limiting the amount of money spent, however, it was a success.

As well as reasonably successful implementation of the government's intentions, other changes have taken place in the management of public services as a result of these policy and management changes. The first is that managers and professionals have become more competitive and less collaborative. We look in more detail at the impact of the competitive régimes in Chapter 10. The reduction in collaboration had negative effects. The first was the reluctance to share skills, knowledge, information and good practice. In the case of schools and surgery, institutions which compete with each other do not like to share their successes. The same is true in the case of the competing and privatized government scientific laboratories. The second effect is that organizations in the private and voluntary sectors which may in the past have been collaborators are now seen as competitors. Professionals whose previous way of working involved caring for the service users and sharing good ideas have become focused on revenues and the competition for them. The 'modernisation' may well have the impact of making professionals spend more time listening to service users.

The third effect is that professional discretion is reduced and managerial power increased. The centralization of policies and procedures reduces the autonomy of the professionals but at the same time increases the influence of managers. Service commissioning has been one way of achieving this objective. If central direction in the form of procedures is to be followed, it is the managers who transmit and interpret the procedures from the centre (whether the Ministry, Inspectorate or whatever) to the local organization. Whether the managers were previously professionals or not, the power they acquire derives from their relationship with the centre rather than their professional expertise or knowledge. Centralization shifts the balance from the professions to the managers.

The Labour government tried to correct some of these negative effects by taking the edge off some of the market solutions and encouraging collaboration. An assessment of these efforts is made in Chapter 8.

A fourth effect was the residualization of many state services. The state pension is now a residual benefit for pensioners. Community care is increasingly a last resort. The least well-resourced schools have an atmosphere of simply surviving, rather than generating confidence and pride in their pupils. The effect of this on people working in the state sector is that they know that they are no longer doing the best possible, rather the best possible in the circumstances. Social workers, for example, spend a great deal of their time either telling clients that they cannot have the services which they need and thought they were entitled to, or arguing to get access to those services. These results were accepted by the Labour government and some efforts were made to correct them, adjusting pensions, recognizing the over-targeting of social services and trying to turn around the worst schools.

A fifth effect is a greater concentration on measurable results. The emphasis on output-based funding means that managers and workers have to concentrate on the relevant numbers. We will see that the Labour government strengthened this process and strengthened inspection systems through an ever greater emphasis on measurable results.

Notes

For weblinks relevant to the issues discussed in this chapter see www.sagepub.co.uk/flynn.

1 Set out in Department of the Environment, Transport and the Regions *Modernising Local Government* (DETR, London, 1999).
2 Commission for Social Care Inspection, *The State of Social Care in England 2004–05* (CSCI, London, 2005) p. 47.
3 Michael Freeden, 'The Ideology of New Labour', *Political Quarterly*, 70, 1, (1999), Jan-March.
4 Department of Social Security/Department of Employment, *Jobseeker's Allowance*, Cm 2687 (HMSO, London, 1994), p. 4.
5 News release 10.2.2000.
6 'Department of Work and Pensions, *A New Deal For Welfare: Empowering people to work*, Cm 6730 (HMSO, London, January 2006).
7 The proportion of people of working age who are in work.
8 Rowntree Foundation, *The Future of Work: A Contribution to the Debate, Policy Summary 7* (Rowntree Foundation, York, 1996), P. 3.
9 Tom Clarke, Andrew Dilnot, Alissa Goodman, et al. 'Taxes and Transfers 1997–2001', *Oxford Review Economic Policy*, 18, 2(2002), pp. 187–201.
10 Department of Health, *NHS Plan, a plan for investment, a plan for reform* (DoH, London, 2000), para. 6.3.
11 Department of Health, *The New NHS, modern, dependable*, Cm 3807 (DoH, London, 1997).

12 King's Fund, *An Independent Audit of the NHS Under Labour (1997–2005)*, (King's Fund, London, 2005), p. 11.

13 (in England – we saw in Chapter 1 that there is a different structure in each country in the UK).

14 Speech 13 December 2005.

15 Audit Commission, *Early Lessons from Payment by Results* (Audit Commission, London, 2005), p. 10.

16 Causes of the overspend are not clear, at the time of writing. Pay rises for NHS employees under Agenda for Change, in excess of predicted salary budgets, probably accounted for 60% of the overspends.

17 Audit Commission, *Early lessons*.

18 Ibid. p. 15.

19 Department of Health, *A short guide to NHS Foundation Trusts* (HMSO, London, 2003), p. 4.

20 *British Medical Journal* 2.9.2000, p. 563.

21 'Independent Sector Treatment Centres', in which the government invested £1.5 billion.

22 Audit Commission, 'Taking Stock: Progress with Community Care', *Community Care Bulletin* No. 2, (1994), December (HMSO, London).

23 CSCI, *The State of Social Care*.

24 Office for National Statistics, *Community Care Statistics 2004–05: Referrals, Assessments and Packages of Care for Adults, England: National Summary* (ONS, London, 2006b).

25 K. Wright, *The Mental Health (Patients in the Community) Bill, Research Paper 95/71* (House of Commons Library, London).

26 Home Office, *Statistical Bulletin 20/95. Statistics of Mentally Disordered Offenders England and Wales 1994* (Government Statistical Service, London, 1995).

27 Figures from Department of Health *Tracking Progress in Children's Services: An evaluation of local responses to the Quality Protects Programme, Year 2*, (DoH, London, 2000b).

28 Ibid., para 32.

29 CSCI, *The State of Social Care*.

30 Child Support Agency Annual Report and Accounts 2004–05.

31 The Academy sponsored by Amey, Unity City Academy in Middlesbrough, was soon declared a 'failing school' by Ofsted.

32 Department for Education and Skills, *A Short Guide to the Education and Inspections Bill 2006* (HMSO, London, 2006), p. 1.

33 N. Ferguson, P. Earley, J. Ouston et al. *Improving Schools and Inspection: the Self-Inspecting School* (Paul Chapman/Sage, London, 2000).

34 Peter Malpass, *Housing and the Welfare State: the development of housing policy in Britain*, (Palgrave, Basingstoke, 2005), p. 193.

35 J. Ford and S. Wilcox, *Affordable Housing, Low Incomes and the Flexible Labour Market*, (National Federation of Housing Associations, Research Report 22, London, 1994).

36 K. Barker, *Delivering stability: securing our future housing needs, the Barker Review of Housing Supply – Final Report* (HM Treasury, London, 2004).

37 140,000 in 2004, the peak of the building boom.

38 P. Prescott-Clarke, S. Clemens and A. Park, *Routes into Local Authority Housing: A Study of Local Authority Waiting Lists and New Tenancies* (HMSO, London, 1994).

39 Home Office, Northern Ireland Office and Scottish Office, *Inquiry into Police Responsibilities and Rewards*, Cm 2280 (the 'Sheehy Report'), (HMSO, London, 1993).

40 F. Leishman, S. Cope and P. Starie, 'Reforming the Police in Britain', *International Journal of Public Sector Management*, 8, 4(1995).

41 M. Lewis, S. Long and A. Williams, 1995, 'What to Do with What You've Got', *Policing*, 11, 4 (1995), pp. 261–71.

42 B. Loveday, 'The Police and Magistrates' Court Act', *Policing*, 10, 4 (1994).

43 D. O'Connor, HM Inspector of Constabulary, 'Closing the gap: a review of the "fitness for purpose", of the current structure of policing in England and Wales' (Home Office, London, September 2005), p. 6.

44 Targeted Performance Initiative Working Group, *Modernising the Management of the Prison Service: An Independent Report* (Home Office, London, 2000).

45 Known colloquially as 'Strangeways'.

46 W. Halward, 'Manchester Prison: Mounting a Successful In-house Bid' in Prison Reform Trust, *Privatisation and Market Testing in the Prison Service* (Prison Reform Trust, London, 1994).

47 *Howard Journal of Criminal Justice*, 33, 3, (1994), p. 354.

48 D. Faulkner, 'The Criminal Justice Act 1991: Policy, Legislation and Practice' in D. Ward and M. Lacey, *Probation: Working for Justice* (Whiting and Birch, London, 1995), p. 63.

49 Home Office, Department of Health, Welsh Office, *National Standards for the Supervision of Offenders in the Community* (Home Office Public Relations Branch, London, 1992 and 1995).

50 V. Dews and J. Watts, *Review of Probation Officer Recruitment and Qualifying Training* (Home Office, London, 1994).

51 Under the Crime and Probation Act, 2000.

52 Home Office, *Prisons Probation: Joining Forces to Protect the Public*, (Home Office, London, 1998).

53 Patrick Carter, *Managing Offenders, Reducing Crime* (Cabinet Office Strategy Unit, London, 2003).

Part Two

Introduction

Part Two is about the variety of arrangements that successive governments have implemented to manage and control public services. The full range of available options has been tried, some more than once: for example, competitive internal markets have been introduced, abolished and re-introduced in the NHS, the rail network was privatized and effectively re-nationalized. Various forms of competition and contestability were tried, whether by compulsory tendering in local authorities or market testing in the civil service. The public utilities, which are discussed in Part 2, have also had a full range of policies applied to them, from privatization and regulation, competition and even (water in Wales) renationalization under a novel form of ownership. The private sector has been encouraged to get involved in running schools, has been offered huge incentives to invest in water and sewerage infrastructure and the chance to participate in the financing and building in the biggest public investment programme for thirty years.

A casual observer might think that the array of management and market methods was randomly assembled from experiences from business, other countries' experiments, management consultants' handbooks and presentations, and implemented in a programme based on trial and error. One of the Ministers at the head of the second term changes in the NHS was Alan Milburn. In a speech on NHS Foundation hospitals he said that the process had to be continuous:

> Reform is not a process that starts one day and ends the next: it must go on and on and on.[1]

We saw in Chapter 4 that by the third term, some of the reforms that had been abandoned in an earlier period were brought in again, as if they would be more successful a second time around, in an increasingly anxious search for effective solutions to persistent problems. The continuous reform programmes were designed to solve at least four sets of problems. At different times and sectors some of these problems were more important to the government than others.

For the Conservative governments of the 1980s and 1990s a dominant problem was the size and role of government: for ideological reasons the Thatcher and

Major governments believed both 'public bad, private good' and that markets were the only way to organize the allocation of resources. All solutions therefore had to incorporate privatization and/or cuts in public spending. These two solutions were not always compatible: for example the privatization of the railway resulted in increased public subsidy. But the direction of change had to be towards the greater use of markets and the reduction of the proportion of national output that was used by the public sector.

Governments seek popularity. Since the 1990s politicians have been trying to find ways to control public services, to make them popular with the people who use them and with the electorate in general. The Blair governments took this process further, putting satisfaction ratings both of services and of the government at the centre of decision-making. Focus groups and opinion polls were consulted extensively from 1997 on, to inform the government how people were reacting to what they were doing. Naturally, this objective could easily contradict the first: privatization of the railway, of power and of the water and sewerage industry was never popular.

We saw in Chapter 3 that cuts in spending, and especially in capital budgets, dating back to the mid 1970s left the assets of the public sector in a decrepit state. Victorian water and sewer networks, un-maintained train tracks and signalling, a very old estate in education and health, prisons designed for a different era and scale of penal policy, all presented an increasingly urgent problem: how to get these assets restored to good working order after decades of neglect. Solutions to this problem that were compatible with solving the first two, reducing spending and gaining popularity, were to be preferred.

A fourth problem concerned the relationship between government and public servants. Governments were faced with the problem of how to get the five and a half million people employed in public sector jobs working hard and doing what the government wanted them to do. Successive governments, of both parties, were suspicious of the motivation and performance of public servants, from street sweepers to Permanent Secretaries. How could people be persuaded to work harder, increase their productivity, and act in the government's interests rather than their own? The need for efficiency improvement, defined as reducing unit cost however measured, is a more common way of defining this issue. As the level of public spending was raised after 1999, the government was concerned that the extra spending would be dissipated in higher costs, whether of labour or of goods and services bought in. A study in 2003 showed that they were right to be concerned.[2] It showed that overall the outputs of the public sector failed to keep pace with the increase in spending after 1999. A graph from the study (Figure Intro Pt. 2.1) illustrates the point.

What Figure Intro Pt. 2.1 shows is that as the volume of inputs increased, productivity actually fell. It is not clear precisely why this happened; it was a combination of spending being absorbed by higher pay, higher prices and higher costs of capital. We saw in Chapter 1 (Figure 1.1 on page 11) that the numbers of employees in the public sector rose steadily from 1998, especially in the NHS, education and 'public administration'.

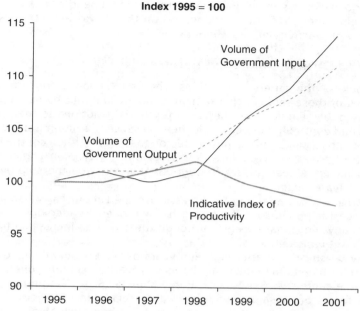

Index 1995 = 100

Figure Intro Part 2.1   Government productivity 1995–2001

Table Intro Part 2.1   *Average earnings index 2000–2005 (2000=100)*

	Public Administration	Education	Health and Social Work	Whole economy
2000	100.0	100.0	100.0	100
2001	104.4	105.1	106.1	104.5
2002	108.4	109.4	113.0	108.2
2003	113.1	115.2	119.3	111.9
2004	118.4	119.3	126.6	116.7
2005	124.1	123.8	132.5	121.5

Source: Office for National Statistics, 2006

The level of pay in the public sector clearly has an impact on the amount of output produced per pound of public spending. Between 1997 and 2000 public sector pay rose by 12%, while private sector increases amounted to over 15%. After the spending increases from 1999, public sector pay rises overtook the rest of the economy, especially in the health and education sectors. Table Intro Pt 2.1 shows the average earnings index for Great Britain 2000–2005.

From the government's point of view, growth in expenditure as well as the number of employees and their earnings meant that it was essential to find ways of improving productivity across all inputs.

Part Two A: Directly managed services

Part Two looks at the variety of solutions. The first section is concerned with the management of those services that remained mostly in public ownership and were provided by public employees. They are managerial solutions to the problems of motivating and controlling direct employees. The second section is about the management of those parts of the public sector that were either contracted to the private sector, privatized completely (such as power, water in England, the railway), or managed, at least partly, through some form of partnership between the public and private sectors.

Solutions came from a range of sources. Once the Labour Party had abandoned its preference for public ownership and had wrapped its ideology in Third Way eclecticism, anything was possible, although there was an increasing tendency to look for market-type solutions.

What may be surprising after eighteen years of the Conservatives' enthusiastic pursuit of reforms and management changes is that the Labour governments still diagnosed the same set of problems. Prime Minister Blair's emotional condemnation of the 'forces of conservatism' in the public sector[3] included criticism of both professionalism and conservative bureaucracy: '... the British Medical Association and other professional organisations ... are there to represent and promote the interests of its members ... the Government is there to govern for all the people.' And 'people in the public sector are more rooted in the concept that if it's always been done this way it must always be done this way than any group of people I've ever come across ... It's not that there aren't wonderful people now with a tremendous commitment to public service, but you try getting change in the public sector and public services – I bear the scars on my back after two years of government.'

One formulation of the general problem of controlling and improving the performance of was 'public choice theory'. An import from the USA, this set of ideas was never explicitly claimed as a guiding paradigm, but it was implied in many government actions. The idea is that all people act in their self-interest and respond to incentives. Public servants will build empires, waste money and be lazy if left to their own devices. The extreme solution to this problem is to minimize the scope for such behaviours by minimizing the role of the public sector and leaving the allocation of resources and provision of services to the market, where selfish behaviour produces beneficial results. Where the state is involved, it should structure incentives, both for employees and contractors to produce the results that it desires. The contract, setting out as many aspects of the services required and their results, is the preferred solution, whether for employees or for out-sourced service providers.

All of the solutions examined in Part Two of this book rely on markets or contracts as the main mechanism for managing performance, controlling costs, ensuring desired outcomes. In the case of services provided by employees, the solutions are based on contractual relationships between the government and its constituent organizations and between those organizations and their employees. Chapter 5 examines the performance management frameworks that have been put in place. A hierarchical system of targets, agreements with incentives and punishments and measurement systems has been developed, sometimes with great effort, over a long period. The system is designed to prevent the sorts of behaviours, such as shirking and cheating, predicted by public choice theory. The system has been refined in two principal ways over the years. First, there has been an increasing emphasis on the outcomes of activities, assessed by various measures of results, rather than simply measuring activities. Secondly, there has been an attempt to attribute cause and effect to professions, organizations and individuals. For example, if pupil performance is mostly determined by social class, then the impact of schools on pupils has to be separated out from the impact of the socio-economic background of the schools' intake. The chapter shows that on a small sample of measures, in health, education and crime, the management system has produced largely positive results. While the system has been, at least in part, successful as a way of managing, it has not had a proportionate impact on public satisfaction. Unlike successful management in the private sector, producing more customers and better profits, successful management in the public sector apparently does not, of itself, produce public satisfaction.

Chapter 6 is about how public services can be designed. Comparing public services with ideas from service marketing in the private sector, it looks at the differences between the two and what can be done to design customer and citizen oriented services. It explains that public service users and citizens do not have the same needs and expectations as customers of businesses, nor are they equivalent. The paradox that was discovered, that better performance does not necessarily produce more satisfaction, may be addressed by taking account in service design of democracy, active involvement and the entitlements that come with citizenship. For the government, there was another solution, 'personalisation', the idea that services can go beyond the period of mass production to a period of individually designed services. Beyond the speeches, it was not clear how this might be achieved in practice. Choice of provider, a small part of the solution, is a long way from individually designed services.

Chapter 7 turns to another tool, or set of tools, that governments have used to manage and improve public services, the audit and inspection functions. It finds that governments have made increasing use of these two institutions both to assure the citizens and service users that services achieve pre-defined quality standards, and as devices to push standards up. In the extreme, where inspection reports are used to close down institutions such as schools and hospitals or parts of local authorities, these devices are used in place of an economic regulator. The inspectors do not simply assure standards, or help improve service quality: they can ultimately decide who is and is not entitled to deliver services. The main government efforts towards these functions have been to bring about structural changes, merging the eleven main inspectorates into four, rather than clarifying the different purposes of inspection and audit.

One of the consequences of centralized control and the use of targets and inspections is that people are judged and managed on the basis of a narrow range of activities, those in which they are directly engaged. Services may be well managed without addressing the multiple needs of their users or the communities they serve. 'Joined-up government' was a slogan of the first Labour government and various efforts were made to ensure that services were co-ordinated. Various institutions were established at the centre, such as the Social Exclusion Unit, to think about and devise solutions to the problems of fragmentation and narrow focus that centralized management produced. Partnership became the order of the day, with dozens of schemes and projects, usually 'pathfinders' followed by 'roll-outs' to make service deliverers act together. Often there was compulsion, usually there were incentives to behave, or at least appear to behave collaboratively. Chapter 8 addresses this question of collaborative management.

Part Two B: Outsourced services

The book then turns from the management of those services that are controlled by direct management of employees, the great bulk of services, to those that are provided by private companies or voluntary agencies. These include contracted-out services, allocated to companies after competition, such as outsourced back-office functions, physical tasks such as refuse collection and street cleaning, and some management functions. In addition, some services are run, at least in part, by market mechanisms. For example, the NHS provides about 90% of health care through employees but they have been forced, in various ways over the years, to operate in market-type conditions. Local authorities and the civil service have also been subjected to competition and 'market testing' in various forms. The services discussed in Part 2B also include those produced by post-privatization companies that are still subsidized and/or regulated by government. Power generation, distribution and supply are all in private hands but the state intervenes in their management. Water and sewerage services have been privatized in part of the UK, renationalized in Wales, kept public in Scotland.

Chapter 9 questions why and how markets are used to regulate and control public services, the nature of the markets that have been established, and how managers behave in those markets. It discovers that there has been a great variety of market structures and mechanisms and consequently a range of managerial strategies and behaviours to cope. Competition was often a prelude to privatization, as parts of government activity were prepared for the market by subjecting them to competitive cost pressures.

When services are still the responsibility of government, at various levels, but provided by companies and voluntary organizations, the cost and quality of those services depends on how the competition is organized and then on how the contracts are managed. Chapter 10 is about the different forms of contract and supervision arrangements that have been devised and used. It shows that different forms of contract are appropriate in different circumstances, but that there is a tendency towards the use of adversarial, 'arm's-length' arrangements between government and contractors. Such arrangements did not prevent the expensive contracting disasters in the Information Technology sector.

Chapter 11 includes another disaster, the attempt to run the post-privatization railway through a series of contracts among a large number of companies, by some estimates over 1,000 if all the subcontractors are included. It discusses the regulation of the post-privatization utilities and transport networks, including London Underground. Another set of arrangements of a slightly different kind are represented by the Public–Private Partnerships. The chapter traces the history of PPPs and follows up examples from Prisons and the NHS. It shows that PPPs have been used to reduce public borrowing by transferring the financing of public buildings to the private sector, but also to provide an alternative method of managing the services themselves: in the case of Prisons the whole custodial service, in the case of hospitals falling short of medical services.

Notes

1 Alan Milburn, speech 22 May 2002.
2 Alwyn Pritchard, *Understanding government output and productivity*. (National Expenditure and Income Division, Office for National Statistics, London, 2003).
3 Speeches in February and July 1999.

Part Two A: Directly Managed Services

5

Managing performance

Introduction

The public services are mostly delivered by 5.5 million state employees. The desire to get high levels of productivity and quality from these staff has generated a performance measurement and management system that stretches across the whole of the public sector.

Performance measurement and management are important both for the accountability of organizations and individuals and to enable targets to be set and monitored. As we saw in the previous chapter, centralization of control has been common across all public services, requiring a centralized performance management system. Accountability is more than a process of showing how money is spent: it also involves demonstrating that money has been used efficiently, effectively and for the purposes for which it has been allocated.

This chapter examines the performance management system and how it is used. It also asks whether the system, especially that based on Public Service Agreements, has improved performance and whether in turn public satisfaction with services has been affected by that performance.

Why measure and manage performance?

Accountability

Public sector organizations are in principle accountable to the public for three things: that money has been spent as agreed and in accordance with procedures;

that resources have been used efficiently; that resources have been used to achieve the intended result. At the same time politicians are supposed to be accountable for the policy decisions they make while holding the management of the organizations to account for their actions. Government has been increasingly willing to make explicit, measurable promises.

Accountabilities require ways of measuring performance. Accounting for how money has been spent is relatively simple despite the mysteries of accountancy. This measure, how much money was spent and on what, is still an important part of managers' lives, however sophisticated the other types of accountability become.

Whether resources have been used efficiently is a question which requires some measure of the output or value of services provided, which can then be compared with the cost of provision. Here the problems of measurement begin: how to measure the outputs of schools, hospitals, prisons and so on?

The third question – did the service achieve what it was supposed to? – requires an assessment of what works best in the particular service, or indeed what works at all. Here the relationship between management and professionals or experts is important. One aspect of the specialized occupations in public services is that people claim to know what works and what does not, without necessarily being able to explain or demonstrate it. When politicians, through their managers, take control of public services away from the professionals, they need evidence of what policies and services produce the desired results and a system of measurement and monitoring to make sure that people are doing what they are told and achieving what the government wants them to.

Promises and targets

The Labour governments were brave enough to make specific electoral promises, using targets whose achievement could be verified in areas such as class sizes in primary schools, waiting lists for medical treatment. They also published targets that were less easy to pin down to policy or service delivery, such as the incidence of cancer and the rate of teenage pregnancy. They took the work of the previous governments on target setting through the Citizen's Charter initiative and, in the first term, made 'Service First' an important part of their toolkit for delivering measurable improvements in public services. The government's critics from the Left dismissed this attempt as 'managerialism', using methods derived from management rather than politics to run state services. Rather than electoral accountability through local government and parliamentary elections, it chose the methods of 'management by objectives' to make and monitor promises. There is no doubt that the government had a belief that management methods could improve the standard of public services. Specific targets were set for the level of attainment in literacy and numeracy in schools, backed by a measurement system and given priority through the introduction of literacy and numeracy hours in schools. The same was true of the campaign to reduce the numbers on waiting lists for surgery: simple targets, made a priority and given resources, can usually be achieved. The question is whether the overall standard of services can be improved by using multiple targets, some of which may conflict with each other. For example, waiting lists may be reduced by offering shorter hospital stays resulting in more re-admissions, or may be achieved by exceeding budgets. Literacy and numeracy may be improved at the expense of physical fitness. Targets concentrate managers' and professionals' efforts on those specific items that politicians define as important.

Having made such explicit promises to the electorate, the government then faced the problem of how to make a contract with the managers and employees of the public services that would allow the government to achieve the targets and therefore gain and retain public support. While the Labour governments continued to use markets, strengthened the inspection and monitoring agencies and took powers to punish poor performers and replace their management, in some cases by private companies, the main control mechanism was a series of internal contracts setting out targets, mostly expressed as outputs and outcomes, which have been formalized as Public Service Agreements (PSAs).

As the Audit Commission put it, 'Each department's PSA was in effect its contract with the Treasury: linking increased investment arising from the CSR to improved productivity and outcomes; and with the public: articulating departmental priorities and setting clear targets for improvement over the next three years.'[1]

Implicit in the government's actions is the belief that through targets, publication of results and the threat to managers that they will lose their jobs, and to whole institutions that they would be privatized or replaced in some other way, managers and workers would behave as required by the government. At the same time incentives, often in the form of performance-based pay, were established for those meeting the targets. Sometimes these incentives were at the level of the institution: if they perform well they are rewarded with higher budgets and a 'light touch' inspection régime. What exactly was the problem that government actions have been designed to solve?

Shirking

A particular problem in public services, and especially those produced by professionals, is that the required behaviour is unobservable: it is unrealistic to have an inspector for every teacher, nurse, doctor and in any case, how would the inspectors be monitored? The main solution was to produce a set of targets and ways of measuring their achievement and an incentive system to back them up. Individual performance-based pay was introduced to tackle the individual shirking problem. Schools were heavily inspected to tackle the institutional shirking problem and in extreme cases could be put under a régime of 'special measures' or in very extreme cases closed down altogether.

Standards

A frustration for politicians and managers trying to run thousands of service delivery operations from Ministries in London, or the Scottish Executive in Edinburgh, is that if only those at the bottom of the performance scale would behave like those higher up the scale, output and quality could be increased at no extra cost. Performance improvement by emulation of the better is one solution to the problem. Closure of the 'plants' (schools, hospitals, prisons etc.) at the bottom end would, in principal, improve average performance. Even without closures, median performance or top quartile performance can be used as a benchmark for all the units in the service.

Standards go beyond measures of efficiency and include cycle times, courtesy, accessibility and other aspects of quality. All public services have been subjected to quality improvement programmes, the most frequently used being the European Quality Foundation model. Since this work on quality was in large part concerned with the quality of interaction between the service and its users, objective measures are not easy to establish: while cycle times and telephone answering times can be measured, the quality of the interaction can only be gauged by asking the customers how they feel. To translate this into a binding contract, resort was made to clauses about the percentage satisfaction level as measured in customer surveys.

A perennial problem with public services is the difficulty in measuring efficiency and improving productivity. Since most of the outputs have no independently measurable value, tracking changes in the cost per unit value of output is hard. One solution in contractual terms is to reduce the overall budget by a fixed amount per year while requesting that output is held constant. Thus, budgets are agreed, then an adjustment made for 'efficiency savings' or 'productivity improvements', despite the likelihood that the outputs cannot be measured accurately enough to ensure that the volume of production is not reduced proportionately. When budgets were increased, the government was especially concerned that the extra spending should increase the volume of services produced, rather than be absorbed in higher pay and prices.

A 'principal–agent' problem

The problems that the governments have tried to solve through the performance management system are those defined as the 'principal–agent problem'. Originally formulated to explain the relationship between business owners and business managers, the principal–agent relationship is conducted through a series of instructions and attempts to control and measure the behaviour and performance of the agent by the principal. While the language of 'principal–agent' was not explicitly used, the performance system devised was based exactly on such ideas.

The literature[2] on the principal–agent problem predicts that agents will seek ways to act in their own interests, whatever contracts are written and whatever monitoring is put in place. Such opportunities exist when performance control systems are implemented in the public sector. An example is the case of secondary schools whose rewards are derived from their pupils' achievement: the obvious way to improve performance is to select out the potentially poor performers and attract potentially good performers. Such behaviour does nothing for the overall standard of education (the overall aim of the system) but produces the required results for the school. Once this behaviour starts, another contractual solution has to be found: in this case the measures used are not performance by pupils but 'value added' or the gain in performance from whatever starting point.

Individual and organizational performance

Almost all public servants have an appraisal process through which their individual contribution to their organization's performance is assessed. While the appraisal process has other objectives, such as to identify people's training and development needs, the emphasis is normally on individual performance, sometimes with an element of performance-related pay. In principle, the targets which individuals are assessed on should aggregate into the performance targets of the organization as a whole. In centrally managed services there is a direct relationship between targets set by ministers and the targets in individuals' work plans, targets and assessments. Sometimes the individual targets are not related to those of the organization itself, especially if managers are free to decide their own priorities.

The three 'E's

Both the Treasury and the Audit Commission encouraged the achievement of the 'three E's': economy, efficiency and effectiveness. Economy is about the cost of the inputs used, and making economic use of them. Efficiency is concerned with the cost of producing outputs. Effectiveness is defined as producing results. People concerned with equality of access to services have talked of a fourth 'E', equity, and argued that it should be included in any scheme of performance measurement.

In those parts of the public sector in which there are markets, it could be argued that measures of economy and productive efficiency are taken care of: competition eliminates those producers whose costs are too high, or forces them to reduce their costs. There is no need for any independent measurement or analysis of their costs. There may be targets and measurements related to resource use, such as return on capital employed. Where there are no markets, public accountability for the use of resources would require that those given stewardship of public money should demonstrate how well they are spending it. Measurement and reporting of efficiency is an essential part of public accountability and needs to be independently validated.

The most important aspects of performance management are not technical issues divorced from the real world of politics. Managers operate in a political environment, and ignore politics at their peril.

Economy

At its simplest, performance measurement looks at how much money was used up by the organization over a period. At first sight this might seem trivial and say nothing about managerial or organizational performance. In practice such measures are given importance by the dominance of the budget process. Budgets are cash limited and in many cases are projected from one year to the next with the expectation of an 'efficiency saving' of a certain percentage of the last year's budget. The notion of the annual efficiency saving relates to a general expectation that productivity, especially labour productivity, increases constantly. Technology changes, improvements in work organization, enhancement of skill levels all contribute to a trend improvement in the value of output per worker. Even if outputs cannot be measured, because these processes of improvement are going on in the public sector, it can be expected that productivity will improve every year. Hence budgets can be reduced in real terms without loss of outputs. In those cases where the output either cannot be measured or where the quality varies with cost, what this means in effect is that the main performance target is staying within the budget.

Staying within budget means both not spending too much and not spending too little. The fact that budgets have normally to be used up in a financial year (with some exceptions) means there is sometimes a need to stop spending in the tenth or eleventh month, while in other cases, there is a rush to ensure that money is spent at those times to ensure that budget targets are met. This necessity overrides other, more sophisticated aspects of performance management. A manager who can demonstrate that the services were effective, the service users were delighted and the other stakeholders were satisfied will not last long if the budget is consistently overspent.

Reporting systems reflect this. Financial management reports of actual expenditure against the projected spend are sent out, usually monthly. While there are variations among sectors and within them, there are two remaining problems even with this most simple measure of performance. The first is that the details of the projected spend are sometimes produced after the year has begun, which means that managers are not sure against what figures they are monitoring the spending. The second is that monitoring systems are still often based on cash outflows in each period. In many services, a decision taken in one month may represent a commitment to spend money for many months or even years. For example, if a social services department assesses a child aged 12 as needing residential care, they undertake a potential commitment to looking after that child in a residential home for four years. A monthly financial report which says that this month £4,000 was spent on the child does not give a picture of the continuing commitment.

Efficiency

In economics there are two definitions of efficiency. Productive efficiency is measured by the average cost of producing goods and services. Allocative efficiency is measured by the extent to which the economic system produces that mix of goods and services which reflects people's preferences as expressed by their consumption decisions. There is an argument that markets promote both types of efficiency. Competition generates the need for producers to reduce their price to that of their competitors. Choice allows consumers to influence producers in their decisions about what to make: if nobody wants what is on offer, producers have to make something else.

For most services, it is possible to devise a measure of volume. Universities can measure the number of hours of student contact the staff have or the hours of staff contact the students have, hospitals can measure the throughput of patients, libraries the numbers of books issued and reference materials referenced, pest control the number of rats captured or cockroaches killed. All that remains to produce a measure of efficiency is to find out how much each one cost, and then make comparisons, either with other producers, or over time.

Such comparisons have to be interpreted with care. The accounting mechanisms used in making the calculations have to be the same: the allocation of overheads, for example, may be made using different methods. The nature of the 'product' may also vary: the fact that Rochdale educates primary pupils for half the cost of doing the same thing in Lambeth may be because the education system is twice as efficient there, or because the quality of the education is half as good, or some position in between.

A different consequence of such comparisons might be that those with high costs will concentrate on finding reasons for the differences: council tax is harder to collect in areas where there is a high turnover of population, for example. Such comparisons should be used to raise questions about apparently poor performers, rather than be accepted simply as a certain indicator that one organization is performing better than another, and the factors affecting the comparative figure should be looked at.

Barzelay[3] argued that the emphasis on measuring and improving efficiency has been a mistake. He argues that the scientific management approach to performance improvement is based on how manufacturing is managed, where the product is easily defined and measured, whereas public service 'products' are not so easily measured:

> Since it excluded the concept of product, reformers' influential conception of efficient government was trouble waiting to happen. It encouraged the notorious bureaucratic focus on inputs to flourish and it permitted more

specialized functions to become worlds in themselves. More specifically, an increase in efficiency could be claimed in government whenever spending on inputs was reduced, whereas it was much easier to argue in an industrial setting that cost reduction improved efficiency only when it led to a reduction in the cost per unit of output.[4]

The other definition of efficiency is whether the organization produces the range of services which reflects the preferences of citizens or their representatives. At an aggregate level, this is a question of the distribution of resources among the main services: defence, social security, education, health and so on. The notion of Pareto optimality is that there is an allocation of resources which produces the most possible benefits. To move resources from one activity to another would diminish the total of benefits. Classical economists would argue that the market achieves precisely this optimal position: the sum of individual purchasing decisions and the response by producers will produce the best allocation of resources, in this Pareto sense.

However, the question of allocative efficiency poses a different problem. If there are markets in which consumers have a choice of what to buy and from whom, it might be argued that there is an automatic process of matching supply to demand or even need. But what if there is no choice? Political processes of resource allocation substitute for the market. How do we then know whether those choices reflect demand, preferences, or even need?

In practice, allocative efficiency is never measured: there are no mechanisms for measuring whether the result of the resource allocation processes reflect either any individual's set of preferences or any sense of a set of collective preferences. In any case different classes of people have different preferences.

Effectiveness

But what of effectiveness? Given that the success of the allocation process is difficult to measure, is it possible to measure the degree to which those resources which are allocated to services produce the desired results? Progress is being made towards measuring effectiveness in those areas where there is agreement on what a desired outcome is, such as improved health status or acquired knowledge and skills. The issues about measuring effectiveness are partly technical. There are two broad categories of outcome. One is a change in *state*. The purpose of the service might be to improve the quality of a person's health, the durability of a road, the cleanliness of water. While there may be arguments about what to measure, there are numerous examples of how to measure. The second sort of outcome is a change in *behaviour*. The criminal justice system aims to change the offending behaviour of people convicted of crimes. Interventions by social workers are sometimes intended to change the behaviour of parents or children. Such changes may be more difficult to measure than changes in states, although offending rates and rates of abuse can be measured and monitored.

Measuring effectiveness is concerned with finding out what services produce the desired outcomes. The outcomes of services may be different for different stakeholders. As Peter Jackson[5] says:

> Because different stakeholders have different interests in the performance of public sector departments, the stakeholder approach helps to force the question 'whose value for money is being considered?' Value for money will mean different things for different individuals. Often these different perspectives will come into conflict and will need to be resolved. This is the business of politics. Value for money is not a technocratic value-free concept.

There are many examples of the differences in opinion about what outcomes are desired from services. For example, applicants for planning permission want to be able to carry out their developments, while neighbours may not.

The Labour government was very keen in the idea of specifying outcomes and measuring their achievement. The Introduction to the Public Service Agreements for 1999–2002 said:

> The amount spent or numbers employed are measures of the inputs to a service but they do not show what is being achieved. While the number of new government programmes established or the volume of legislation passed are often critical milestones on the path to achieving change, they are only a means to delivering the real improvements on the ground that this Government wants to see. What really matters is the effectiveness and efficiency of the service the public receives. That is what makes a difference to the quality of people's lives.
>
> The targets published in this White Paper are therefore of a new kind. As far as possible, they are expressed either in terms of the **end results** that taxpayers' money is intended to deliver – for example, improvements in health and educational achievement and reductions in crime – or **service standards** – for example, smaller class sizes, reduced waiting lists, swifter justice. The Government is therefore setting specific, measurable, achievable, relevant and timed (ie SMART) targets, related to outcomes wherever possible. Moreover, as experience of this new approach develops, it hopes to further refine and improve future target-setting.

A hierarchy of contracts

The solution to the performance problem that governments chose, in almost all cases, was to move towards contracts that are as complete as possible, specifying as much as can be specified. Incomplete contracts depend on a high degree of trust between the parties: where there is low trust, contracts become more and more elaborate in their search for completeness. The quest for the complete contract results in increasingly elaborate definitions of outputs and outcomes.

Incentives

At the bottom end of the hierarchy of principal–agent relationships is normally an employer–employee contract. The incentives that have been put in place are of three kinds:

- Financial: both institutional and individual incentives were put in place, including extensive use of performance-based pay. Great efforts were made to line up the incentives with the performance measurement and management systems, individual appraisals being based on the targets for the unit, then with the organization as a whole. In the Health Service managers rather than professionals were put on performance-based contracts. In the education service, all teachers were eventually persuaded to accept performance contracts, although in practice few teachers are excluded from the performance element of pay. In the case of education targets, the government introduced a system of performance pay for teachers, who would be paid up to £2000 per year extra if they crossed a 'performance threshold.' At the same time schools had to install performance management arrangements with targets for pupil progress and the professional development of staff. Annual appraisals include setting targets for each teacher in line with the school's targets for the coming year. In the event almost all teachers passed the threshold tests and the scheme was used to raise overall pay subject to a performance constraint, rather than improve individual performance.
- Moral: public praise and public humiliation are blunt instruments with which to hold people to account, and have been widely used. Performance tables are published and those at the top singled out for praise and the award of symbolic prizes (for example being named as a 'beacon') and cash prizes. Those at the bottom might be defined as a 'failing school' or a 'red light hospital' and have very public denunciations of their management, which could either be 'helped' or replaced.
- Managerial autonomy: managers demonstrating success are rewarded with the chance to do their job with less outside interference and inspection than their less successful counterparts. In a development in 2003/4, hospital Trusts that could demonstrate their managerial prowess were awarded 'Foundation' status, giving them certain freedoms from the central planning régime of the Department of Health but still subject to Treasury financial controls. Similar relaxations in exchange for success were used in other sectors, such as prisons.

Sanctions

Each level in the principal–agent relationship hierarchy also has sanctions.

- Termination of contract or quasi-contract: it has long been known that internal agreements are not 'contracts' in the legal sense, especially with regard to the process to follow if one side is found to be in breach. However, even quasi-contracts have administrative sanctions that can be brought into force, which have the same effect as a real contract.

- Financial penalties: budgets can be withheld or not increased in subsequent periods if performance targets are not met.
- Termination of employment contract: at the top levels of management there is widespread use of short-term contracts, the government having the impression that short-term contracts allow greater leverage on managers than long-term permanent contracts. In practice many have benefited from generous compensation terms for premature termination, but this is balanced, in the government's opinion, by the ability to get rid of poor performers.
- Change of ownership (either privatization or nationalization): for extreme failure the sanction is a change of ownership: in the case of the Prison Service, for example, the threat of privatization and the threat of bringing the prison back under Prison Service management are available to the service if either public or private prisons do not meet the required standards. Failing local education authorities have had their management removed and given to private companies. Failing hospital trusts have been merged with other, more successful trusts. Individual parts of services are also subjected to periodic exercises of market testing with private contractors. The threat of privatization, or of re-nationalization, makes a large proportion of public services contestable.

Performance management and policy evaluation

Once it has been decided that a set of outcomes is the objective of the organization, the next question is how their achievement is to be measured. There are two approaches to this. One is to search for some global indicator, such as the quality of life changes as a result of a service, such as a health intervention, or an environmental improvement. Employment policy may be measured by the level of unemployment in an area. This is essentially a top-down approach in which the change in the state of a person or a population is defined by the organization and then measured.

The other is to start with the individual service encounter and start a discussion between the service provider and the service user about what outcomes they expect from the service. A good example of this has been the health authority in East London which developed outcome measures for the treatment of leg ulcers by asking nurses and patients what results they expected from treatment. Or the employment service can measure the numbers of people with whom it deals who find employment, rather than measuring the level of unemployment in its area.

Once the problems of defining the desired outcomes have been solved, there is then a third question: the organization needs to evaluate how best to achieve those outcomes. Here the distinction between policy and management is not clear. Politicians may decide on the services to be provided, such as sentencing policy on criminal justice, that education should take place in particular sorts of institution, or that health treatment should take a particular form. After those decisions have been made, managers implement them. However, the policies themselves may have as big an impact on the outcome as the way in which the service is managed. Even the best-managed workhouses probably had negative effects on their residents.

This aspect of performance management is the process of policy evaluation. This might involve scientific studies of the impact of medical interventions, teaching methods, treatment of people convicted of crimes. It also involves dealing with the opinions of politicians about what works and what does not work. It may be politically attractive to favour harsh treatment in prisons even if criminologists can show that rehabilitation produces lower recidivism rates. Mixed-ability teaching may be shown to produce better overall educational outcomes but some politicians believe in streaming. Low public transport fares may reduce road congestion and improve passenger movement but politicians may prefer balanced budgets for transport operators.

Evaluation has two aspects. One is to find out what works best in producing the desired outcomes: this may indeed be technocratic. Although professionals may continue to claim that only they know what works, because only they have the training and experience to make judgements, empirical scientific methods can produce results which allow people other than professionals to use their own judgement about policy choices. Such science is normal in the medical professions, where blind testing of drugs and treatments gives a good idea about the effectiveness of different approaches to diseases. In other services such an approach may be less appropriate if the outcomes are less measurable, although if outcomes are definable, it ought always to be possible to see whether they have been achieved. Indeed it could be argued that if outcomes cannot be identified, the service has no purpose and should not be provided.

The second aspect is the preferences which service users have for different services. For example, police forces claim that deploying their resources into 'rapid response' units with cars produces higher rates of crime detection and solving than having foot patrols. Surveys have shown, however, that visible police have the effect of reassuring people about their safety. The same is true for certain aspects of school education: parents have preferences for styles of discipline, uniforms and teaching method which are not scientifically-based judgements.

The Labour government's pragmatism to some extent promoted the idea of policy evaluation. The idea that ideology or populism should not distract services from 'what works' was widely promulgated. 'Evidence-based' practice was to be preferred to prejudice. The nature of the evidence on which practice was to be based was contested. The government's view was that evidence was represented by a national view of all evidence, rather than local experience, and that 'what works' should be defined from above and handed down. National Service Frameworks for treatment in the NHS are an example, as are the guidelines for probation services. Centralized interpretation of policy analysis became another way of controlling the organizations delivering services.

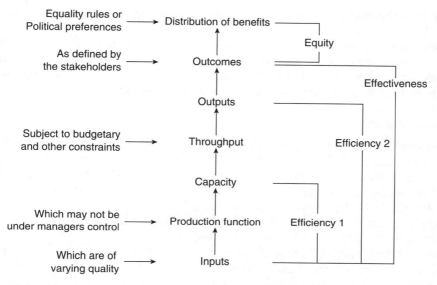

Figure 5.1   Elements of performance measurement

Managerial discretion

Performance information is used for two main purposes: to judge the effectiveness of policy and the performance of organizations and their managers. Managers may also use measurement to judge and improve their own performance. The degree to which measures are able to offer a judgement of managerial performance is partly determined by the degree of discretion which managers have. Figure 5.1 represents a simple flow from inputs to outcomes. The ratio between inputs and outcomes or results is a measurement of a mixture of policy effectiveness and managerial performance. If the choice of outputs to achieve the outcomes is made by either politicians or professionals, then managers can be judged only on the efficiency with which they produce the outputs. If managers have little discretion in the choice and arrangement of inputs, any judgement on their performance is in practice a judgement of how well they manage a given set of people and equipment.

For example, let us consider what is being judged in a league table of school examination results. If a headteacher has no control over which teachers are hired, what equipment is purchased and how the school buildings are built and maintained, his or her discretion is limited to the organization of the school and the motivation and skills of the staff. As personnel policy and budgets are delegated to schools, more discretion is given to headteachers and governors about the uses to which the budget is put and the results achieved are more subject to their efforts.

Satisfactory performance management requires a balance among all of these elements. Organizations that concentrate on a narrow range of targets, especially efficiency targets, are likely to look away from important elements of their work, such as the nature of their relationships with their service users.

League tables

Comparative performance information is published for most services. Schools and education authorities have their examination results made public each year. The local authority indicators are available to the public. The NHS has produced the Health Service Indicators since 1983. Universities are judged and ranked on the quality of their research and teaching.

The publication of these tables can have two effects. Managers may make efforts to achieve the targets contained in the league tables, to the detriment of other aspects of performance. In practice, there are trade-offs between elements of performance. For example, the Benefits Agency has targets for both the speed and accuracy with which benefits are paid. Accuracy can take more time. Universities teach and do research. Since resource allocation has been based in part on research output, some universities have recruited staff with a high volume of research output and not asked them to engage in much teaching: results in the research assessment exercise are improved, with a negative effect on the quality of teaching for students.

The second effect is that managers may try to find out how they can improve their performance by looking at how people above them in the tables work. One way of organizing this is through 'benchmarking', the systematic comparison with the best performer in a group. Benchmarking was first used by companies faced with competitors who could achieve much lower costs than themselves. It consists of comparing elements of the production process against a 'benchmark' performer. The benchmark may not necessarily be in the same industry. Benchmarking has grown in the public sector, both internally and using private sector benchmarks.

There is a national benchmarking project, based on the 'business excellence model' of the European Quality Foundation. Public sector organizations can check their performance on a range of criteria against each other and against those private sector organizations that have also signed up to the scheme.

How well did departments meet the targets and how satisfied was the public with public services?

Answering the first question is not as straightforward as it might be. Targets change from year to year and targets in one instrument of measurement and control are not necessarily used in the rest.[6] As the system of measurement and control developed, managers and politicians were feeling their way with little precedent. When the Executive Agencies were established there were 'Framework Agreements' that set out the basis of a contract between the departments and the agencies, including definitions of managerial discretion and overall targets. Agencies then had to produce corporate plans and business plans as part of their corporate governance. Later the Treasury introduced targets, often consisting of service outcomes, into the Spending Review, the three-year financial planning process. These targets were explicitly set in exchange for the cash allocation. Local authority targets have similarly developed in sophistication and in the formality and explicitness of the cash for performance bargain. In the process of developing the governance mechanisms unworkable targets were dropped, outcomes targets were refined and large amounts of technical work done to produce a set of unambiguous and reliable targets. A comprehensive system of Public Service Agreements generates targets and annually reported performance.

There are five main sources of information on satisfaction. The government has surveyed customer satisfaction with government services since 1998. A 'People's Panel', in practice a sample of about 1000 individuals, was set up to provide market research information about how satisfied people were with public services The panel stayed in existence until 2002. The report on the 'Final Wave' of the panel was published in June 2002.[7] Questions were asked about 29 services across a range of providers, from central government agencies to local authorities and privatized transport operators. The 2002 report also made comparisons with levels of satisfaction in 1998 and 2000.

A further source is the British Social Attitudes Survey,[8] an annual survey of a wide range of attitudes, including attitude to public services. The Scottish Executive conducted a poll on attitudes and satisfaction with the NHS in Scotland in 2004.[9] The British Crime Survey collects information about the number of crimes committed and public attitudes towards crime, fear of crime and the criminal justice system. The National Consumer Council[10] conducted a survey of attitudes and expectations towards public services.

Three examples of public services will be used: crime, health services and school education. First we show how some of the indicators of performance have changed in recent years, and then look at evidence of public attitudes towards the services.

Crime

The trend in number of crimes committed since the 1997 election, as reported to the British Crime Survey (BCS), is downward, as shown in Table 5.1.

Longer term trends for BCS crime are shown in Figure 5.2.

The survey asks people whether they think that the crime rate has increased during the previous two years. Despite an overall fall in crime over the two years,

Table 5.1 *% change in incidents of crime reported in BCS, 1997–2003/4*

Incident	% change
Vandalism	−14
Burglary	−42
Vehicle theft	−40
Bicycle theft	−32
Other household theft	−37
Common assault	−33
Wounding	−18
Robbery	−15
All household crime	−32
All personal crime	−26

Source: Home Office, 2004

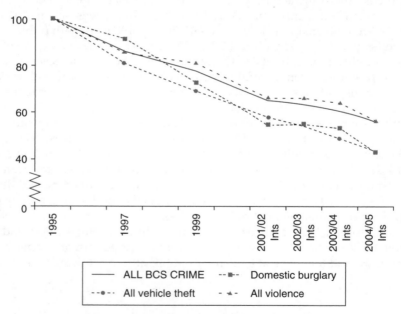

Figure 5.2 Trends in BCS crime 1995–2004/5 (indexed 1995)

Source: Nicholas et al., 2005

61% of respondents believed crime had increased, with 27% believing it had increased 'a lot'.[11] Despite this perception, the fear of crime had decreased since the previous survey. Public confidence in the criminal justice system, recorded by the BCS, dipped between 2001/2 and 2002/3 and then improved slightly in 2003/4 and continued to improve in the 2004/5 survey.

'People's Panel' satisfaction levels with the Police fell from 63% net satisfied in 1998 to 49% net satisfied in 2000 and 38% net satisfied in 2002. There is apparently no connection between the actual level of crime and the satisfaction with the police forces. This leaves a dilemma for government: if it makes promises on policy to reduce crime and delivers on that promise, how does it then generate satisfaction with police services? One answer could be to concentrate on those aspects of police services, behaviour and attitude that impact directly on those people with whom they come into contact. For the rest of the population, who have no direct contact with the police, selling, persuading, explaining and generating engagement through democratc processes might be part of the answer.

Education

Central government control of schools is exercised through national curriculum, standards, tests, public examinations and inspections. Targets are published for attainment at all levels of education and tables are published of schools' attainment. These are aggregated into national targets and national data. Two examples of aggregate targets and attainment are shown in Figures 5.3 and 5.4.

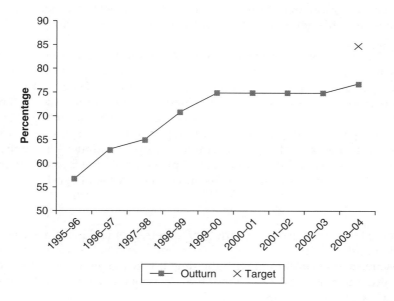

Figure 5.3   Percentage of 11-year-olds achieving level 4 in English

Source: Department for Education and Skills, 2005

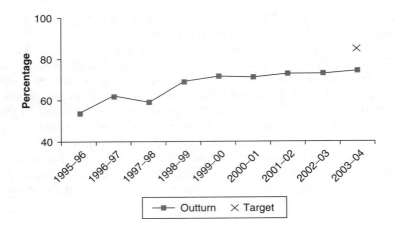

Figure 5.4   Percentage of 11-year-olds achieving level 4 or above in maths

Source: Department for Education and Skills, 2005

What these two examples show is an improvement in performance of 11-year-old children in English and Mathematics from 1995 to 1999 and then a flattening of the rates of achievement. In both cases the targets for 2004 proved to be optimistic.

Public satisfaction with primary schools, as reported by the People's Panel, stayed at the same high level (83% net satisfied) between 1998 and 2000 and improved by a further 2 percentage points between 2000 and 2002, despite the flattening of performance as measured by the National Curriculum Assessments.

People's Panel scores for secondary schools declined over the 1998–2002 period, from net satisfaction of + 74 to + 65. Over that period there was a slow but steady improvement in the indicators, for example of pupil attainment in English and Mathematics at age 14 and the proportion of pupils achieving 5 passes at grade C and over in the General Certificate of Secondary Education at age 16.

Health

The National Health Service has a variety of targets, grouped into three categories: service standards, health and social care outcomes, and value for money. Service standards are mainly concerned with the time it takes to get to see a local doctor or be admitted to a hospital. On both of these counts the service levels have been improving, as shown in Figures 5.5 and 5.6.

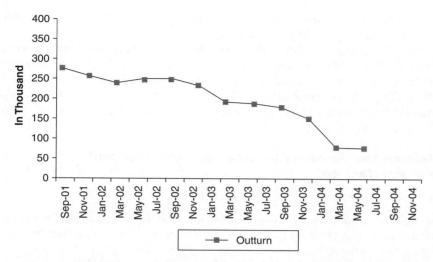

Figure 5.5   The number of people waiting longer than 6 months for inpatient treatment

Source: Department of Health, 2005

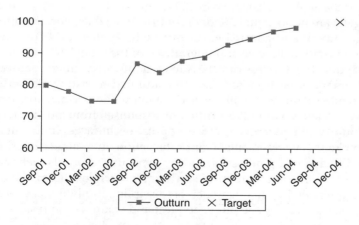

Figure 5.6   Percentage of patients able to see a GP within 2 working days

Source: Department of Health, 2005

The targets on outcomes and value for money were only set in 2002 and the department has yet to publish trend data on them.

People's Panel data on satisfaction with hospitals improved from net +69% in 1998 to net +71 in 2000 and then fell sharply to net +62% in 2002. The British Social Attitude Surveys[12] also tracked an improvement in satisfaction from 1997 to 1999 and then a fall in satisfaction after 2000. The proportion of respondents expressing themselves 'very' or 'quite' satisfied with the NHS went from 37% in 1997 to 42% in 1998 and dropped to 40% by 2002.

Explaining the disparity between performance and public satisfaction

Performance does not create satisfaction

There are two possible explanations for the fact that the trends in performance and satisfaction can and often do go in opposite directions. The first is that the matters that generate satisfaction are not those that are measured in the performance management systems. We have direct evidence of this from MORI,[13] which found the highest correlations with satisfaction were whether people thought they were being 'treated with dignity and respect', the level of relative deprivation of the area in which the service and its users are located, and the degree of ethnic diversity of the area. People in deprived areas are generally less satisfied with services, whatever their performance levels, and satisfaction in racially mixed areas is lower than in racially homogenous areas.

A survey for the Scottish Executive in 2004 suggested that waiting times (one of the main targets) are important: 'The data confirms (sic) that shorter waiting times for contact, treatment and admission correlate with higher levels of satisfaction, with both the individual service and overall use of the NHS.'[14]

The case of education has less direct evidence about what creates satisfaction. In the case of primary education, satisfaction continued to rise while performance levelled off, while satisfaction with secondary fell while performance improved. There are two issues: there will be different responses from people with direct experience (pupils and parents) and the population at large; both categories of people will make their judgements about satisfaction on a variety of criteria. The population will have its opinions formed by exposure to pupils' behaviour outside school and by media attention to stories about schools. Pupils and parents may be more interested in matters such as discipline, bullying, extra-curricular activities, etc. as much as by the published test and examination results.

Whatever the explanation for the apparent paradox, it is clear that the measures and targets used to manage the education system are probably not precisely the same set as would be required to improve satisfaction.

The same division between service users and the public at large applies in the case of the police and the criminal justice system. In the UK it has long been the case that satisfaction with the police is lower among those who have dealings with the police than those who have no dealings, unlike most other services where satisfaction among service users is generally better than among people who have no contact but form their opinions in other ways. While perceptions of the level of crime are not the same as satisfaction with the police (the police do not, after all, cause crime levels directly) it is a paradox in the BCS evidence that people have a view that crime is increasing when it is in practice decreasing.

Satisfaction with the encounter with the police is determined by the manner in which the encounter is handled, whether with the victim or the suspect. There has been an attempt to create a 'customer focus' among the police in the UK[15] and the largest force, the London Metropolitan, have appointed a senior member of staff to improve customer care and customer satisfaction. The main elements of improvement are telephone answering speed, language and treatment of people reporting crime, follow-up actions with victims and general police visibility on the streets. None of this effort will necessarily have any impact on the performance targets used by management: clear-up rates, arrest rates and the level of crime. In fact, spending more time with victims and walking the streets may reduce efficiency in achieving the performance targets. This presents management with a dilemma: whether to aim for public safety or public satisfaction. Managers' response to the dilemma will depend on how the incentives are structured: if resources and rewards are allocated according to the performance targets they will be given priority.

There is other evidence that suggests that satisfaction with services is a function of satisfaction with government. The British Social Attitudes Survey referred to above found that there was a link between political affiliation and satisfaction with the NHS. ' ... the surge in net satisfaction with the NHS between 1997 and 1999 was wholly due to increased satisfaction among *Labour* identifiers after Labour's election victory ... since 1999, the *erosion* of net satisfaction has been due to Conservative identifiers becoming more dissatisfied with the NHS.'[16] This finding turns the argument on its head: Labour voters are satisfied with services because they are happy with the government, rather than happy with the government because they are satisfied with the services. Their political opponents take the opposite view – they express dissatisfaction with services because they dislike the government. They conclude: ' ... this suggests that general attitudes towards the NHS may tell as much about government popularity as they do about the NHS *per se*.'

Satisfaction is a result of the relationship between expectations and experience

It has long been known in the service marketing literature that customer satisfaction with services depends on the extent to which expectations are met. The

National Consumer Council[17] tested this proposition. Using discussion groups and a quantitative survey of the public and opinion leaders at the end of 2002, NCC found that few people thought that the quality of public services had increased over the previous five years: 50% of the sample of the public thought they had stayed the same and 22% that they had got worse. In reaction to the statement 'Increased investment has raised the quality of public services in the UK over the last five years', 36% agreed and 48% disagreed.

Paradoxically, the survey found that people believed that they had improved information about services than they had before (68% agreed), that 'frontline staff have become more customer-focused over the last five years' (61% agree), that 'public service managers take more account of public expectations now than five years ago' (51% agree, 34% disagree). Given these responses, it might be expected that satisfaction levels would also increase.

One clue to this paradox comes from the response to the statement 'It's not that the public services have declined over recent years, but that people now demand and expect more of them.' 69% of the sample of the public agreed with this statement and only 23% disagreed.

One of the NCC's overall conclusion from the research was:

> The findings show that the general public often expects to receive poor quality public services (based on what they hear both in the media and from the people around them). However, service users are often satisfied with the services they receive. These high satisfaction ratings are often attributed to low expectations ... (p. 24)

Appleby and Rosete[18] also found that satisfaction with the NHS was much higher among people with recent experience than among those without. For example, 44% of those with recent outpatient experience were 'satisfied or very satisfied' with the NHS, compared with 34% of those without experience.

This finding is in line with the Parasuraman et al.[19] proposition that the level of satisfaction is a function of the relationship between the perceived services and the expectation. However, the findings reveal another contradiction: while people report that expectations have risen over the past five years, they also claim that expectations are low and that when people experience services they are pleasantly surprised. One possible explanation is: expectations generated by exposure to the media are relatively low; satisfaction generated by personal experience of services is high. This fits the proposition that (apart from the case of the police) service users are more satisfied than the public at large.

Is 'satisfaction' the right target?

These dilemmas could be resolved by aligning the managerial targets with those matters that generate satisfaction. While clearly satisfaction has different roots for users and non-users of services, it should be possible to devise a system of measures aimed at both sets of people. The high-volume services used by a large proportion of people, such as the NHS or the education service, would clearly be able to concentrate on customer-focused activities, while low-exposure services, such as the police, the courts, Customs and Excise for example, would need to work on generating satisfaction among non-users to maintain public support.

But it is at least worth asking the question whether this approach would produce the services that 'society' 'wants'. Individuals might be more satisfied as the result of having 'better' experiences. But what if, for example, doctors' spending more time with fewer patients creates more satisfaction for those who receive the service? Or what if the police create happier crime victims at the expense of catching the perpetrators? What if pupils can be made 'satisfied' with easy tests and an unchallenging curriculum?

In practice choices are not so stark, but the direction of management effort can skew services in one way or the other. Collectively society may prefer a reduction in crime or an increase in clear-up rates to more customer-friendly police, but it has no means to express that preference. The consumer model implied by the 'customer satisfaction' approach treats service users as individuals with needs for satisfaction, rather than as a collectivity with needs for public safety, health and education.

Why has there been such an emphasis on 'satisfaction'? One answer is that this is what the consumer-oriented approach throws up. It is a very crude, aggregate term. Even in a relatively simple service, defining and measuring satisfaction is complicated. For many public services it is further complicated when the specifics of satisfaction are considered. First, there is the question: with what is the service user satisfied or dissatisfied? Inadequate social security payments are not cancelled by polite treatment in the claim process. Being treated with dignity and respect by an overworked and under-resourced nurse may produce admiration and sympathy rather than satisfaction or its opposite. The real problem with separating consumer satisfaction from all other opinions and feelings about public services is that it fails to capture the whole of the relationship between the service user and the service provider.

Abandon the customer paradigm?

There is an alternative argument: that the business–customer relationship is not analogous to a government–citizen relationship and the techniques of service design and management and customer satisfaction are inappropriate. An example is the Catalyst pamphlet by Catherine Needham[20] who argues that the customer–service relationship built around the passive customer and their experience of the service is inappropriate in a democracy: 'Consumerism is a model that prioritises the individual over the community, encourages passivity, downgrades public spaces, weakens accountability, and privatises citizenship.' (p. 33)

Her solution is to shift the emphasis from satisfaction to two other elements: customer co-production and voluntarism. Customer co-production, ironically, has been at the heart of service marketing for two decades or so and recognizes that the users of services are rarely passive recipients but have to take an active part in the production process. The key to a satisfactory co-production relationship is that the customer has the amount of production to do that they expect and are comfortable with. Voluntarism is seen as an expression of solidarity and belonging, in contrast to the individualism and isolation generated by a customer relationship. Together with active involvement in politics, especially at local level, Needham defines this approach as 'civic republicanism'.

The view gathers some support in a study by Clarke and others on the development of citizen-consumers in the United Kingdom in three public services, health care, policing and social care. Clarke concludes that there has been too great an emphasis on the consumer to the detriment of the citizen: 'So, at one point, we may be the individuated, self-directed choosers of public services (articulating our needs, expecting them to be met), but we may also act collectively as a group of users (activists making demands), or as citizens (lobbying political representatives; demonstrating against policies) ... None of these are exclusive and situational factors may tip us from one to another.'[21]

If this alternative view of the relationship between government and consumers and citizens were to be the basis of the management of public services, the balance of management and political effort would need to be tilted towards citizenship and away from consumerism. There are some signs in recent opinion surveys in the United Kingdom that satisfaction levels are creeping up again after their dip, but that performance against targets is remaining flat. If this is the case, then factors other than performance are affecting satisfaction. We return to this issue in the discussion of service design in Chapter 6.

Conclusions

Performance measurement and the use of performance indicators are at the heart of the efforts by government to take central control of services. The Labour governments staked their reputations on performance targets and their achievement. They believed that they could create a unified hierarchy of control systems with a set of performance targets and indicators that flowed from manifesto promises to individual performance targets for workers. In addition, there was a strong belief that improving public services in measurable ways would generate public and electorate support for the party that delivered those improvements.

The development of the performance management system was impressive, and managers' and professionals' responses have been broadly in line with government expectations. There were some disappointments. The examples shown in this chapter reflect a tendency for performance improvement to level off after a while, once the initial easier changes are made. Productivity improvement seemed to be a problem during the spending increases of the early 2000s, as extra cash was not turned into commensurate extra services, some of the money being absorbed in higher pay and prices.

The biggest disappointment for government must have been the disconnection between improvements in performance and the level of public satisfaction. When polled, members of the public base their opinions of the standards of public service on factors other than the measurable performance targets carefully crafted by government. While the government has apparently treated the management of the 5.5 million public servants as a 'principal–agent' problem, the public do not apparently see it the same way. Their expectations, experiences and expressed opinions do not fit neatly into the hierarchical managerial system that governments have devised.

Notes

For weblinks relevant to the issues discussed in this chapter see www.sagepub.co.uk/flynn.

1   Audit Commission, *Performance measurement as a tool for modernising government: Using the PSAs to drive continuous improvement* (Audit Commission, London, 1999).
2   For example, J.-J. Laffont and D. Martimort, *The Theory of Incentives* (Princeton University Press, Princeton and Oxford, 2002).
3   M. Barzelay, *Breaking Through Bureaucracy: A new vision for managing in government* (University of California Press, Berkeley, 1992).
4   p. 120.
5   Peter Jackson, 'Reflections on Performance Measurement in Public Service Organisations' in P.M. Jackson (ed.), *Measures of Success in the Public Sector* (CIPFA, London, 1995) p. 4.
6   For a description of the evolution of central government controls, see C. Talbot, 'Executive Agencies: have they improved management in government?', *Public Money and Management,* April (2004), pp. 104–112.
7   Office of Public Services Reform, *Monitoring Satisfaction: Trends from 1998–2002* (HMSO, London, 2002).
8   A. Park, J. Curtice, K. Thomson, L., Jarvis et al. (eds), *British Social Attitudes: The 20th Report* (Sage, London, 2003).
9   Scottish Executive, *Public Attitudes to the National Health Service in Scotland – 2004 Survey* (2004), www.scotland.gov.uk
10   National Consumer Council, *Expectations of Public Services* (National Consumer Council, London, 2003).
11   S. Nicholas, D. Povey, A. Walker et al., *Crime in England and Wales 2004/2005,* (The British Crime Survey), (HMSO, London, p. 21).
12   J. Appleby and A.R. Rosete, 'The NHS: keeping up with public expectations?' in A. Park, J. Curtice, K. Thomson et al. (eds), *British Social Attitudes: The 20th Report* (Sage, London, 2003).

13 MORI, 'Frontiers of performance in the NHS', London, June 2004.

14 Scottish Executive, *Public Attitudes*, para. 10.5.

15 L. Westmarland and N. Smith, 'From scumbags to consumers: customer service and the commodification of policing', output from *Creating Citizen Consumers; Changing Identifications and Relationships* (Open University, Milton Keynes, 2004).

16 Appleby and Rosete, The NHS: Keeping up, p. 31.

17 National Consumer Council, *Expectations.*

18 Ibid.

19 For example, A. Parasuraman, V. Zeithaml and L. Berry, 'A Conceptual Model of Service Quality and its Implications for Future Research', *Journal of Marketing*, (Fall, 1985) pp. 41–50.

20 Catherine Needham '*Citizen-Consumers, New Labour's Market Place Democracy* (Catalyst, London, 2003).

21 John Clarke, 'Citizen-Consumers: the trajectory of an identity'. Conference of the Canadian Anthropological Society, London, Ontario, 2004.

6

Service design and customer–citizen orientation

Introduction

The purpose of this chapter is to look at ways in which public services can be made more sensitive to the requirements, preferences and expectations of the people who use them. There has been a progression in government policy towards service design and customer care. The introduction of the Citizen's Charter by the Major government represented an approach based on predetermined standards and a measurement system designed to find out whether those standards had been met. The standards were publicized, often in posters in places where the public receive services. Keeping to the standard won the organization a plaque and a pat on the back from ministers.

While initially the standards were set by the organizations themselves, there was a gradual adoption of consultation, to see what people wanted from services and which aspects of service quality were important to them. Matters such as speed, privacy, being treated with dignity and respect are weighted variously in different services.

We saw in Chapter 5 that improvements in service quality, objectively measured, do not always produce improvements in satisfaction. Towards the end of Labour's second term, around 2004, 'choice' was chosen as the key to customer satisfaction. An essential element of service design, wherever feasible, was to be choice, of service and of service provider. While this had not arisen from customer surveys, it was seen by senior government people as an essential element of 'modernisation'. Uniform standards and standardization were old-fashioned; variety and choice were modern. So, famously, the 'bog-standard comprehensive school'[1] was condemned to be replaced by specialist schools, whether specializing in languages or arts or sport or science, or by City Academies. Patients were to be given a choice of at least four hospitals for their non-emergency treatments. Few other services were to get the choice treatment: one social security system, state pension, foreign service, court, etc. All had to continue to try to improve customer service without the added ingredient of choice.

Not all users of public services are 'customers' in the normal sense of the word. There are many relationships between public service organizations and those they serve, although managers in many services have decided to use the idea of a customer as a metaphor that staff can easily understand. While perhaps not technically accurate, the thought of claimants of social security, for example, as customers implies that they should be treated with respect, politeness and dignity.

People using public services can be offered control over those services in a variety of ways, from consultation to direct decision-making. Managers and politicians have devised a range of procedures to make services more sensitive, including in a limited way the use of vouchers to enhance choice, market research to find out what people think, and charters which set out standards and what people can do if those standards are not achieved, readering the politicians' task of making decisions about services more meaningful and a holistic approach to the design of the service delivery system.

While each of these approaches has been used, there remain some contradictions in trying to develop a customer- or service-user orientation, including the difficulty of doing more with less and the distancing from the service users which is implied by contracting out service delivery.

Approaches to customer orientation

Customers, voters and citizens

It has become common for managers of public services to try to make them more 'customer-oriented'. This applies both to services which are for the public and to those which are for internal 'customers', such as personnel or accountancy services. A pure definition of customer would exclude many of the relationships between public organizations and the people who use their services. Customers normally have a choice about what to buy and from whom, they provide the revenue from which businesses generate profits, and they have certain rights as customers. These conditions only apply to a small proportion of public services. There is a wide range of relationships between public services and the people who use them. At one extreme is the prison–prisoner relationship in which the prisoner is an unwilling user of the service with no option of exit. At the other extreme, users of public sports facilities have many of the attributes of customers: they pay for at least part of the cost, they can choose to go elsewhere or do something else. In between are relationships with varying degrees of ability to exit: if geography permits, children can change schools, patients can change general practitioner. In practice, choice is limited: inner city areas, for example, have fewer GPs per head of population than the suburbs; travel prevents choice of primary school in rural areas; the district hospital system provides a natural catchment area for hospitals in small and medium sized towns.

The right to exit is an important determinant of the way in which competitive businesses treat their customers. If they can go to another supplier when dissatisfied, they will. One measure of customer satisfaction is whether they come back or not. Without the option, there is neither the direct incentive to generate satisfaction nor the obvious measurement of whether it has been achieved. That is not the same as saying that competition and a customer relationship are sufficient to produce customer orientation: whole sectors can be equally poor at customer service. Nor does it imply that competition is necessary for customer orientation: there is no reason in principle why monopolies could not be responsive to their customers – in the case of many public services which are a monopoly, this is indeed the management task.

In addition to the question of whether or not there is a choice of provider, relationships vary according to the nature of the service. Some services are protective (fire, child protection) while others are concerned with organizing access to entitlements (social security), yet others are concerned with helping people to have fuller lives (adult education). These services all require different ways of thinking about developing and maintaining a relationship which gives the recipients or users of the service as much control over the service as they want (and can be allowed to have). It is not necessarily the case that services can be more responsive if there is a consumer relationship than if the relationship is one of dependency. A consumer relationship might be very responsive in a monopoly (the only library in the village, the only golf course), if there are empowered and sensitive managers.

Box 6.1   Customer orientation in a monopoly

A manager in a social services department was given the task of organizing a meal for frail older people every day in a rural area. The standard solution would have been to have pre-cooked meals delivered (a 'meals on wheels' service). She asked the people what they would prefer and found that social contact was an important element in their needs. She organized a service by publicans cooking and serving meals to those who were able to get to the public house. A London Borough with a large number of different ethnic groups among its older people organizes cooking by restaurants and delivers the meals.

The question is, how to organize the process of listening to the service users and responding to their needs and preferences in each of these different relationships?

Bureaucratic paternalism by agency	Information provision	Seeking opinions	Discussion of proposals	Consumer/ citizen exploration of issues, goals and choice	Joint decision making	Decisions devolved to consumers/ citizens

Figure 6.1   A spectrum of consumer/citizen control

Source: Skelcher, 1993, p. 14.

Even the most coercive services such as the prisons can respond to needs and preferences in areas such as education and training.

Responsiveness can occur at different levels. At its most trivial, a customer care approach is limited to providing a welcoming attitude, including a smile and a presentable reception area. While this may be pleasant it makes only a small contribution to the service. A more responsive approach would be designed to 'deliver' the service in a way which reflects people's wishes. For example, whether they have to travel to get it or it is delivered at home, whether transactions are carried out by letter or by telephone. Even greater responsiveness would give the service user control over the level of service they can receive, such as the frequency of home help services.

Chris Skelcher[2] has argued that there is a spectrum of degrees of power for consumers/citizens. His categories are shown in Figure 6.1. He argues that agencies are less willing to devolve power about fundamental or strategic questions. Once the organization goes beyond the more trivial degrees of responsiveness, the difference between public services and private services becomes apparent: choices have to be made about what services are provided and who should be eligible for them. Fundamental decisions such as these are made through some sort of democratic process, rather than through a market. Democratic decisions, whether at local authority level or at the level of parliamentary legislation, are not then negotiable with individuals or groups of citizens. The boundary between the negotiable and the non-negotiable is not always either clear or fixed, however. Some managers use the fact that a service is 'statutory', or defined by law, as a reason for not allowing the users of the service to have a choice.

Given this variety of relationships and degrees of responsiveness, managers of public services have a subtle job to do in making their services responsive. Sometimes they have no control over the fundamentals of the service: managers in social security offices do not decide the level of benefits and teachers do not choose the national curriculum. The fundamental decisions are made in some part of the political process, while informed by managers.

Citizenship and entitlements

T.H. Marshall[3] argued that citizenship has three elements: civil rights (liberty, freedom of thought and speech and religion, the right to own property and make contracts, etc.); political rights (to participate in the exercise of power) and social rights (the right to economic welfare and to participate in the prevailing level of civilization). Social rights could be exercised either by working, through the family or by state provision for people who could not work. If it is the case that people have a right, as a citizen, to a certain level of access to income and services, this places a duty on the state and its workers to seek out citizens and help them to exercise their rights.

This argument emphasizes rights rather than duties and to an extent leaves the definition of the citizenship rights in detail to the people running the institutions of the state. Individuals as citizens cannot individually define and exercise their rights, other than by voting. Citizenship rights are very different from consumer rights. Consumers exercise their entitlements by spending money and by invoking the law. Citizens have recourse to law, to rules and norms occasionally defined by the state and to those elements of redress laid down in the various charters.

There have been legal cases to test the degree of entitlements that people have to community care. It seems that if a local authority assesses an individual as being in need of help because of a disability then they have an entitlement to some service. Given that budgets are cash limited, this has made authorities nervous about making assessments for services which they cannot fund.

The whole question of rights is confused and covered by many different pieces of legislation, for example in education where children have a right to education which is not very closely defined, and in housing where there is an obligation on local authorities to house homeless people but not a guaranteed source of funds to do so. The lack of definition leaves discretion for managers to interpret what entitlements mean in detail.

Vouchers, cash and customer control

There have been examples of the use of vouchers and/or cash to give service users customer control of their services, such as the allowance for people with disabilities to buy their own vehicles, the disability living allowance, or vouchers for home care which are offered in some local authorities. Representatives of people with disabilities argue for the extension of such schemes, rather than having to choose services which have been designed and provided by somebody else. The law[4] allows local authorities to make direct payments to people assessed as needing community care, but as we saw in Chapter 4, very little use was made of this power in practice.

At various times, there have been arguments for vouchers for education and they were introduced for nursery education in 1996. Voucher schemes or cash

Table 6.1   *Benefits Agency Customer Survey: Reasons for dissatisfaction with outcome of interview at local office*

Claim refused/couldn't help	47%
Query not answered	30%
Length of time taken	26%
Wanted more money	13%
Incorrect payment/calculation	13%
Staff unknowledgeable	12%

Source: Chandler, P., 1994

allowances work if certain conditions apply. First, supply has to be available in a way that offers choice. Without that, the voucher is simply a token of funding. For example, if there is one nursery school in an area, the introduction of vouchers simply adds form-filling and paperwork to the previous process of applying for a place. Second, for equity the voucher must be adequate to cover the cost of the service. If vouchers require additional payments, services are available according to how much money people have, rather than need. Third, people should be both willing and able to organize services for themselves, researching the options, making choices, entering agreements. Tradition and familiarity play a part here. Not everyone is used to the idea of acting as a consumer in relation to doctors or schools, or home helps or residential homes.

Where these conditions do not apply, other mechanisms are required to enable people to exercise power.

Market research

There is now widespread use of market research to find out what users of public services think of them. Local authorities regularly research both general levels of satisfaction and attitudes to individual services. Various Agencies also conduct research to find out how to improve satisfaction. For example, the Benefits Agency commissions National Opinion Polls every year to find out what its customers think of their services and how they might be improved (see Table 6.1).

Market research allows people to express their preferences and reactions to services. It can be done by survey, either by focus group or by interview with service users. Without market research, approaches to customer satisfaction or quality are likely to be based on managers' ideas about what is important, rather than service users'.

Charters and standards

In the mid-1980s several local authorities, such as the City of York and the London Borough of Islington, took an interest in service design and the specification of service standards. They published the standards by which services should be delivered, which were expressed as a 'contract' between the local authority and the citizens.

In 1991 the government published the Citizen's Charter. In the Preface, John Major was careful to point out that the charter was not simply a statement of entitlements:

> The Citizen's Charter is about giving more power to the citizen. But citizenship is about our responsibilities – as parents, for example, or as neighbours – as well as our entitlements. The Citizen's Charter is not a recipe for more state action; it is a testament to our belief in people's right to be informed and choose for themselves.[5]

The charter was not only about accountability and standards. The principles of public service set out consisted of seven items: standards, openness, information, choice, non-discrimination, accessibility and redress. To implement these principles, the government decided that there should be nine mechanisms: more privatization; wider competition; further contracting out; more performance-related pay; published performance targets; publication of information about standards achieved; more effective complaints procedures; tougher and more independent inspectorates; better redress. This list illustrates the range of ideas about the use of the public sector. Privatization and contracting out are seen as positive in themselves, whether or not there is competition. Standard setting is purely a matter for the service providers: they will set standards, an inspectorate will monitor them and the citizen may receive redress if they are not met. As the charter initiative developed, more attention was paid to service users' expectations and preferences.

As well as the principles and mechanisms, the Charter Initiative included the introduction of the Charter Mark, a competition in which public service providers who could demonstrate their quality of provision would be awarded a certificate (and plaque).

Following the publication of the overall charter, individual charters were produced for services. These are published and in many cases, such as at service points for the Employment Service and Customs and Excise, they are on public display. The idea was that the Charters would focus managers' and workers' attention on service standards and draw citizens' attention to what they could expect. On occasion, the publication of standards seemed to be directed towards depressing expectations: for example the NHS standards state the times by which all patients should be admitted to hospital, broken down by ailment. Early standards included 18 months waiting times for serious procedures, such as heart by-pass operations.

The Labour governments continued the use of charters and standards together with awards. The Chartermark was retained by Labour and used to promote good

customer service. The criteria are wide-ranging, encompassing financial management as well as customer service and customer choice. The criteria[6] are:

1 Set standards and perform well
2 Actively engage with your customers, partners and staff
3 Be fair and accessible to everyone and promote choice
4 Continuously develop and improve
5 Use your resources effectively and imaginatively

Standards and charters may or may not be customer-oriented. They can be based
on service users' expectations, or they can be devised in isolation. Customer satisfaction occurs when the service as perceived matches the customer's expectation. Even criterion 2, about consultation with customers, staff and partners, does
not specifically require an assessment of expectations.

Meeting standards which do not themselves match expectations will not produce satisfaction. Parasuraman et al[7] argued that dissatisfaction arises from a gap
between the expectation of a service and the customers' perception of it. The
expectation comes from a range of sources: past experience, word of mouth, need
and the advertising which the service provider produces. The managers' task is to
find out what the expectations are, produce a specification which matches them
and then organize service delivery according to the specification. They found that
dissatisfaction was as likely to be caused by misinterpretation of the expectations
as by the failure to produce the service according to the specification. The performance element of the Citizen's Charter and the related departmental charters
started with standards devised internally, but many have progressed to include
customer expectations.

Democracy

A more difficult managerial task is to assist the political process to make the big
decisions about what services to provide and to whom. This is especially difficult
at times when funds are being cut: decisions about what to subtract are harder
than those about what to add.

The elements of support for the political process are: an evaluation of services
and their impact, rather than only budgets and the way in which they are spent;
distributional impact of changes in services (geography, gender, age, race);
options among which political choices can be made. The elements which make
the process more difficult for politicians are: shroud waving, a process by which
managers tell of the worst consequences of changing or withdrawing a service;
recourse to untrue legal advice, in which managers speak of 'statutory responsibilities' which are in practice vague and professional obstacles, in which reference
is made to professional judgements which override political choice.

Customer-oriented service design

Services are intangible and therefore quality standards can only be measured by the customer's perception. While standards of manufactured products also have to meet customer requirements, once that requirement has been defined there are objective measures of whether they have been met. This is true of services only to a limited extent, through measuring response times, for example. In fact response times and waiting times are a common element of all charter-type standard setting, precisely because they can be measured. Other aspects of the service experience, such as the degree of anxiety caused, the confidence the customer has in the abilities of the service provider, the politeness or empathy level during the transaction, are all important parts of customer satisfaction but cannot be measured continuously. Because of that, people designing and managing services have to find ways of ensuring that the exchanges take place in a consistent way without being able to check on every member of staff all the time.

The second main difference between services and products is that services cannot be stored, but have to be made available when the customers want them. Matching the timing of service availability with customer preferences sometimes requires work outside 'normal' hours and often requires seasonal variation in supply. More recently, people have come to realize that most industries have a service element to them, whether this consists of after-sales service or the service elements of the process of buying a product, and many of the ideas of service management have been applied in sectors which are not service industries at first sight.

These developments have been commented on and supported by academics and consultants on service management and service marketing. They need careful interpretation in public services because of the different relationships between the organizations and their service users and because of the frequent need for equitable treatment and the exercise of entitlements which derive from citizenship rather than the market.

Who is the customer?

The first aspect of service design which managers in the public sector have had to cope with is the definition of the 'customer'. While the people who receive the services are the most obvious customer, public services have other people to satisfy. For example, the Benefits Agency decided early that claimants of social security benefits should be called customers and treated as such. Managers argued that the customer relationship was an appropriate one as a model for the way in which claimants should be treated, even though some of the features of the supplier–customer relationship were absent. They said that the respect, politeness and concern which good customer service implies were appropriate and would be well understood by staff dealing with members of the public. They also had to acknowledge the interest in the service relationship of ministers, the Treasury and other parts of government.

Box 6.2   Redefining the customer

A dog warden service in a London borough was unpopular and expensive. Children threw stones at the wardens' vans and dog owners resented having their dogs picked up as they roamed the streets. The managers decided to orient the service towards the dogs as customers, rather than the general public. The service concept became one of secure and happy dogs, rather than protection for the public. The delivery system was changed from catching dogs and taking them to Battersea Dogs Home to finding the owners, or a substitute owner. Owners were offered counselling in how to look after dogs. As a result fewer dogs were destroyed, costs were therefore lower, grateful substitute owners made donations to the service and the children stopped stoning the vans.

Similarly, the Probation Service has a relationship with offenders which has elements of a customer–supplier one. At the same time, the service is reliant on magistrates to give non-custodial sentences. The service also has had to respond to the Home Secretary's ideas about what probation orders are, as we saw in Chapter 4. Service design therefore has to take account of the expectations and preferences of a range of 'stakeholders' or people who have an interest in and influence on the organization.[8]

Service concept

Different stakeholders have their own ideas about the benefits of the service being provided. While people on probation may see the service as an intrusion, magistrates see it as a way of preventing reoffending and the Home Secretary sees it as a punishment. The service concept is defined by Normann[9] as the benefits of the service as defined by the customers. Clearly the public sector, with its multiple stakeholders, has to design services for many different definitions of benefits.

Market segment

As well as having multiple stakeholders, public services have service users with different characteristics. One of the dilemmas which managers face is how to meet the different expectations of different types of service user while maintaining equitable treatment. Should doctors give as much time to people with minor ailments as they do to people with serious complaints? Fairness would suggest that everyone should have the same time spent on them, while creating an equal outcome would dictate that the serious cases get more time. In social security, should all claimants have the same access arrangements or should routine enquiries about pensions and child benefit be dealt with differently from social fund applications? Should gifted children receive more attention from teachers than children with difficulties?

Service delivery system

Once the service concept has been defined, and differences between groups of service users identified, the service delivery system can be designed. The delivery system has many elements: physical things, such as buildings, vehicles and telephone systems; staff; processes of access and rationing. Most services can be seen as having 'core' and 'peripheral' elements. The core is those parts of the service without which the service would not happen at all, while the peripherals may be designed to make the services attractive or accessible.

In the private sector, a lot of the competition among service organizations is based on the quality of the peripherals. Airlines, for example, have similar service cores: aeroplanes which take people from one airport to another. They differentiate themselves from each other partly by their schedules, so that people can go where they want at the time they want, and partly by the peripherals. The booking system can be very easy or tortuous. Treatment on the ground can vary: some airlines provide business class passengers with chauffeurs from their office to the airport; they build special lounges at the airports. Treatment in the aeroplane can also vary, with different grades of food and drink and entertainment. The no-frills airlines compete on price and schedules.

The public sector attitude to the peripherals is somewhat different, especially in periods of budget cuts. Managers and professionals defend the core services more than the peripherals against cuts. So, if there is a choice between reducing the number of staff and delaying redecorating the waiting area, the core service is preserved.

Where there is competition for customers, these attitudes change. Schools which have to attract pupils to maintain their budget often concentrate on the attractive peripherals, as well as the core service of teaching and learning. Uniforms, school plays and music lessons may not be essential to the core service but they differentiate one school from another in the eyes of parents and potential pupils. Specialist schools all teach the national curriculum. What distinguishes them from each other and from the bog-standard is the extra facilities available to help teach their specialisms.

The call centre is a cost-effective way of providing access to services. It represents a relationship with the customer that is in practice entirely impersonal, although it has some superficial aspects of real human contact. Call centres handle calls for a range of businesses, and workers can access information databases on customers and services during the conversation. Banks, utilities, cable companies and many others operate their customer interface through this method. The Blair government saw call centres as the 'modern'[10] way to provide services. It established NHS Direct in 1998, a way of accessing advice from the NHS over the phone as an alternative to visiting primary care providers.

The National Audit Office reported on the use of call centres by government in 2002.[11] The report found a high degree of public satisfaction with the 133 call centres that were operated by both direct employees and outsourcing operators. Service quality and customer satisfaction are measured in a variety of ways, including measuring the time it takes to answer a call (84% are answered within 20 seconds), satisfaction polling (satisfaction ratings ranged from 71% to 100%), mystery shoppers and call monitoring.

The government has also set targets for the proportion of services that can be accessed through the internet. In 2000 the Prime Minister pledged that by 2005 all services that could be accessed through the internet would be. Promoting this access was one of many tasks taken on by the 'Office of the eEnvoy', a post created in 1999 (and deleted in 2004 when the function was transferred to the Prime Minister's Delivery Unit) to co-ordinate investment in information and communication technology in government. The portal through which services would be accessed (DirectGov) was launched in 2004 and by 2006 was getting 2 million visits a month and included links to 11 government departments. In 2006 responsibility for DirectGov was taken over by the Central Office of Information, as a main route for communication with citizens.

Customer co-production

All services involve a partnership between the service provider and the service user. In fact the expression 'service delivery' implies that the user of the service is a passive recipient who has the service delivered to them. School children have to participate in the education process, doing most of the work, or the service will fail. Medical services also require active participation by patients to effect a cure. The degree to which service users wish to participate varies, and sensitive service design and management will take this into account.

Image

The fourth element of service design is how the organization is to present itself to the outside world. In private services, designers work on the whole set of ways in which an organization communicates with its customers, from the appearance and attitudes of staff, through the colours used in the premises, to the letterheads used for correspondence.

Many public sector organizations have had similar design makeovers. The creation of NHS Trusts, grant-maintained schools, competitive white-collar services and Executive Agencies has promoted the flourishing image management industry, producing logos, 'corporate dress' (staff uniforms), glossy brochures and repainted signs.

Just as the other elements of design need to be interpreted in a public sector context, so does image management. The reasons are also similar: different messages may be appropriate for different stakeholders. Even glossy brochures may give the impression of profligacy to funders while instilling confidence in service users. The police have a particular problem in projecting a consistent image to members of the public, transgressing drivers and criminals.

Values

There is a debate about the role of values or organizational culture in service design and management. Normann, for example, argues that without shared values, service delivery cannot be of high quality and consistent. If there is to be discretion at the point of contact between the organization and its customers, that discretion cannot be exercised by reference to a rulebook, rather to the customer service ethos of the organization. When price competition called for cost reductions, rulebooks about the limits to customer service were introduced.

The opposite view is that if there is a high turnover of staff and especially if they are poorly paid and uncommitted to their organization, staff cannot be expected to use their discretion and express the organization's customer service values. Rather they can learn routines of behaviour which match most customer expectations. This is especially true in services which are relatively routine and where little discretion is required. Operatives in fast food outlets have not internalized an ethos of desiring general well-being when they tell us to 'have a nice day'. They have learned a routine, in which communication with customers is as regimented as portion size and uniform clothing. Such routine service produces customer satisfaction because it matches expectations.

In the public sector, there may be values and a collective ethos which are more than a desire for customer service: many public sector workers say that their motivation for working is to provide a service for people, to high standards and with equity. If, together with these values, they also have the necessary skills, then the service management process can rely on their appropriate use of discretion.

However, if the people in contact with the service users are not inspired by a desire to serve the public but regard the work as 'just a job', and a low-paid one, managers have a dilemma. Do they try to engender an appropriate set of values, perhaps through a training programme, or do they design a set of behavioural routines which simulate a good ethos? Approaches such as quality circles, in which people collaborate to find better ways of doing things, rely on the willing and perhaps enthusiastic participation of people in service improvement. If willingness is in doubt, such approaches are a failure.

Once these elements are put in place, they reinforce each other. The delivery system reinforces customers' expectations. The image reinforces staff attitudes to the organization. Different segments have a modification of the delivery system. In well-managed services there is consistency among the elements.

Quality

Public service organizations have all had initiatives about service quality. There are two main approaches to quality, implied by two definitions of it. One is that quality is defined as 'conformance to specification', a definition clearly derived from manufacturing. Management's main effort, using this definition, is to make sure that the specification is met, either by employees or contractors. Quality control, through inspection and monitoring, will ensure conformance.

Another definition is 'fitness for purpose', which implies that it is the person using the service who makes the judgement about what would make it fit for the purpose and whether that has been achieved. This approach implies that service users are involved or control the quality assurance process, reacting with those providing the service to ensure that it does what it is supposed to do. This implies that the specification may be ignored or modified, to make sure that the service is what the user wants. Inspection of conformance to specification would not achieve this.

Quality assurance is an approach to quality which emphasizes the importance of making sure that all the processes and activities involved in producing services are working properly, from planning to delivery and feedback. There are certification procedures, such as the international quality standard ISO 9001, which check whether all the right sorts of procedures are in place. Many firms and public authorities will only deal with organizations which have such a certificate.

A survey[12] was carried out in 2000 on the quality approaches used by government departments, local government, Training and Education Councils and the NHS. The survey found that Investors in People was the most commonly used approach. The answers to the question about which tools were used are shown in Figure 6.2.[13]

Citizen-oriented service design

We have already seen that a private sector service design and management model cannot be directly applied to the public sector without interpretation. The underlying reason is that people who use public services are citizens as well as customers. Their access to services is frequently a right which derives from meeting eligibility criteria, or simply from being a citizen, rather than from the ability to pay.

There are several implications of this. First is that overstretched services may not wish to make themselves too attractive, because they cannot cope with existing demand. On the contrary they may want to engage in 'demarketing' their services, especially to those in least need. Second, in those services that are

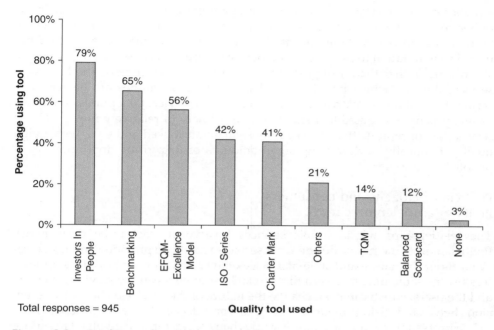

Figure 6.2   Quality tools used in UK public service
Source: PricewaterhouseCoopers, 2000

available as a right, the organization cannot decide that they do not want to provide a service for a particular individual or group. Inclusiveness may obstruct good service design and delivery. Third, decisions about what to produce, in what quantity and for whom are not in the hands of the managers. All public services are ultimately under the control of politicians, whether directly or indirectly. A pure customer orientation is affected by politicians' attitudes.

In addition, accountability is more diffuse in the public sector. Managers of private services are accountable to shareholders for attracting enough customers at the right price to make a profit. Public sector service managers are accountable, ultimately, to their customers through the political process. They are also accountable to people who are not customers but taxpayers, and to their elected representatives.

Contradictions in customer/citizen orientation

Budgets and quality

These special characteristics of public services present managers with dilemmas. One is the balance between service quality and cost. In private services, generally, a higher quality service can command a higher price and stay profitable. In the public services, high quality does not necessarily generate more revenue, but may be more expensive. If there are insufficient resources to meet overall demand, there is a temptation to provide a mediocre standard of service to as many people as possible, rather than a high standard to a few. An example is the homecare service, through which people with disabilities or infirmities are helped with certain tasks at home. With a given budget for this service, the options are to give as many people as possible a small amount of help (a relatively low quality of service) or concentrate the service on those in greatest need and give them a high quality. Politically, withdrawing small amounts of help from large numbers of people is unpopular.

Politicians, citizens and consumers: limits of arm's-length control

The relationships within public services involve at least three participants. Politicians vote the funds, decide what services should be provided and take decisions about the nature and style of service delivery, as representatives of the electors. At the same time there is a direct relationship between the service providers and the users, which can itself change the nature of the services. There can be tensions between decisions made by politicians and decisions made by managers.

The problem is even more complicated when contractors are involved in service delivery. Politicians do not have direct control over the operations of contractors, which are managed through a series of contracts and specifications. Contractors have to refer to the specification and the purchaser before changing a service in response to a service user's preferences or requirements. It is more difficult to have a responsive service in these circumstances.

Equity, equal treatment and customization

Another serious dilemma is that between equity of treatment and customization.[14] David Miliband, schools standards minister, called for more customized approaches to education, and the Prime Minister included 'personalised learning' in his speech to the Labour Party conference in 2003. Miliband said:[15] 'It means building the organisation of schooling around the needs, interests and aptitudes of individual pupils.' He did not go into detail about how this might be done in the classroom.

Private sector services can be customized, as long as the customer is willing to pay and is satisfied with the result. If the service design is to recognize and respond differently to different sorts of people, the implication is that managers and workers respond in different ways to each group, or even to each individual, which implies a greater degree of discretion than standard, routine treatment. Some people have described the process of designing services for individuals, rather than producing a standard service, as 'post-Fordism', an analogy with flexible production methods making manufactured products more individual.

Box 6.3   Customer service, choice and rationing

At a seminar for managers of community care services, the proprietor of a private homecare service said that one of her workers had arrived at a client's house to carry out her normal routine of work. The client said that she would rather use the time, and money, being assisted to go to a bingo game. The worker agreed. The public sector homecare managers said that this could not have happened in the public sector. The client could not have been assessed as 'needing' a bingo game. Such use of funds and time would be depriving someone else of their service. In any case, had she won the jackpot, her ability to pay for the service would have to be re-assessed. The reason that it could happen in a private transaction was that the client was paying for herself.

It is possible to overstate the existence of such individual treatment. An example sometimes quoted is the creation of 'packages of care' in community care. The range of alternatives to residential care is in practice not large: the combinations may be individual but the services are quite limited in scope. In other services there does not seem to be a trend towards customization. Standardization through national standards and procedures leads to less individual treatment, and the growth of contracting leads to less flexibility.

Conclusions

The relationship between public service organizations and their users can be more complicated than that between a company and its customers. People have rights as citizens as well as customers and in any case may be unwilling users of the services. There is a choice of ways of making services more sensitive. Managers are sometimes asked to use many methods at once, if their organization decides that customer service should be the subject of some sort of initiative. However, good service design is an important element of the managers' task and can make the difference between satisfied and dissatisfied customers, even when resources are limited.

One of the differences between managing public services and managing a business is that the business has an obvious measure of customer satisfaction, which is repeat business and profitability. These factors are rarely available or appropriate in the public sector as neither the health nor prison services, for example, are pleased to see their customers again. What is clear is that creating customer satisfaction with public services does not happen automatically by target setting or by setting up market-type mechanisms. Targets only reflect managers' views about the service, and virtually all the markets established stop short of giving customers power. Service design and delivery require a close relationship with the service users, whether through real empowerment or just by consulting them through market research.

Notes

For weblinks relevant to the issues discussed in this chapter see www.sagepub.co.uk/flynn.

1 A phrase coined by the Prime Minister's communications advisor, Alastair Campbell, in 2001.
2 C.K. Skelcher, 'Involvement and Empowerment in Local Public Services', *Public Money and Management*, (July–September, 1993).
3 T.H. Marshall, *Sociology at the Crossroads* (originally published 1950), (London, Heinemann, 1963).
4 The Community Care (direct payments) Act, 1996.
5 Cabinet Office, *The Citizen's Charter* Cm 1599 (HMSO, London, 1991), p. 2.
6 Cabinet Office, 2004, *Chartermark Standard* (HMSO, London).
7 We introduced this notion in Chapter 5. See A. Parasuraman, V.A. Zeithaml and L.L. Berry, 'A Conceptual Model of Service Quality and Its Implications for Future Research', *Journal of Marketing*, 49 (Fall 1985), pp. 41–50.
8 For an analysis of the stakeholder approach to public services, see J. Bryson, *Strategic Planning for Public and Not For Profit Organizations*, 3rd edn. (Jossey Bass, San Francisco, 2004).
9 R. Normann, *Service Management*, 2nd edn (Wiley, Chichester, 1991).
10 I asked a senior manager of a major outsourcing company if they ran call-centres for government. 'Ah,' he said, 'you mean the modernisation agenda.'
11 'Using call centres to deliver public services', report by the Comptroller and Auditor General, HC 134 Session 2002–2003, 11 December 2002.
12 PricewaterhouseCoopers, *Report on the Evaluation of the Public Service Excellence Programme* (PWC, London, 2000).
13 Ibid. p. 6.
14 Demos, the think-tank, published a pamphlet by Charles Leadbeater called *Personalisation through participation* (Demos, London, 2004) with a preface by David Miliband.
15 In July 2006 at an OECD conference.

7

Audit and inspection

Introduction

If governments want to run services in a centralized, hierarchical way, they need a system to inform them of how services are being delivered on the ground. If they wish to set national standards, they need intelligence to find out the extent to which those standards are being met. A central function of inspections is to report to government on how well managers and professionals are performing. In addition, since the establishment of the Audit Commission governments have used audit and inspection to bring about improved standards, or improved ways of working. We saw in Chapter 5 that contracts or quasi-contracts are at the heart of the centralized control system. Inspection and some aspects of audit are one of the tools used to enforce those contracts, especially the Public Service Agreements.

Heavy reliance on inspection produced a growth in the numbers of inspectorates and the cost of the processes. The assessment of external review by Ian Byatt and Michael Lyons[1] reported that external inpection of local authorities, for example, cost £600 million in 2000–01. The proliferation of inspections led to duplication and overlap and a need to rationalize the approach. Byatt and Lyons recommended better co-ordination and a system of whole organization review. Their report also spelled out the purposes and limitations of external review as a way of improving performance.

In this chapter we look at the changing purposes of audit and inspection as part of the control process and the impact of inspections on management.

Regulation, audit and inspection

The National Audit Office and the Audit Commission have attained a central position in assessing efficiency and evaluating effectiveness on behalf of the government. The Audit Commission has also become more like a management consultancy, with powers to impose management methods on local authorities as well as assessing and reporting on their performance.

This role is different from the traditional, narrow audit function. Audit is concerned to look at processes and procedures in things such as ordering materials, signing cheques, handling cash to make sure that money is handled honestly. Audit as an effort to stop fraud and waste has a very long history. It also checks that accounts are produced in the correct way and produce a 'true and fair view', or some equivalent phrase, of the organization's financial position. If the accounts are not satisfactory they might be 'qualified'. Staff trained to follow procedures clearly set out in audit manuals carry out such work. Measuring and comparing unit costs is not a big step from traditional audit. It uses accounting techniques to establish costs and is concerned with measurable things. 'Value for money' work by the Audit Commission and the NAO is based on a foundation of comparative cost performance.

Governments have used inspectorates to keep an eye on public employees for centuries. In Britain, such bodies as Her Majesty's Inspectorates of Prisons and of Schools have long traditions. They are charged with making sure that employees are doing what they are supposed to do: that standards are maintained and that results are acceptable.

The Audit Commission has offered definitions of the elements of regulation, useful for understanding the different parts of the process. 'Quality regulation comprises activity aimed at improving services or at assuring service users and others that minimum service standards are being achieved ... It overlaps with economic regulation when an element of the role of the quality regulator is the granting of authority to provide the service in question, or to remove this authority in circumstances where minimum quality standards are not being met.'[2] Inspection, they say, is a sub-set of quality regulation with three purposes: to provide assurance that standards are being met; to provide information to the public; and to improve standards. Performance assessment includes inspection but relies on a wider framework. Economic regulation applies where there are markets and applies to prices, consumer protection and competition policy. These distinctions are useful when designing or using the various instruments that regulatory and inspection bodies use to influence, judge and control public organizations.

Government policy on inspection was set out by the Office for Public Services Reform in 2003[3] and followed the definitions above, stating that inspection's purposes are to provide assurance and to generate improvements. Inspections should be based on the following ten principles:

a) Pursue the purpose of improvement;
b) Focus on outcomes;
c) Take a user perspective;
d) Be proportionate to risk;
e) Encourage self-assessment by managers;
f) Use impartial evidence, wherever possible;

g) Disclose the criteria used for judgement;
h) Be open about the processes involved;
i) Have regard to value for money, including that of the inspection body;
j) Continually learn from experience.

To enable inspections to take account of the degree of connection among departments and agencies for service delivery and to rationalize the organization of inspection, the Government announced, in the 2005 Budget, mergers of inspectorates, reducing their number from 11 to 4, to implement this policy on inspection. The four new inspectorates were to cover, from 2007: children's services, education and skills; adult and social care and health; justice and community safety; and local services.

The inspectorates

The mergers set out for 2007 produce bigger and more wide-ranging inspectorates than previously existed. These brief descriptions cover the functions of the organizations before the mergers.

The Office for Standards in Education was established in 1993 to take over the schools inspection function and was made responsible for four elements:

- The quality of education provided in schools
- The educational standards achieved in schools
- The way in which financial resources are managed
- The spiritual, moral, social and cultural development of pupils.

OFSTED inspects processes, outputs and outcomes, defined as the impact of the education process on pupils.

The Social Services Inspectorate was concerned with a similar range of matters, inspecting how services are delivered and assessing their impact on the users of the services. Largely as a result of scandals involving abuse or loss of clients the Labour government strengthened the social services inspection arrangements, through the Care Standards Act. The National Care Standards Commission was established from April 2002 to regulate and inspect residential and nursing home care for adults and children and domiciliary care, fostering and adoption services. All care sectors were, for the first time, regulated within the same framework.

'Best Value' inspections of local authorities by the Audit Commission[4] are very different from audits and are conducted by different people. They are based on a model of management practice, especially in relation to benchmarking, competition and continuous improvement. The process is illustrated in Figure 7.1.

One characteristic of inspectors is that they are generally recruited from the profession or occupation of the people they are inspecting. There are some exceptions, whereby lay people are included in inspection teams to bring a dispassionate view.

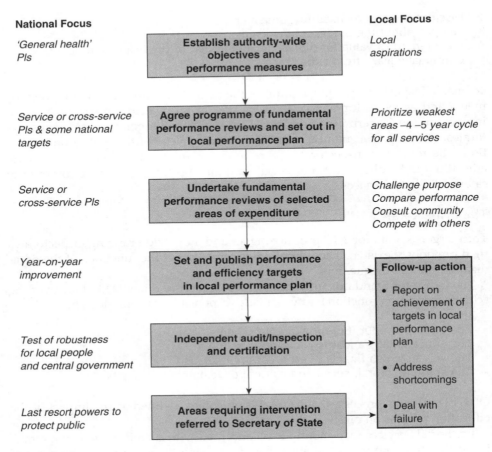

National Focus

'General health'
PIs

Service or cross-service
PIs & some national
targets

Service or
cross-service PIs

Year-on-year
improvement

Test of robustness
for local people
and central government

Last resort powers to
protect public

Local Focus

Local
aspirations

Prioritize weakest
areas –4 –5 year cycle
for all services

Challenge purpose
Compare performance
Consult community
Compete with others

Establish authority-wide
objectives and
performance measures

Agree programme of fundamental
performance reviews and set out in
local performance plan

Undertake fundamental
performance reviews of selected
areas of expenditure

Set and publish performance
and efficiency targets
in local performance plan

Independent audit/Inspection
and certification

Areas requiring intervention
referred to Secretary of State

Follow-up action

- Report on
  achievement of
  targets in local
  performance
  plan

- Address
  shortcomings

- Deal with
  failure

Figure 7.1   Best value inspection

Source: Audit Commission, 1999

Some of the inspectors' experience of doing the job may be in the distant past, and that has proved to be a problem especially for school and social services inspectors whose relevance to current conditions is sometimes questioned by current practitioners. However, in principle they have relevant experience. This may not be the case for the auditors, although as they have expanded their role they have tried to recruit people with direct experience of managing the services they are inspecting.

The consequence of this shared experience is that there can be a shared idea about what is good practice and at what level standards should be set. This might not be the case when what is being inspected is management processes on which there may be no consensus. The distinction between auditors' inspection of management arrangements and the inspection of professional practice is not absolute. In the case of schools inspections, there are differences among teachers about how to teach and teachers may not have the same ideas as inspectors about what is best. But the notion that an inspector or an auditor can claim to have a superior grasp of management than the people being inspected is in principle different from an inspection of professional practice such as providing teaching, prison custody, residential care and so on.

Styles of inspection

The two main audit bodies, in their role in performance improvement, have expanded their activities into work that cannot be done following a set manual of procedures. When the Audit Commission was established by Michael Heseltine to improve 'value for money' in local government it set about trying to find a framework for its analysis and recommendations. Its first framework came from McKinsey, probably because the Director was an ex McKinsey employee. The '7 Ss' framework (Structure, Strategy, Systems, Staff, Skills, Style, Super-ordinate Goals) was modified slightly and taken around the country in the auditors' briefcases. It was uncomfortable for some of the people who had spent their career in audit. Following an audit trail and looking for errors or fraud was a very different task from looking for 'style'. What were they supposed to do if they found a lack of 'style'? It did not matter which managerial template was used, the problem was that this outside body had its own ideas about what constituted good management practice (and later, good political practice) and was expected to impose those ideas on independent local authorities. The job was not made easier by the fact that the authorities had to pay the fees for this work.

Inspecting for the quality of management and, in the case of local government, the quality of the political decision-making processes requires special skills and a report that is different from the report on the inspection of lessons or what goes on in a prison. Prison inspection reports are full of details about what the prisoners do during the day, how much time they spend out of their cell and how useful or productive the activities are. They also report on how clean or otherwise the toilets are and other easily observable things. Descriptions of 'strategic direction' by a local education authority or the 'leadership qualities' of a management team are harder to formulate and adduce evidence for.

The different traditions and the variation in services provided have produced a varied set of inspections and inspection reports. The different inspection régimes also have incorporated in them different powers for the inspectors and different consequences for those they inspect.

The Prison Service has been the subject of every government initiative to improve performance. It was made into an Executive Agency, had a geographical management structure imposed with hierarchically set and monitored targets (see Box 7.1). It has been subjected to market testing and privatization. It has a robust régime of inspection and has had a series of outspoken inspectors. It has been forced to manage certain aspects of its work in collaboration with others, eventually being merged with the Probation Service into the National Offender Management Service. Despite all this managerial effort, many prisons are a disgrace to a civilized society, variously plagued by insanitary conditions, inhuman routines, brutality and suicide, widespread substance misuse, racism including racist murders and very poor efforts at education and rehabilitation.

Box 7.1   Prison Governors' guidance

Prison governors will find their work constrained and directed by the following:

- Government's Crime Reduction Strategy
- Criminal Justice System Strategic Plan 1999–2002
- Criminal Justice System Business Plan 1999–2000
- Home Office Business Plan 1999–2000
- Home Office – Aim 4 Business Plan 1999–2002
- Home Office Public Service Agreement
- Correctional Policy Framework
- Prison Service Framework Document
- Prison Service Corporate Plan 1999–2000 to 2001–2002
- Prison Service Business Plan 2000–2001
- Prison Service Vision
- Prison Service Aim
- Two Prison Service Objectives
- Six Prison Service Principles
- 15 Key Performance Indicators
- 42 Key Performance Targets
- 67 Performance Standards

Source: Bryans, 2000, p. 7

The Chief Inspector of Prisons who retired in August 2001, Sir David Ramsbotham, continued his predecessors' tradition of publishing damning reports if he found cause. In January 2001 he said that Brixton Prison had been in decline for four years and was 'failing', with no workshops, no education centre and a gym outside the perimeter walls. In 1999 he described Feltham, Europe's largest youth jail, as 'rotten to the core and unacceptable in a civilised society.' He supported a Children's Society report that recommended that 15- and 16-year-old offenders on remand should not be held in prison custody.

In an interview in January 2001 he expressed doubts about the purpose of inspection. 'I have never seen an organisation with so many rules, operating standards, instructions, visions and mission statements. You name it. It is a horrendous amount of bureaucracy, it is not hands-on management. In the Army, the purpose of inspection was to ensure that the organisation being inspected was ready for its operational purpose. If not, you asked why not. This presupposed that someone was listening, which is not always the case in Whitehall.'[5] Extracts from one of Sir David Ramsbotham's inspection reports, on HMP Wandsworth, are shown in Box 7.2.

Box 7.2   Extracts from HM Inspector of Prisons report on Wandsworth, October 1999

... invariably, I find myself asking how Prison Service line management, with its Visions, Statements of Purpose, Prison Rules, Operating Standards and so on, quite apart from all that it publicises about its aims and performance – all of which profess exactly the opposite of what we have found – can have allowed such treatment and conditions to exist, let alone become established in the first place ... .

I am saddened at the number of times I and my teams go into prisons, and find practices which are far removed from what the Prison Service itself preaches, about which, when they are exposed, the Director General expresses surprise. This appears to be not because he does not know what he wants prisons to deliver, but because the information that he is given about them is not about the quality of outcomes for prisoners but about budgets, Key Performance Indicators and measurements of the quantity of laid down processes. In other words I fear that the agenda on which I and my team are required to report to Ministers, based as it is on an Act of Parliament, and the Prison Service's own Statement of Purpose that lays down how prisoners should be treated, is far removed from one governed by budgets and Key Performance Indicators and processes, which concentrate on completely different outcomes ...

Regrettably I have to report that, in no prison that I have inspected, has the 'culture' that we found caused me greater concern than that in HMP Wandsworth. This is not just because of the grossly unsatisfactory nature of the regimes for many different types of prisoner that are described in the report, but because of the insidious nature of what the 'Wandsworth way' – as the local 'culture' was described to us – represents, in terms of the attitude of too many members of staff to prisoners and their duty of care for them.

(Continued)

(Continued)

What we observed, and learned, confirmed that too many staff do not seem to think that the phrase 'look after prisoners with humanity', enshrined at the heart of the Prison Service Statement of Purpose, applies to them, and continue to pursue an agenda which, if it ever was authorised, is not only long out of date but far removed from current and acceptable practice.

There can therefore only be one 'way' in prisons, and that must be the 'Prison Service way'. Those who think, or presume otherwise, preferring such as the 'Wandsworth way' should get out, or be got out, of the Prison Service now, and leave it to the decent minded majority, who hate what is happening, but feel, or have been rendered, powerless to do anything about it ...

This may suggest that I envisage a long haul, but I would be wholly wrong if I suggested that anything approaching a 'quick fix' was either possible or appropriate.[6]

Sir David Ramsbotham
Her Majesty's Chief Inspector of Prisons
October 1999

Inspection reports on prisons are based either on planned or unannounced visits and include physical inspection, interviews with prisoners, staff, the governor and prison visitors. They are very detailed and include recommendations about detailed arrangements and routines. Often the reports produce improvements that are acknowledged in subsequent inspections but sometimes, as in the case of Brixton, inspection reports simply plot the decline of the institution. These reports, while designed to follow the government's subsequent policy that they should aim towards improvement, have apparently limited value for such a task.

School inspections have more clearly laid out consequences. While the inspections involve observation of teaching, they also take account of the management of the school, the role of the governors and the general ethos of the school. A report on a well-run inner city school, which was previously not doing well, includes the following general statement:

Queensbridge School is well led by the Headteacher, the Deputy Headteacher and members of the Senior Management Team, working with a committed and active Governing Body. The Headteacher has...gradually brought about a marked change of emphasis in the management of the school in order to address the complex and varied learning needs of the pupils in a corporate manner. Since the last inspection, the school has improved in identified areas of its life and work, although significant aspects require further attention. Both pupils and staff are proud of and dedicated to their school. There is a strong and caring ethos, in which pupils feel valued and which supports their progress and attainment. Behaviour in lessons and around the school is usually good. Relationships and support for individual pupils are a particular strength of the school community, recognised in full by the parents who attended the meeting before the start of the inspection.[7]

The report contains assessments of the quality of lessons in all subjects, standards at Key Stages 3 and 4, public examination results, spiritual, moral, social and cultural development and the management and efficiency of the school. In the case quoted above, the management is given a favourable report: the development plan is said to be 'clear and explicit about the priorities facing the school and is under-pinned by extensive documentary support for staff. Consultation processes are full and involve governors, committees and the school's middle managers ... structures and procedures provide a model of management that gives all staff clear roles and responsibilities.' There was a suggestion that the devolution of responsibility to what is described as 'middle managers' requires more attention. At the end of the report there is a list of five 'Key Issues' that should be addressed 'in order to raise further standards of attainment.'

This style of inspection report is helpful and supportive of the school and is designed to find things that have made a good impression and those that still need to be put right. It was presumably not too stressful an experience either for the inspectors or the school.

When a school is not in such good shape, inspection is not such a happy experience. In November 1999 there was an Ofsted inspection of Kingsland School in Hackney. The inspectors managed to find two positive things to say, that there is 'harmony between pupils from different races, nationalities and creeds' and that there are 'pockets of good teaching, especially in music, business studies and Turkish'. The report then lists fourteen weaknesses, including fundamentals such as poor teaching, unsatisfactory curriculum, assessment procedures and leadership of the school and financial planning and control.

The inspection resulted in 'special measures' under the School Inspection Act 1996. Under this the governors had to produce an action plan detailing how they intended to put right the list of matters that were unsatisfactory. Shortly after the school failed to respond to special measures it was closed down and replaced. In this case inspection was part of a process that led to the replacement of the school, but it was not effective, apparently, in bringing about improvements.

Reports on education authorities can have similarly clear consequences. A report by Ofsted and the Audit Commission on Brighton and Hove LEA in June 2000 had some very specific recommendations for improvements in areas such as funding, school improvement, support, monitoring and challenge, use of performance data, improvement in ICT support for schools, special needs provision, contracted-out services, admissions planning, exclusions and attendance.

In contrast, a report on Hackney LEA, the authority responsible for Kingsland, in 2000 found that despite the efforts of the education department's management team to provide stability and protect it from the damage caused by budgetary and management failure in the rest of the authority, the performance of the LEA was unsatisfactory:

> the corporate context still does not provide conditions which are sufficiently stable, secure or supportive to education. This is dramatically illustrated by the current circumstances in the authority. Sudden and unpredictable budgetary constraint across the council has created nervousness and insecurity among teachers. Poor handling of issues, such as those which led to the resignation of the Director of Education, who was the principal architect of improvement and who had won the trust and confidence of the schools, officers and elected members, impedes progress and undermines schools' confidence. Too much of the time of senior management in schools is still spent in attempting to compensate for poor performance in some services. The morale of some headteachers is consequently very low, and the recruitment and retention of teachers create significant problems for many. This situation is all the more injurious to morale, because the education department's current senior management team has provided effective leadership and has successfully brought increasing discipline and stability, together with pertinent and rigorous analyses of the problems. More than that, the team brought a degree of hope to Hackney schools that the LEA was in the process of becoming a source of support, rather than a burden. Elected members and schools had begun to trust the senior officers and had more than a glimmer of the benefits which a successfully functioning partnership could bring. What should be a period of stability and consolidation of improvements has become a time of further turmoil. The agenda for improvement set by the previous two inspections has been immense. We found evidence of progress which has been hard won. That progress is not sufficient to enable us to conclude that the LEA is now functioning effectively overall. Nor do we believe that the progress made can be sustained. The resignation of the director of education and her senior colleagues is only the latest in a series of crises resulting from the continuing ineptitude of the corporate management of the council. We do not believe that Hackney LEA has the capacity to provide a secure, stable context for continuous educational improvement. The time has come for radical change.

The radical approach was to outsource the management of the LEA to a private company. The two examples from Hackney, the school and the LEA, show inspection resulting in the existing management being removed, and in effect the school and the LEA were prevented from providing education services. This falls more closely into the Audit Commission's definition of an economic regulator, deciding who shall and shall not have the right to continue to provide services. The process, though, was performed as part of quality regulation.

This option, to remove the right to provide the service, is also open, in principle, to the Prison Service. The Minister for Prisons in the first Labour government, Paul Boateng, made a reputation for threatening privatization if standards in individual prisons did not improve. The opposite threat, bringing the service back into public management, was the solution for one prison, Blakenhurst.

The Home Secretary does not have the option of privatizing the Police Service as a consequence of an adverse inspection, although proposals published in 2001 included the use of private security forms for patrolling. Inspections of police forces are mainly concerned with reporting the achievement of statistical targets, for crime, detection, call management, traffic, public order and community relations. Inspections also include a management element, which is very specific in relation to the Best Value régime in the Police Service. While the 'challenge' part of best value, in which every service has to be considered for outsourcing, does not apply to the Police Service the rest of the process does, and the police were involved in the pilot efforts to implement Best Value.

An example of an inspection report that criticized the lack of consultation as part of the management process was the report on Greater Manchester Police published in 1999.

> Her Majesty's Inspector understands the difficulties of consulting (and communicating) within a large organisation and he accepts that the Force is making efforts to improve the situation. Based on his discussions with staff, he urges the Force to focus those efforts at section, unit and relief levels to engage supervisors in the process to generate involved discussion and interest from 'front line' staff. If these staff can be made to feel genuinely included, with feedback and clear signs that they can make an impact, then he believes that business plans will be more effective working documents and performance review of progress will be positively accepted rather than disdainfully received. The issue of internal consultation is closely linked to that of internal communication. Again, systems are in place but effort is needed to make them work. A large amount of information is passed down the hierarchy but little appears to be read or listened to. Meanwhile, the voice from the 'front line' reported difficulty in making itself heard (i.e. 'bottom up') and again a question is raised as to who listens actively rather than merely hears passively.[8]

This was an explicit endorsement of a consultative style of management and a criticism of the lack of enthusiasm for the style in this particular force. An inspection report on the West Midlands police force in the same year found that consultation was satisfactory: 'A clear priority is also given to internal consultation ... The consultation involves OCU[9] commanders and focus meetings based on OCU. It is encouraging to note that the Chief Constable or the Deputy Chief Constable attend each one of these focus group meetings, a fact that is well received.'[10] The West Midlands inspection report also commented favourably on the Force's use of a small number of performance indicators, and of its successful partnership meetings with other statutory bodies.

The style of reports in these different services varies. School inspection reports are evaluative, lessons scored on a three-point scale, judgements made about management style. Prison reports have detailed descriptions of what is observed as well as recording the performance indicators. Police force inspections are mainly concerned with indicators but also comment on what officers say about management style. Best Value inspections are mainly concerned with procedures and with service standards against comparators. The assessment of teaching quality in Universities is based on assessing the paper evidence of procedures of student feedback and interview opinion from students, resulting in an overall score, also on a three-point scale. The inspection processes have developed independently and were introduced for different purposes. They are also carried out by different sorts of people. Schools, police forces and social services departments are visited by full-time inspectors who have previously worked in middle to senior management positions in the services that they are inspecting. The same is true of prison inspectors, apart from the Chief Inspector who is not always a prison professional. Best Value audits are done by people who may have had management experience although for any one service, only one auditor will be from the service being looked at. University inspections are done by 'peers', a team of teachers from other universities who teach the subjects they are inspecting.

One explanation for the differences in style may be that there is a variable degree of consensus about how things should be done between the inspectors and those being inspected. If inspection is used as a way of changing unwilling people's practice, there will be a hostile reception for the inspectors. If the teaching style preferred by the staff of a school is challenged by the inspectors, then the process is not one of scoring performance against an agreed set of criteria.

The exasperation that Her Majesty's Inspector of Prisons exhibits comes from a frustration with the inertia of the system. Standards and procedures are agreed formally but repeated inspections of the worst jails show little improvement. Diagnosis by the inspections includes the powerlessness of governors, the quick turnover and short tenure of governors and other senior managers and the power of the Prison Officers Association, the trade union of the prison workers. There is not much the inspector can do about these causes of bad performance or, apparently, about their effects.

In the case of local authorities, the diagnosis of the problems of the performers produces a set of detailed recommendations in a letter to the authority. There are powers, not necessarily in the hands of the inspectors, to intervene if the problems persist. The same is true in schools if they are deemed to be 'failing'.

The managerial consequences of inspection

Senior managers have to cope with a wide range of scrutiny, whether audit, inspection or someone telling them how to do their management job. While the Public Audit Forum works towards consistency and tries to avoid duplication, from the manager's point of view not all of these interventions are useful, cost-effective or the best use of time. Nobody wants a bad report which, in the extreme, can lead to a career-limiting intervention and replacement of the local management. As the Audit Commission said: 'Centrally imposed targets and the associated performance monitoring and intervention are perceived to stifle innovation, addressing the failures of the worst performers while holding back the majority.'[11] In any case, there may be insufficent powers in the inspectorates to ensure that improvement takes place.

The Audit Commission called for 'greater incentives for improvement through a more varied approach which recognises the different starting points of different local authorities and which recognises too that local government is not just about the delivery of services.'[12] This was a polite plea that there are insufficient incentives available to the inspectors, in this case the Audit Commission, to bring about improvements. We have seen the frustration of the prison inspectorate on this same issue.

There are differences in approach according to whether the scrutiny is a professional inspection, an audit or a management inspection. While excuses may be found for poor professional practice, the only acceptable argument is a lack of resources, such as cash or trained staff. A standard response to adverse reports on individual prison performance is to use the report to make the case for more money or staff. The only credible response to criticism in an audit report is to put things right or even better to claim that things have been put right between the audit visit and the report.

Strategies for coping with scrutiny on performance or the quality of management, such as the Best Value inspections, are more complicated. One approach is to join in wholeheartedly with the latest initiative and try to become a shining example, or beacon. This brings prestige and possibly extra resources and should be good for a manager's career. To achieve this the organization needs to get involved early, become a pilot for whatever the initiative is and take part in shaping the process. This requires that the existing arrangements are in line with the current thinking and that the existing managers are well connected with the scrutineers.

Less adventurous is a policy of conformance whereby the manuals are studied and the procedures followed in preference to existing ways of managing. In practice this should not be too difficult as the prescriptions offered are not usually too far removed from existing practices in well-managed organizations. Conformance involves work on presentation, possibly representing existing processes using the new language. For example local authorities have been doing various forms of performance review for decades and it should not be too hard to present this as the sorts of performance review implied by the Best Value process. The response of the Chartered Institute of Public Finance and Accountancy[13] to the government's consultation on inspection reform included this warning:

CIPFA is concerned that performance inspection regimes may distract focus away from improvement towards 'inspection compliance'. For example, many

> senior managers in local government ... have developed a very detailed knowledge of the Audit Commission CPA [Comprehensive Performance Assessment] framework. They know exactly where additional points need to be earned in order to secure a more positive overall rating for the authority.[14]

Inspection compliance is a sensible reaction to inspection used as a way of assuring conformance to pre-set standards. If the purpose is improvement, then compliance will not be enough.

Less submissive is an approach that involves a dialogue with the scrutineers to persuade them that there are viable alternatives to their prescriptions. This requires confident management and an evaluation process that enables it to demonstrate that its ways of working are producing results. It also requires some political courage if the régime being imposed has strong government backing, but if the local authority members think that what they do has value, they need to protect it from the visitors.

So far, the strategies described have been feasible only for self-confident and well-managed organizations. What should managers do when they know that they are failing, not only by the standards of the latest initiatives but other standards of cost and service quality? At the extreme, managers are just overwhelmed by day-to-day events and whatever the scrutineers say, they cannot do any better. This seems to have been the case in Hackney LBC, where the main effect of adverse reports by the Audit Commission was the resignation of most of the senior officers and their replacement by a new team. Cynics in Hackney would say that they have seen all that before as well, and will remember when the failing and resigning team were the new team brought in to fix the problems left by the previous failures.

Less drastic organizations can harness the external influences to help bring about change. Often managers know what should be done but they need help to overcome obstacles to change. An adverse report can be used to get extra resources. When the Benefit Fraud Inspectorate make a visit they are very explicit about the resources required to combat fraud and specify the shortfalls in staffing. Similarly the capacity of management is a legitimate reason for non-compliance and can be used to strengthen the management team. A report can also be used to gain legitimacy for changes some managers wanted to make in any case. An alliance can develop between like-minded people among the managers and the scrutineers.

Management style and inspection

The degree varies to which the inspectorates comment on management style. The Audit Commission clearly has a codified version of how management should be done, and managers seeking a good report know what they have to do. Benchmarking, outsourcing, consultation, continuous improvement, decisions made in small groups are the words that represent the management style currently in favour. The style should preferably be backed by some externally validated process, whether Investors in People, the Business Excellence Model or ISO 9001-accredited quality procedures.

Police inspectors have a view that management style should include devolved responsibility and a consultative decision-making process. This is slightly surprising, since the police have developed as a hierarchical, disciplined uniformed force. Training emphasizes rank and obedience rather than initiative and imagination. At constable level, however, there has always been a high degree of discretion and individual initiative, as officers have to act on their own or in small numbers in response to incidents.

School inspections also favour management devolved to 'middle managers', as subject or year heads are designated. Participation in decision-making and clear planning processes and target setting are the aspects of management that inspectors are looking for.

In social services, especially in children's services, and in the Probation Service the emphasis is on following procedures and keeping records. In both cases the purpose of this is to codify and control the behaviour of social workers and probation officers. Children at risk and people on probation are protected by detailed conformity to procedures. Consultation and participation are not a priority.

Conclusions

How successful are audit and inspection as a mode of control of public services? Clearly, well-established procedures for audit provide protection against fraud and corruption. When external inspectors are concerned with service standards and efficiency, different techniques are required. In some cases the technique is to produce a set of comparative indicators and then urge those at the lower end of the comparative tables to emulate the performance of those at the top. The question then arises, what is it that the best performers do that can be transferred to the less good? At this point the inspectors have to take a view about what works best. While auditors can devise procedures for matters such as how cash is handled and payments are made, inspectors of management processes have to seek universally applicable prescriptions for a variety of circumstances. At a high level of generality, there can be agreement that managers should know what is expected of them, should be aware of the results of their actions and should have sufficient control of resources to achieve results. Beyond that, solutions may not be so obvious. The problems found by the various inspectors have a wide range. For units that are performing at or near the average, the route to better performance might not be very clear. A standard template to all units is unlikely to cure the variety of problems. The inspection of Kingsland School referred to above found that one of the main reasons for the problems of the school was that a neighbouring school had recently been closed and a large group of boys had suddenly been inserted into Kingsland. It was not at all obvious how the school should have dealt with this problem. The inspection of Wandsworth prison found such bad practice that the only solution was to get rid of the prison officers who refused to conform to prison service norms of behaviour. The inspection of Hackney Council found that lack of political will, high rates of turnover of senior staff, strong and resistant trade unions and cynical staff led to overspending and loss of control. In all these cases the problems were complicated and deep rooted. In no case was the application of a standard management template likely to solve the problems. If an organization is out of control, standards very bad and finances overspent, then probably a period of 'turnaround' management is required. This implies centralization of spending authorization, the imposition of discipline and probably the replacement of staff who are unwilling or unable to change their behaviours. The very opposite prescription may be appropriate for a middling performer trying to raise its standards. Here, a process of quality improvement through consultation and 'empowerment' is likely to improve performance.

The implication of these differences in diagnosis and prescription is that the inspection is not itself a solution. Checking standards and procedures may show some of the symptoms of the problems but the particular solution lies with the organization itself. The experience of the attempts to turn around schools by importing a 'super-head' was informative. The charismatic leader replacing 'failing' management in 'failing' schools in no case produced satisfactory results. Institutions fail for complex and varied reasons. Inspection can identify and define failure but is limited in its scope for putting it right.

Notes

For weblinks relevant to the issues discussed in this chapter see www.sagepub.co.uk/flynn.

1   Sir Ian Byatt and Sir Michael Lyons, *Role of External Review in Improving Performance* (Public Services Produ ctivity Panel, London, 2001) footnote 7, p. 23.
2   Audit Commission, *The Future of Regulation in the Public Sector*, Corporate Discussion Paper (London, March 2006).
3   Cabinet Office/Office of Public Services Reform, *The Government's Policy on Inspection* (OPSR, London, 2003).
4   The process is described in Audit Commission, *Seeing is Believing* (Audit Commission, London, 2000).
5   *Daily Telegraph*, 16.01.2001, p.15.
6   Sir David Ramsbotham, Her Majesty's Chief Inspector of Prisons, October 1999.
7   From the Introduction to Inspection Report on Queensbridge School, Birmingham, May 1998.
8   Her Majesty's Inspectorate of Constabulary, *Report on Greater Manchester police 1998-99* (TSO, London, 1999), paras 2.6–2.7.
9   Operational Command Unit.
10 Her Majesty's Inspector of Constabulary, *Report on West Midlands Police, 1998–99* (TSO, London, 1999), para 2.7.
11 Audit Commission, *The Future of Regulation.*, p. 4.
12 Ibid., p. 30.
13 The main accounting body for the public sector in the United Kingdom.
14 CIPFA (Chartered Institute of Public Finance and Accountancy) *Response to ODPM Consultation on Inspection Reform*, CIPFA homepage.

8

Collaboration

Introduction

One of the negative consequences of trying to manage the public sector through a combination of markets and centralized management is fragmentation. Competitive units looking out for themselves are not likely to search out solutions that might involve loss of their own resources. Management systems that emphasize individual and organizational performance, defined by units of output and unit costs rather than overall results, concentrate the mind on the organization and its products and services rather than social results among the client group or wider population.

The problem is analogous to the business problem of emphasizing vertical integration at the expense of horizontal integration. Vertical integration makes managers and workers concentrate on getting and keeping costs down. Production is internalized to make sure that each process is under direct control and management can concentrate on each part of the production process. It may make managers and workers fail to consider either quality or how the product range is seen by the customers. Horizontal integration makes for a positive approach to such things as the customer experience as a whole or to the brand being portrayed by the product range. Whether production is in-house or outsourced is not important, since managers concentrate on the quality of the end product and how customers see, buy and use it. The search for efficiency or cost reductions can produce a preference for vertical integration, or at least adversarial contracting processes that drive down costs. The search for solutions to policy problems and for better services from the citizens' point of view made politicians and managers look for better ways to achieve horizontal integration.

This chapter looks at the reasons for promoting collaboration and finds that the argument applies both to service delivery and to policy making. It then looks at how managers have responded to the demand for collaboration and finds that there is a spectrum of behaviours, depending on how close the collaboration has to be. It then looks at the case of collaboration between the private and public sectors and at some of the companies that have grown as a result of the increasing use of outsourcing as a management tool.

Why collaboration?

There are two main reasons for promoting collaborative working. The first is that the management arrangements that promoted performance orientation for individual units produced unintended negative consequences. Examples include the pursuit of efficiency targets in hospitals: throughput per bed and income derived from procedures performed as targets promote efficiency, but do not necessarily make for an allocation of resources that would produce the best health outcomes. Or targets for educational attainment for those who will pass public examinations do not necessarily produce the best overall results for the school population. Collaboration among agencies involved in promoting the health of the population in an area, or the educational attainment of the whole school population, is one possible solution to this problem.

The second reason is recognition that policy outcomes cannot be achieved by institutions working on their own and therefore nobody can be said to be accountable for results. The police forces are not responsible for many of the causes of crime, schools cannot control the extraneous variables affecting pupils' performance, nobody is solely responsible for controlling the effects of substance abuse, and so on. Some of the reasons for policy failure will never be attributable to any organization, such as social inequality, family breakdown or attitudes to authority. In those cases where there are several institutions involved in contributing to service delivery towards a policy objective, then some arrangement that encourages them to work together and be accountable jointly for effectiveness would be preferable to them working in isolation.

Collaboration and managerial behaviour

Experience shows that it is not a simple matter to change people from being competitive and concerned with their own organization's success and resources into enthusiastic collaborators. Setting up collaborative structures and co-ordinating mechanisms does not in itself guarantee success. The incoming Labour government first set about solving the problems of isolated ministries, departments and policy areas with a programme of setting up new organizations and mechanisms for people to collaborate with each other. Some were concerned with joining up policies, such as the Social Exclusion Unit and the new regional Development Agencies; others were about joining together services, such as Sure Start, and the encouragement of prisons and probation to work together.

As well as establishing formal mechanisms or organizations, the main effort went into designing incentives for collaboration. There were many examples of funding being tied to collaborative efforts, such Health Action Zones and Education Action Zones. Other area-based approaches include economic regeneration, which has been approached through partnership working for at least 30 years under a bewildering variety of titles. Regeneration policy generated a number of partnership arrangements, usually starting with a 'pathfinder' programme, followed by a 'second pathfinder' programme before being 'rolled out' or forgotten. In 1998 the New Deal for Communities was launched, an area-based initiative initially in 17 pathfinder partnerships, with 22 more added in 1999, with three-year funding adding up to £2 billion. In 1999 Education Action Zones were launched with modest funding of £750,000 per annum and an expectation that private funds of a further £250,000 would be raised. In 2000 the Social Exclusion Unit recommended Neighbourhood Management, a scheme to co-ordinate services in local deprived areas. The scheme was started in 2001 with a pathfinder programme of 20 partnerships, each with funding of £200,000 or £20 per head of population. In 2004 15 more pathfinders were added. Local Strategic Partnerships were launched in 2001, eventually spreading to 350 partnerships. Although voluntary, LSPs were compulsory components of a bid for Neighbourhood Renewal Funding.

By 2001 there were at least 30 area-based initiatives requiring partnership working in regeneration.[1] Announcing a consultation on the continuation of one of these, the Local Strategic Partnership, the Office of the Deputy Prime Minister said that there was a need, now, for a partnership of partnerships:

> As indicated above, the LSP must take an oversight role, ensuring that the lines of responsibility between partners and thematic sub-partnerships are clear and that duplication is avoided. In essence the LSP needs to be the 'partnership of partnerships' encompassing all thematic partnerships in the area. For example Children's Trusts will be expected to be integrated within the LSP system of partnerships whilst retaining their responsibility for coordinating children's services.[2]

Faced with incentives to collaborate, managers had to work out their strategies, just as they had to work out what to do when they were asked to compete for the first time.

A collaborative spectrum

In practice there has been a wide range of approaches to collaborative working (Fig. 8.1). In many cases collaboration is a requirement of funding. To get funding for a zone and other area-based initiatives, a joint bid is required. Normally there is a leading body responsible for organizing the bid and that body is responsible for calling the partners together and submitting the bid. The government department allocating the funds requires evidence of joint working.

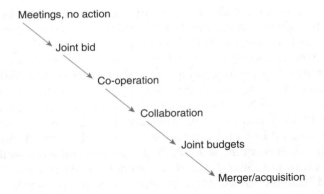

Figure 8.1 A collaborative spectrum

At its worst, the process produces unproductive meetings. People are invited as representatives of their organization or as tokens of their sector or community. The lead organization proceeds to write the bid document and the criterion by which collaboration is judged is whether the meetings took place, whatever their content or outcome.

A more authentic form of collaboration is a real joint bid. Partners bring their experience and interests to the process and the bid for funding reflects the collection of positions. Meetings to arrive at the bid are real exchanges, and joint analysis of problems and proposals are made. There are examples where this is the end of the process of collaboration. Once the bid is made, even if it is successful, people revert to their previous competitive behaviours. The collective agenda is forgotten and people compete for their share of the joint funds. If there was a lead organization putting the bid together they become custodians of the cash (for accounting reasons) and think of it as their money.

Neither case is real collaboration. The first point on the spectrum that represents real collaboration is co-operative working. Here each organization retains its own specialism but works with the others on projects or programmes but retains staff under their previous management arrangements. They may co-ordinate activities, especially in relation to client contact, but there is essentially no change to the management arrangements resulting from the co-operation, although there needs to be agreement about the objectives and values of the project.

According to an evaluation of Local Strategic partnerships conducted in 2002, some struggled to find a common agenda:

> Establishing shared priorities, influencing the agendas of partners and agreeing action is exercising many LSPs. Some LSPs are still at the stage of developing a shared vision, others are dealing with the realignment of partners'

service delivery plans. The main difficulty appears to be identifying and focusing on a limited number of priorities, as well as resolving conflicting priorities within a broad and complex agenda. Mention was made of the difficulty of getting individuals and organisations to give ground to support joint aims. A specific issue is the tension between the medium to long term aims of the LSP, and the mostly short term aims of elected members.

Many LSPs are trying to establish a role and purpose. This is hampered by a lack of clarity about the long term role of LSPs, their powers and resources. Others mention the need to demonstrate that they are adding value, and ensure that they deliver. Mainstreaming is seen as an issue especially in terms of the need to link partner activities and plans to the community planning process, and so influence changes in core service delivery.[3]

While generally positive about Local Strategic Partnerships, their members seemed to be unclear about what they were for (other than being a necessary condition for neighbourhood renewal funding, a purpose stated by 23% of respondents). Partnership became, partly, an end in itself. In the same survey many respondents listed as a benefit of the partnership the contact among partners.

An evaluation of Neighbourhood Management, published in 2006 by the Office of the Deputy Prime Minister, emphasized the limited expectations of such arrangements:

It is also important to be realistic in our expectations of what a small, modestly funded neighbourhood partnership can achieve in respect of neighbourhood renewal. Neighbourhood management may be able to add value, but it cannot, alone, deliver neighbourhood renewal objectives. When assessing the value of neighbourhood management as a tool for change therefore, we must assess the benefits against the scale of investment to achieve them.[4]

Funding for Neighbourhood Management was protected ('ring-fenced') until 2006, when the funds were re-allocated back to general local authority funding. The evaluation pointed out: 'If it fails to convince, it will join many other regeneration initiatives that come and go'.[5]

Collaboration involves a shared task with shared management and supervision of staff. People move from their parent organization and become attached to the collaborative venture. If they come from different professions they find they have to adjust to others' professional values and ways of working. In a collaborative venture people may become more attached to the collaborative activity than to their parent organization, especially if they are seconded full-time to the venture.

Legal problems have hindered the development of joint budgets for collaborative efforts. It took years to develop joint community care budgets between health and social services. Very often, budgets are the reason for the behaviours that contradict collaboration. Hospitals discharge elderly patients because they cost too much to keep in a hospital bed, and thereby transfer the responsibility to social services. If the budgets were combined there would be no such incentive and the most efficient solution could be pursued by both health and social services. The same applies to the funding of nursing provision and care provision. Frail and sick old people are subject to the definitional niceties about the boundary between nursing and social care because these come out of different budgets and different rules apply. The almost theological debate about these definitions went on for many years because they were part of the definition of the state's liability to older people: 'health care' was part of it while 'personal care' was not. In Scotland the state was more generous and abandoned the distinction.

An extreme form of collaboration is the merger. Mergers of public organizations have happened for a variety of reasons, whether rationalization and economies of scale in management or service synergies. Over the years the functions of helping people find jobs and paying benefits have been merged and demerged. Ministries split and fuse like cells as fashions for large and inclusive and small and specialized come and go. Local government reorganization sometimes involves previously independent authorities merging, and sometimes involves authorities taking on functions previously the responsibility of another tier. Single-tier government, which is now in place in many towns and cities, is an example of a multi-functional merger.

Take-overs have been fairly common in recent years. There were cases of NHS Trusts, Training and Education Councils and Further Education Colleges in which take-overs were seen as the solution where individual institutions had failed and been taken over by others considered more capable. The Education Green Paper of 2001 allowed for similar things to happen in schools, failing schools being taken over by successful ones. This use of merger to solve the problem of failing institutions comes from private sector practice in which an ailing company is bought by a successful one and 'turned around'.

Conditions that promote successful collaboration

Guy Peters studies co-ordination at national government level, and concluded that 'The first lesson is that mere structural manipulations cannot produce changes in behaviour, especially if the existing behaviour is reinforced by other factors in government.'[6]

Eugene Bardach[7] looked at case studies of inter-organizational collaboration among public agencies in the USA. Various studies have also been made in the UK following the government's espousal of what became known as 'joined-up government'. Reports by government departments in England and Scotland also looked for the factors that make collaboration work. Lessons about collaboration had also been learned in the private sector. Towards the end of the 1990s collaboration became fashionable among business writers and apparently among businesses as a source of competitive advantage.

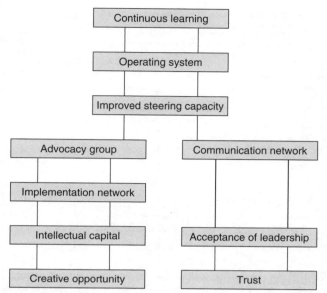

Figure 8.2   Developing inter-agency collaborative capacity.

While the contexts for co-operation and collaboration varied greatly in the private sector, from joint ventures to entering new markets to synergies among technologies and sharing of distribution networks, there are some general lessons from both the public and private sectors about what helps collaboration to work and what inhibits it.

Bardach proposed a model of what he called 'platforming', building 'inter-agency collaborative capacity' on twin platforms of trust and creative opportunities. His model is summarized in Figure 8.2.

The main conclusion is that the two, or more, collaborating organizations have to start their collaboration by jointly defining the opportunity and learning how to work together, rather than starting with operating systems and rules.

Similar analysis was made by the Manchester Business School[8] study of collaboration in health services in Britain. They concluded that collaboration required a 'nurturing environment', including:

- A synergy of interests between management and practitioners and therefore between 'quality' and financial objectives
- An organizational system which encourages active communication with users and frontline staff
- A cohesive senior management team
- The involvement of committed medical staff
- Performance and measurement systems sensitive to emergent practice and staff learning.

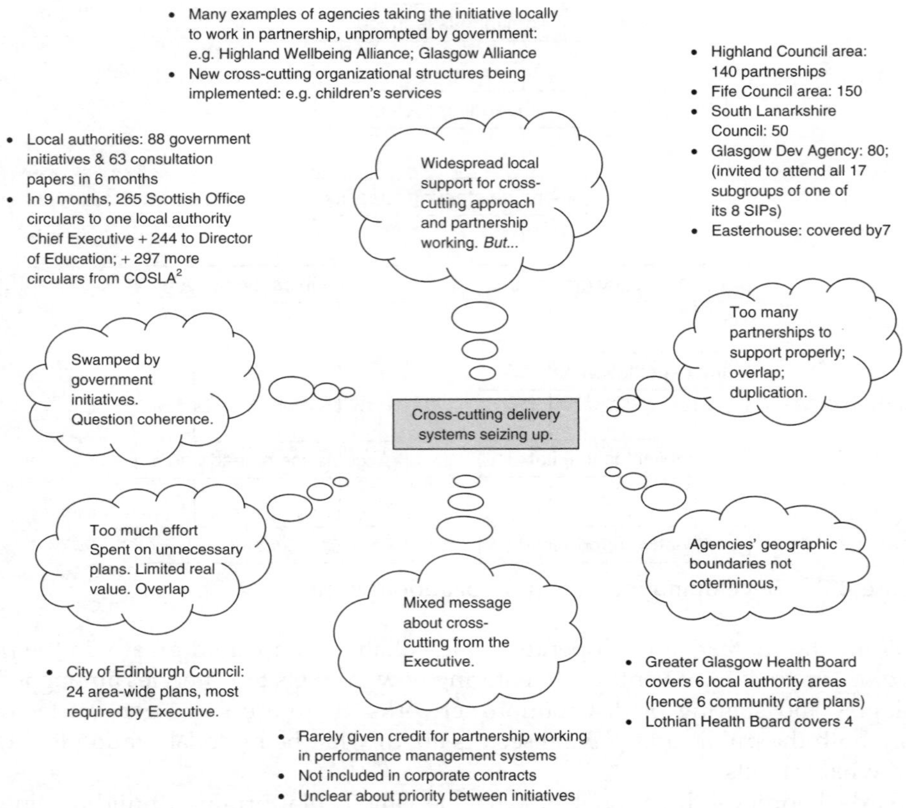

- Many examples of agencies taking the initiative locally to work in partnership, unprompted by government: e.g. Highland Wellbeing Alliance; Glasgow Alliance
- New cross-cutting organizational structures being implemented: e.g. children's services

- Highland Council area: 140 partnerships
- Fife Council area: 150
- South Lanarkshire Council: 50
- Glasgow Dev Agency: 80; (invited to attend all 17 subgroups of one of its 8 SIPs)
- Easterhouse: covered by7

- Local authorities: 88 government initiatives & 63 consultation papers in 6 months
- In 9 months, 265 Scottish Office circulars to one local authority Chief Executive + 244 to Director of Education; + 297 more circulars from COSLA[2]

Widespread local support for cross-cutting approach and partnership working. *But...*

Too many partnerships to support properly; overlap; duplication.

Swamped by government initiatives. Question coherence.

Cross-cutting delivery systems seizing up.

Too much effort Spent on unnecessary plans. Limited real value. Overlap

Mixed message about cross-cutting from the Executive.

Agencies' geographic boundaries not coterminous,

- City of Edinburgh Council: 24 area-wide plans, most required by Executive.

- Greater Glasgow Health Board covers 6 local authority areas (hence 6 community care plans)
- Lothian Health Board covers 4

- Rarely given credit for partnership working in performance management systems
- Not included in corporate contracts
- Unclear about priority between initiatives

Figure 8.3 Cross-cutting policy in Scotland: the view from delivery agencies

Source: Hogg 2000

In other words, for collaboration to work, the collaborators need to work on the processes required as well as the structural and formal arrangements. That is not to say that systems are unimportant. At the least collaborative end of our spectrum, it is likely that there are few incentives or rewards for people to really collaborate, whereas if there are joint budgets, performance systems that measure and praise the achievement of joint targets and an accountability structure that makes it clear what is expected of the partnerships, success is more likely. The systems need to be congruent with the development of attitudes and behaviours that are needed to make collaboration work.

Conditions that inhibit successful collaboration

It is not always the case that this alignment exists. Experience of collaborative efforts shows that there are many things that inhibit them. A review of collaboration in Scotland from the point of view of people in agencies delivering services produced a fairly negative picture, as summarized in Figure 8.3.

The Manchester study produced another list of inhibitors, mostly the opposites of the factors that encourage collaboration but also including the continuation of a competitive culture in which collaboration was seen as the threat of a take-over, and a political environment that demanded results faster than they could be produced.

Some of these inhibitors and those illustrated in Figure 8.3 reflect the fact that a hierarchy was seeking to impose itself on top of a network of collaborating agencies. The Scottish Executive tries to impose its will on the service delivery organizations by issuing directives and calling for plans. The other category of mistake is the number of joint efforts and the amount of time and work involved for people in going to collaborative meetings. Together these are enough to cause the systems to 'seize up'.

Collaboration between the public and private sectors

The involvement of the private sector in the provision of public services is growing rapidly, through the Private Finance Initiative and Public–Private Partnerships and through outsourcing. The market for providing public services has brought rapid growth in turnover and profits to the companies involved. One of the major players is Capita, a company that was set up by the Chartered Institute of Public Finance and Accountancy (CIPFA) in 1984 as CIPFA Computer Services. A management buyout led by managing director Rod Aldridge in 1987 created The Capita Group. Aldridge became chairman and CEO of the new company, which continued to provide outsourcing services to the public sector, particularly in information technology. The company went public in 1991.

From 1992 to 1996 Capita more than doubled its number of employees every two years while consistently winning management contracts outsourced by the British government's privatization spree. After the Labour Party victory in 1997, Capita saw further growth in business from the public sector, with 75% of its contracts coming from government agencies. It secured the payroll and pension administration for the Metropolitan Police (London) in 1998 and acquired some of its competition in 1999, buying Oldham & Tomkins (information technology) and MPM Adams (project management). In late 1999 and early 2000, the company bought teacher placement firm Capstan Northern, engineering consultants Edward Roscoe Associates, and teaching placement agency LHR. In 2000 the company continued its buying spree, acquiring IRG, a privately-owned share registration business. The Capita Group also formed an alliance with Microsoft in 2000 to provide more Internet services for the education field. Capita's sales are summarized in Table 8.1. By 2005, turnover had trebled to £1.5 billion; profits had grown to £177 million before tax.

Capita's partnerships with the public sector range from what it calls 'partnership support' to service management. The range is illustrated in Figure 8.4, which shows that the profits increase with the degree of involvement in the services. Figure 8.5 shows Capita's interpretation of the relationship structures in outsourcing, partnership agreements and joint ventures or the establishment of new companies in partnership.

Table 8.1   *Capita Sales*

1999 Sales £528.9 million	% of total
Private Sector	34
Local government	30
Central government	19
Education	17
Total	100

Source: Hoover's Company Profiles 02/2001

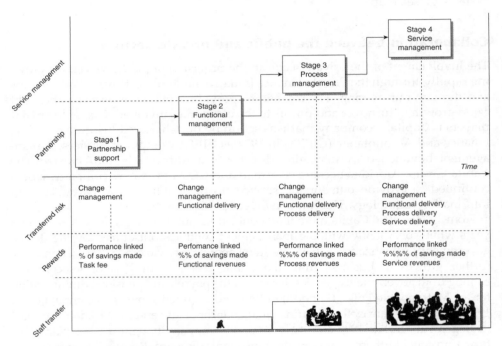

Figure 8.4   Partnership framework

Source: Capita Group plc unpublished presentation

Rod Aldridge resigned as Chairman in 2006, after a controversy over donations and loans to Labour Party funds. Aldridge had personally lent £1 million to the party, on commercial terms.

Another firm that has benefited from outsourcing is Serco, a company that dates back to the 1930s but went public in 1998. It has a history of facilities management for government, including running the Fylingdales missile early warning radar, the National Rail Enquiry System and the Docklands Light Railway. When

Features	Outsourcing	Partnership agreement	Joint venture NEWCO
Client drivers	• Cost reduction • Service improvement	• Cost reduction • Service improvement • Additional benefits • Flexible Relationship	• Cost reduction • Service improvement • Sharing of additional profits • Statutory company position
Control	• Service control	• Partnership rule book • Management board • Joint decision making • Joint change Control	• Company law • Declaration of holdings • Named company directors
Financial management	• Output prices	• Management Accounts • Baseline measurements • Books of account/record	• Statutory accounts
Profit management	• Open book	• Base returns • Profit shares	• Shareholder dividends
Investment management	• Contractor's responsibility	• Partnership agreement – contractor managed	• Shareholder resources
Risk management	• Contractor's responsibility	• Partnership agreement – contractor owned	• Shareholder liabilities
Asset management	• Contractor's responsibility	• Partnership agreement – contractor owned	• Shareholder owned
New-business management	• Contractor's responsibility	• Partnership agreement – joint incentives	• Shareholder driven

Figure 8.5   Relationship structures

Source: Capita Group plc unpublished presentation

large-scale activities were up for outsourcing or privatization, such as the Air Traffic Control sale and the Future Strategic Tanker System, it was well placed to bid for the contracts. 60% of Serco's £430 million turnover is in the United Kingdom and 65% of that comes from government contracts. Another company benefiting from government service contracting is WS Atkins, which has grown from a base in engineering to provide a wider range of contracted services, including part of the privatized Property Services Agency and documentation for a national motorway control system. It moved into education management, taking over the education department of the London Borough of Southwark in 2001 and entering various contracts and joint ventures in education services.

The Labour government is keen for schools to involve the private sector in building and other capital projects. It encouraged Public–Private Partnerships both for complete new schools and for refurbishment and rebuilding.

Conclusions

Collaborative working as a way of managing public services was a central part of the agenda of 'joined-up' government. In most cases what was asked of managers was that they should collaborate while still being competitive. Competition with collaboration as a way of managing public services has not yet produced universally good results. The behaviours that managers and other workers exhibit are conditioned by their environment and especially the rules, motivations and incentives under which they work. In the case of the collaborative way of working that the government has been pushing in many sectors, these are confused. The rules based on a hierarchical system are still in place: the 'centre', whether the Scottish Executive, the NHS Executive, the ODPM or other central government departments, both issue a multitude of instructions and try to devise systems of incentive and reward for their constituent service delivery agencies.

The development of contracting companies and their growth in size is making an imperfectly competitive market for service providers available to public authorities. For very large ITC projects there is a very small number of credible contractors. For outsourcing routine operations, a small number of companies is available. In these circumstances, the mechanisms of adversarial contracting we saw in the previous chapter are not feasible: the threat of switching from one supplier to another is credible only if alternative suppliers are available. Rather, obligational style contracting or collaboration is preferred, the purchaser having good access to the suppliers costs and other information, and a collaborative attitude to problem solving. The same applies to the process of collaborating among public authorities, where information sharing and compatible values are important elements of the collaborative process.

Notes

For weblinks relevant to the issues discussed in this chapter see www.sagepub.co.uk/flynn.

1   Action Teams for Jobs; Active Community Programme; Children's Fund; Coalfields; Community Champions; Community Chest; Community Empowerment Fund; Community Legal Service Partnerships; Creative Partnerships; Crime Reduction Programme; Early Excellence Centres; Education Action Zones; Employment Zones; European Regional Development Fund Areas; Excellence in Cities; Health Action Zones;

Healthy Living Centres; Healthy Schools Programme; Neighbourhood Management; Neighbourhood Renewal Fund; Neighbourhood Support Fund; Neighbourhood Wardens; New Deal for Communities; Playing Fields and Community Green Spaces; Single Regeneration Budget; Spaces for Sports and Arts; Sport Action Zones; Sure Start; Sure Start Plus; Urban Regeneration Companies. List compiled by Stewart Wilks-Heeg, unpublished paper on urban regeneration, 2001.

2 *Local Strategic Partnerships :Shaping their future, a consultation paper* (ODPM/Department for Communities and Local Government, London, 2005) p. 11.

3 Office of Deputy Prime Minister, *Evaluation of local strategic partnerships. Report of a survey of all English LSPs,* Survey conducted in 2002 (ODPM, London, 2003).

4 Office of Deputy Prime Minister, Neighbourhood Renewal Unit, *Research Report 23, 'Neighbourhood Management – at the Turning Point?,* Programme Review 2005–06 (ODPM, London, March 2006) p. 8.

5 Ibid., p. 7.

6 B. Guy Peters, *Managing Horizontal Government* (Canadian Centre for Management Development, Ottawa, 1998 Research paper 21, p. 47.

7 Eugene Bardach, *Getting Agencies to Work Together: The Practice and Theory of Managerial Craftsmanship* (Brookings Institution, Washington DC, 1998).

8 Su Maddock and Glenn Morgan, *Conditions for Partnership* (Manchester Business School, Manchester, 1999).

Part Two B: Outsourced Services

9

Managing through markets

Introduction

A central tenet of the 'new right' ideology was that markets are the only efficient way of allocating resources, reducing costs and improving efficiency. The superiority of markets was an important part of Conservative opinion and part of the ideological effort to counter the post-war development of planning and public services. 'Third Way' thinking was less ideologically enthusiastic about markets but promoted their use as a way of allocating resources: later Blair governments, leaving 'third way' notions behind, were at least as keen on markets as the Conservatives had been.

In practice the markets which were constructed by the Conservative governments rarely conformed with the features of the economists' 'perfect competition', with freedom of choice as to what to purchase and from whom, free entry for new competitors and perfect information for consumers. In fact they were mostly very limited in comparison to this ideal. One reason for this difference is that the motives for establishing markets, whatever the rhetoric, were not only to improve the allocation of resources or efficiency. One motive was to distance politicians from decisions which would be unpopular with the electorate: having a market to blame is convenient, whether for the closure of a popular facility, a reduction in workers' incomes or the number of jobs. Later Labour governments, beginning towards the end of the second in 2004, became keen on the idea of free choice by service users, offering choice of hospital service provider and attempting to offer some choice of schools.

The markets that were created before 2004 mainly excluded the element of free choice of service or supplier for the service user. The market within the NHS was an internal market, transactions being made between NHS employees without involving patients. Under local authority compulsory competitive tendering, the authority rather than the citizen had the choice of service provider. Market testing in central government is an internal matter designed to reduce cost and increase private sector participation in public services. In the community care markets, consumers do have a limited choice of services which is subject to their assessment as being in need.

As well as these internal markets, market mechanisms have also been introduced by getting the private sector involved in financing capital projects and in the market for labour.

The Labour government claimed to be less dogmatic about the advantages of markets and competition: it did not believe in them in principle but rather only if they worked. Very early the new government changed the internal market in the NHS, the competitive tendering regime in local government and the market testing arrangements in the Civil Service. While there was talk about partnerships and trust, the new arrangements subjected at least as many services to market pressures as the old ones and were designed as much to encourage private firms to provide services as to limit the destructive effects of competition.

Why rule by markets?

Ideology

To 'modernisers' the bureaucratic and professional organizations that were built as part of the welfare state, the NHS, local authorities, nationalized industries, powerful government departments, are part of the pre-modernized way of managing the state and delivering public services. The 'Third Way' rhetoric, a prominent feature of the first Labour government, could not simply propose the same market-type solutions but had to find an alternative, apparently softer and more collaborative version. Their coyness about proposing competition soon waned and by the third term, competition had become central to policy again. Towards the end of 2004, in the prelude to the 2005 general election, 'choice' became more central to government policy. Led by Alan Milburn, Minister of Health and a central figure in the election campaign, the new policy put choice for its own sake at the centre of policy. Speeches were delivered berating the lack of choice and 'one size fits all' approach in public sector service provision. In one speech Alan Milburn even used the very old story of council tenants not being able to choose the colour of their own front door as a reason for allowing choice of hospital. Choice was not sold as a way of bringing costs down or quality up, rather as a good thing in itself, which would produce more consumer satisfaction.

Before the idea that choice was a benefit, the main argument was that markets allocate resources more efficiently than bureaucratic rules. Efficiency is defined in two ways. First, goods and services will be produced at the lowest cost. Any high-cost producers will be replaced by lower-cost producers as new entrants seize the opportunity to make profits. Secondly, only those goods and services are produced which people demand. Producers' response to individuals' demands are more likely to produce what people want than some bureaucratic mechanism deciding what people might want or need. The first type of efficiency is known as 'productive efficiency' and the second as 'allocative efficiency'. To enable these two aspects of efficiency to prevail, there are certain prerequisites: consumers must know what is available in the market and at what price and be able to gain access to alternative suppliers; producers must be able freely to enter any particular market; existing producers should not have insurmountable advantages because of their existing operations; capital markets must operate in such a way as to allow investment in profitable opportunities.

Proponents of markets argue that even if these conditions do not prevail, partial market solutions are better than none. If there can be a competition among a small group of producers, this is likely to produce efficiency gains even if there is no free choice for the ultimate consumer. Alternatively, even if there can only be a small element of consumer choice this will make producers more responsive to consumers than if there is no choice. In other words, even if there is not an optimal solution, the less than optimal solutions will be better than having no markets at all.

Anonymous decision-making and arm's-length accountability

There is also a political advantage in market solutions. Just as it has always been one of the perks of a politician's life to open a building and have a name on the plaque, so closing a building has never won any friends. With the exception of the explosive demolition of unpopular tower blocks, the closure of facilities such as an under-resourced branch library, ill-equipped cottage hospital or insanitary elderly persons home always generates a high degree of popular support for those establishments. If the institution to be closed is the oldest hospital in London it can be assured of support not just from the local population but a host of influential friends both from the medical establishment and members of the political élite. Any way of removing the decision from political accountability will therefore find favour. 'Market forces' or Adam Smith's 'invisible hand' are to blame, if indeed blame is due, or the responsibility lies with management who have failed to behave in a sufficiently competitive manner.

The same applies to competitive tendering exercises, in which it is not politicians who reduce the number of jobs and reduce the job security of those remaining, but the 'market' which chooses the winning bid. During the Conservative governments even the Labour Party found this proposition convenient at local government level. Leaders of Labour-controlled local authorities have admitted that efforts to improve customer service and reduce costs in services such as housing maintenance and refuse collection were helped by exposure to competition from outside. Local politicians could not be blamed for asking their workers to produce more output for the same or less pay: a combination of government rules and market forces made them do it. The Best Value régime introduced by the Labour government puts extra pressure on managers to improve costs, quality and competitiveness as well as carry out consultation on the processes.

The market also allows operations to be divorced from policy. Whether a private contractor or an in-house organization wins a bid, there is a fairly clear distinction between the responsibility for setting policy and standards of service and organizing to deliver services. The managers of the service delivery units are clearly accountable for the management of their units and not for the amount of budget allocated to the service that they deliver.

In practice, the markets which have been introduced into the public sector have been a very artificial creation, resulting in rule books rather than anything that might be identified as 'market forces', and the conditions necessary for efficiency have not been established. The particular difference between the ideal type of free market and the artificial creations is the role of the consumer, with free choice and very good knowledge of the options and the ability to switch among suppliers. The reason for this difference is clear: the reason that services such as health, social security and the other major public services are in the public sector is that the market would not work. People who are regularly unemployed could not buy unemployment insurance. Children of poor parents would not be able to afford health care. The rationing system which has to be put in place for public provision immediately restricts the freedom of the 'customer': someone else is always involved in the rationing decision and is therefore likely to be involved in the choices made as part of the rationing process.

Therefore, in the Health Service, there was a possibility of choosing a general practitioner, but referrals to secondary health care have to go through the primary practitioner. In community care, access to services is through the assessment process in which a social worker or other official makes an assessment of need and an allocation of resources. Parents and children can choose schools but only if they can easily travel to them and in some cases, only if the school chooses them.

Whatever the nature of the market, the market mechanisms are combined with government control. The NHS Trusts are subject to Treasury control on capital spending and to a variety of interventions and instructions from the Department of Health. Schools may be more free from local authority control but subject to the Department for Education and Skills and its inspection arrangements.

Markets for services

NHS

The White Paper 'Working for Patients', 1989, introduced market mechanisms to the NHS in two ways. Health authorities were to become purchasers of health services on behalf of the populations of their areas, and people providing services, whether in the community or in hospitals, were to become relatively independent

Trusts which would sell their services under contract to the purchasers. At the same time, general practitioners were to be given the option of having their own budgets with which to purchase medical services on behalf of their patients.

The structure of this administratively invented market varied. In the cities there was the possibility of competition among general hospitals and among teaching hospitals. Any individual hospital could therefore be faced with a range of potential purchasers, and purchasers had some choice of providers. In less densely-populated areas, a single purchaser would be facing a single general hospital and competition would involve patients making long journeys to an alternative service provider.

The market was operated through a series of contracts which specified the services, the volume required and the price. The process of writing and monitoring the contracts was expensive, raising the costs of running services in exchange for the benefits of competition and the separation of the decisions about which services should be provided from the management of hospitals and community health services. The consumers of health services would see no immediate increase in their control over services. Indeed, their choice could be reduced: if their district had no contract with the preferred provider, it would have to be persuaded to make an 'extra-contractual referral' and pay for the service. As Klein said:

> ... there was nothing that the consumer could do directly: there were no decisions, informed or otherwise, to take – except, possibly, to opt out of the NHS and go private ... the consumerism of the internal market was of a very peculiar kind: it was a top–down consumerism.[1]

However, the market did create reasons for managers and clinicians to change their behaviour in response to the purchasers' requirements, especially with regard to the volume of work done for a given amount of cash.

Simultaneously, the reform gave the NHS Executive more ways of controlling and directing the activities of both purchasers and providers, promoting the establishment of Trusts, influencing the appointment of Trust boards and chief executives and promoting ministerial initiatives. In this sense, the changes were both decentralizing and centralizing: managers had to make changes in response to the market as well as in response to the NHS Executive and its regional offices.

The differences between the new arrangements and the free market was that the contracts were not legally binding (there being only one corporate entity); prices had to be based on average cost; there is in practice a geographical restriction on competition; contracts were limited to one year. The Regional Office was felt to be exerting influence through help and guidance and through control of the capital expenditure programme.

The NHS market, therefore, was a mixture of market and central control and direction, both designed to reduce the influence of the medical professions in the hospitals. The abolition of the internal market in the NHS and the introduction of long-term contracts between health commissioners and health service providers was not as radical a break as it was presented. The Department of Health had already lengthened contract periods, and competition was really confined to areas where there was a large number of suppliers. The fundamental reform remained intact, whereby budgets were allocated to people commissioning services rather than directly to those providing them. This was to change with the introduction of 'Choose and Book', whereby patients were given, from 2006, a choice of four alternative providers of secondary health care. Combined with the new system of 'Payment by Results', a system of competition and payment was devised through which hospitals compete with each other – but not on price, which is set by a national tariff. Patients can choose according to their own criteria, based on whatever information they can find about quality and on convenience.

Compulsory competitive tendering and Best Value

Local authorities were subject to a régime of compulsory competitive tendering (CCT) based on the Local Government Planning and Land Act 1980 and the Local Government Act 1988, until the Local Government Act of 1999 established 'Best Value'. The CCT rules made authorities organize a competition with private contractors for any work which it undertook, initially in the areas of building and highways work and then in other 'blue collar' areas such as refuse collection and parks maintenance, followed by 'white-collar' and professional services, including engineering design and legal, personnel, computing and financial services. A market developed as companies formed to undertake local authority work or expanded to enter this new field. In some cases, companies which had previously operated in other countries went to the United Kingdom to tender for the new contracts which were offered.

While the 1999 Act abolished compulsory tendering, it introduced rules and an inspection process that made some form of competition inevitable. As the White Paper preceding the Act said: '…retaining work in-house without subjecting it to real competitive pressure can rarely be justified' (para 7.28). The real competitive pressure did not need to take the old form of CCT, which had been unpopular with many firms because of its long and tedious procedures, but could include partial outsourcing to provide comparative information, outsourcing without an internal bid, forming a joint venture with a private provider, disposal of a service and its assets to another provider. By using these alternative methods, the government thought that 'there is likely to be greater interest from the private and voluntary sectors in working wth local government to deliver quality services at a competitive price' (para 7.30).

Market testing and Better Quality Services

The government introduced a programme of market testing in the Civil Service in 1992. While some services were contracted out to the private sector without an in-house bid, which was called 'strategic contracting out', an expression that survived into the 1997 government proposals, others were to be subjected to competition in a process similar to CCT in local government. Departments and agencies were given targets of the volume of services which would be subject to tendering. In the first year, 389 activities had been subject to testing, costing £1.1 billion. The private sector was awarded £885 million worth of work, of which £768 million was awarded without an in-house bid. Of this £525 million was accounted for by the Inland Revenue computer service and the Atomic Weapons Establishment.[2] The government claims that costs were reduced by an average of about 25% as a result of the competitive process, whether bids were won internally or by contractors. However, we may have a slight doubt about the scale of savings. As John Oughton, head of the Efficiency Unit, said: 'we need to be clear about what the data can, and cannot, tell us. For example, calculating savings is fine so long as there is a clear idea of how much an activity costs pre-test. This is not always the case'.[3]

The market testing initiative was short-lived. The targets for volume of work to be tested were dropped and other initiatives, such as the Private Finance Initiative, were given more prominence. However, departments were still encouraged to consider market testing as part of their search for cost savings. One of the reasons for the falling enthusiasm was the complaint by companies that they had to spend money on making bids, while 70% of work was won by the in-house teams.

The Conservative governments made various attempts to involve companies in the provision of public services in ways which have not involved a competition with the existing public employees. At the same time as the market testing initiative there were contracts with companies which were awarded without the existing employees being allowed to bid. A phrase was invented to cover this behaviour: 'strategic partnerships'. While it was never clear why this was done, there was always a suspicion that it was simply a manifestation of the 'private good, public bad' belief.

The Labour government continued with much the same approach. In 1997 it introduced 'Better Quality Services', which was a combination of performance review, target setting and competition. The guidance for senior managers[4] set out a list of options for the decision about how services were to be provided that was unchanged from the previous government's. The options were:

- Abolish, if the service is no longer required
- Restructure internally, after 'benchmarking'
- Strategically contract out – that is, outsource without an internal bid
- Market test – outsource but only if an external supplier bids successfully against the in-house team
- Privatize

The market for care (community care)

The NHS and Community Care Act 1990 introduced market mechanisms to part of the work of social services departments. The rule that 85 per cent of the special transitional grant (STG) should be spent on services other than those provided directly by the local authority meant that authorities had to trade with the private and voluntary sectors. There were two sorts of transaction: a series of 'block' contracts through which services were purchased in advance, and 'spot' purchasing of services as required by individuals. The Audit Commission estimated that 89% of STG and 21% of total budgets were available for 'spot' purchasing in 1994/5.[5]

This arrangement encouraged some authorities to allocate social services budgets to staff designated as 'purchasers' who could commission care from other staff designated as 'providers'. According to the Audit Commission progress report, this arrangement did not generally apply to the authorities' residential accommodation, which continued to be funded directly. Other authorities decided that it was not desirable to establish such market-type arrangements because the STG was such a small proportion of the total social services budget. The Audit Commission expressed the view that a market-type arrangement 'does not guarantee either greater flexibility or more responsive services. If handled clumsily it can introduce barriers and rigidity'.[6] In cases in which the authorities made a strict division between purchasers and providers, the providers became resentful if their services were not used. In some cases, purchasers found that external providers were both cheaper and more flexible. In the case of homecare in some authorities, for example, agencies could provide staff cheaply at unsocial hours in comparison with direct employees.

The market with the private and voluntary sectors is managed to a large extent by the local authorities. While in the case of residential care individuals have a choice of where to live, within a budget constraint, authorities use their market intelligence to recommend providers of whom they approve. In addition, authorities have been promoting the development of other services by offering contracts to provide homecare and other aspects of non-residential care.

Where budgets are delegated to 'purchasers' rather than allocated to the provision of local authority services, a competition is entered into between the direct providers and their independent sector competitors. However, this competition is normally managed differently from the competitive tendering régime for other services: authorities did not, generally, put their own services at risk by allowing spot purchases of their own services. They were committed to keep the premises and staff, in the short term at least, and would have incurred the expenses whether or not the purchasers in the internal market bought them.

The community care market differs from the NHS market in these respects: in the NHS there is no presumption that a proportion of the budget be spent in the independent sector, although private diagnostic and treatment centres have been established in the private sector; in social services there is no compulsion to organize an internal market for all services.

Markets for labour

Governments have tried to deregulate labour markets, by a series of legislation to reduce the power of the trades unions and the removal of restrictive practices such as minimum wages supported by Wages Councils. In the public sector, they have tried to allow the market for labour to operate more freely, by devolving bargaining to local areas. The idea is that in areas of high unemployment and low pay, public servants can be hired for lower pay than in areas where the local labour market is more competitive. Similar arguments apply to particular occupations. In some parts of the country there are shortages of people with certain skills and premium pay has to be offered to attract people to work. The move towards local bargaining reflects developments in the private sector, where plant-level bargaining or company bargaining has largely replaced whole industry deals, if indeed collective bargaining still takes place.

Markets for capital

Despite the increase in capital spending there is a very regulated market for capital. Local authorities have to obtain permission to make capital expenditures, however they are financed (whether through borrowing or the use of accumulated reserves), capital spending by NHS Trusts is tightly controlled, and in the Civil Service strict control is exercised.

It is inconsistent that markets are established for services, the market for labour has been deregulated, but the market for capital is still very controlled. While the introduction of accruals accounting apparently makes it possible to make more rational choices of investment, in practice the Treasury is always interested in one year's cash flow. There are chances to 'spend to save' or invest to improve productivity but these decisions are generally vetted by the Treasury. Labour continued with these procedures, although some of the names of the funds changed slightly. In addition to the Invest to Save fund there was, inevitably, a 'Capital Modernisation Fund' for approved investments.

The capital funds arrangements for local authorities were thought to be too restrictive and proposals were made to change them.[7] Some of the proposals give more freedom, such as the overall control on borrowing being changed from an approval system to a rule about the rate of growth of debt. However, there are strong views about how capital spending should be done, and that it favours 'strategic partnerships'. The proposals recognize that it will not be able to ensure the growth of such partnerships 'merely by restricting the funding available to authorities and thereby forcing them to seek partners' (para 4.15). However, 'Until private finance achieves more general acceptance, there is a case for continuing to provide ring-fenced grants to remunerate private finance deals' (para 4.16). The government was clearly frustrated by some authorities' reluctance to enter PFI type arrangements because of what it described as their 'proprietorial attitudes to services'.

Markets and managerial behaviour

How have managers responded to the establishment of markets? First we suggest that the amount of change depends on how much competition is introduced, ranging from that which occurs in simple internal market arrangements which involve no competition, through degrees of competitiveness to a market in which buyers have free choice of supplier. In the least competitive position, managers have to define their services and calculate what their unit costs are. More competition, through price testing, makes managers ask questions about cost, while if this is accompanied by real testing against competitors, people start to try to reduce their costs. More change is required if there is an organized tendering process. The most change is required if there is a market in which all purchasers are free to choose their supplier, whether internal or external. In these circumstances, the organization becomes fragmented, jobs are insecure and managers and workers would probably benefit from leaving and setting up their own company. Managers have developed competitive strategies, competing either on price or uniqueness. In general, the argument about quality justifying higher price is difficult to sustain unless quality can be demonstrated.

Sometimes, competition has been a prelude to privatization. There are many examples of organizations developing a successful competitive strategy and then being sold to the private sector. This may be seen by some as positive and by others who believe in publicly provided services as a bad thing.

The chapter then looks at the evaluation of these changes. It concludes that there are probably single reductions in cost as competition is introduced, either through cuts in wage rates or numbers of jobs. However, it is difficult to justify such assessments without an adequate assessment of cost, volume and quality of services before and after the introduction of competition. If the tendering process causes managers to define, measure and cost services for the first time, it is unlikely that true comparisons can be made. However, there have been other results: flexible response to customers may be reduced, the nature of public accountability changes and there has been a growth of public service companies.

A competitive spectrum

As we saw in the previous chapter, markets have been introduced in different forms in different parts of the public sector. It is useful to think of the markets as having degrees of competitiveness which in turn require different responses from managers. This is illustrated by Figure 9.1 At one end of the spectrum the service is outsourced after competition among potential suppliers, but there is no internal bid. The second degree of impact on the competitive behaviour of the internal managers is simply an internal transaction in which each side plays at buying and selling services. At the other end there is a market in which purchasers have a free choice of provider and service providers have to compete. The requirement from managers changes according to how far along the spectrum the markets lie.

Outsourcing with no internal bid

In certain, mainly internal, services a decision was made to outsource to a company without a bid from the internal team previously supplying the service.

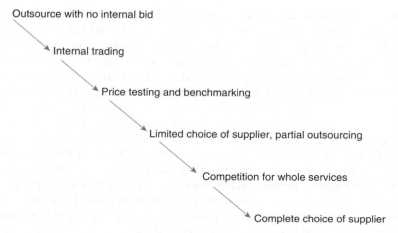

Figure 9.1   Degrees of competition

This applied particularly to central government and some of the information technology contracts between the government and software and facilities management companies. Internal teams were transferred, at least partly, to the new employers and often had the same middle management. The impact was to remove some of the rigidities imposed by internal systems and to make staff make themselves attractive to their new employers, if they wanted to be transferred.

Internal trading

A minimal approach to the development of markets is to establish a supplier–customer relationship within an organization. This idea became fashionable in parts of the private sector during the 1980s as a way of helping people who are not in direct contact with customers, to define what it is they do and for whom. In manufacturing and service industries, the development of internal relationships in this way became part of the quality improvement effort as value chains were defined, each part of the production process being identified as adding value to the product or service and each link in the chain being described as a market relationship. Only the relationship between a 'supplier' and a 'customer' was felt adequately to result in good service or value for money. The idea was applied in the public sector through contracts on the volume and quality of service to be offered. In local government these were called 'service level agreements'.

The first impact of internal trading is that managers have to define their position in the value chain, and decide who is the customer and who is the supplier in each relationship. Sometimes this is very complicated. For example, an accountant working in a local authority may have a large number of customers: line managers for whom s/he provides management information, the chief finance officer who receives finance data, members who receive advice. S/he might also be a customer of the personnel department, the legal department and the car park. Or the chain may be long. A software maintenance person may be a supplier to a school but the school has a contract with a purchasing division of the local authority which commissions work from internal and external suppliers. If in turn the software maintenance section has subcontractors, the supply chain may be longer still. In other cases the process is more simple. Grounds maintenance is clearly a service to a school, personnel advice on disciplinary matters clearly a service to line managers. In these cases the definition of who is working for whom is useful: the school gets its cricket pitch rolled before the match, not after. The process can make the relationships more appropriate for good service delivery: rather than the personnel department dictating what managers can do, they are there to support management. One example is recruitment advertising, which can be a source of long delays for managers trying to replace staff. A customer–supplier relationship can help to ensure that managers are supported.

Once the supply chain has been established, the next task is to define what is being bought and sold. Taken to the extreme, the definition of the service provided by professionals can be an elaborate and lengthy business. However, the process can be useful, especially if it makes it more obvious what professionals do. A negative aspect of professionalism is that individuals can create a mystery. A definition of the service provided both makes the activity explicit and allows others to judge the value of the service. Such definitions also expose the power relationships in the organizations. Traditionally, people in charge of money have been powerful, whether directors of finance or principal finance officers. They have controlled the flow of financial information and in many cases the flow of funds used by people providing services. They have also created the impression of crisis, only to solve the problem by mysteriously finding an extra pocket of money at the last minute. Defining their job as a service to other people in the organization addresses this power and provides a starting point for discussions about who is in control.

The third requirement for an internal market is the need to estimate costs. It sometimes appears odd to outsiders, but it has often been the case that managers have no clear idea about how much services cost: they may know how much cash a department or unit consumes but have little idea of how much a particular service costs. Internal trading forces people to make these calculations. In some cases, the allocation of costs is necessarily arbitrary but even estimates are valuable. The calculation of costs itself puts managers under scrutiny. Even if there is no competition, the fact that costs are known makes people question the value of what is provided for those costs and whether that value could be obtained more cheaply. In some cases, questions are asked about whether the service is required at all.

Once the suppliers and customers have been identified, the services defined and the costs calculated, internal markets can then be accounted for in a series of trading accounts. In traditional public sector accounts, departments or units are allocated funds, usually at the beginning of the year, and the accounts are prepared to show how those funds are spent. Trading accounts are different: they have an income side as well as an expenses side. Credits are made to the account as work is performed according to the contract. In practice, most purely internal trading accounts are fictitious in that income is entered in regular monthly sums whatever work is done. Where the income side of the account represents real transactions, trading accounts become an important means for managers to see whether their trading activity is successful. It is surprising how much difference this change makes: managers no longer see themselves as accountable only for money spent but also for work done and therefore income received. This change in attitude occurs even when there is no competition, although competition brings with it other changes as well.

Internal trading with price testing and benchmarking

A variation on this approach is to make an internal contract and then check the costs of providing that service against what might be offered by an alternative supplier. While there may not be a formal competition, the fact that alternative prices are estimated sets a 'benchmark' figure for the service. For example, it is possible to estimate how much a bank would charge for running a payroll system, which could be compared with the internal charges. It is also possible to define the quality standards that an outside supplier would conform to.

Price testing with outside suppliers generates more change. The costing exercise has to be more precise: if prices are to be compared, the units in which trading occurs have to be defined. For example, if the recruitment part of the personnel function is to be compared with the cost of hiring a recruitment agency, the relevant comparison is between the cost of hiring one member of staff internally and the charge which the agency would make for this. Then, the costs of the department which is hiring need to be included in the total cost of the exercise and the difference in that cost between using the inside personnel department and an agency.

The next step is to compare the internal costs with the external prices. This always starts an argument about the allocation of costs and managers' discretion to affect their own costs. For example, one central government training department had its costs compared with the cost of outsourcing the training function. One of its major costs was the rent it notionally paid on a very expensive central London office, which had a lease signed during the property boom. Unable to vacate the premises or negotiate the rent level, the department was placed at a competitive disadvantage. Similarly, people always argue about the level of recharging for central departments. As more and more services are subjected to internal market régimes, these costs become more visible and what is provided for the money becomes more clear. There is a sequential process of questioning costs: those first exposed to comparison question the cost and value of the services which they receive from others, who in turn begin to ask the same questions of their internal suppliers.

Comparing quality with outside suppliers can also have an impact. In some cases, the internal customers for a service are convinced that the quality of outside suppliers would be higher and it is worth testing that proposition. Conversely it is often the case that existing services are of too high a quality and have too many refinements that internal customers rarely need and do not want to pay for.

Limited freedom to choose suppliers

A further step is when the customer end of the supplier–customer relationship is allowed, within defined limits, to choose an alternative supplier. An organization may have a printing unit, for example, but people who need printing may be allowed to shop around with a proportion of their printing budget. In community care, people making assessments and allocating care may have a proportion of their budget to spend on the open market. Once those exposed to price comparisons are exposed to actual competition, the pressure is even greater. Faced with the threat of losing their job, managers have to look seriously at their costs compared with the prices of the competition.

Both sides of the internal trade also look at the relevance of the services being provided and their quality. Some internal services are of a quality which is not required by the customer: for example, some payroll systems have a level of potential sophistication in reporting which is never used. Line managers question whether they need some services at all. When legal costs are attributed through a service level agreement to a unit which never receives legal advice, they wonder why. If they face competition and those legal costs are a contributory element to their uncompetitive price, they protest. Such activity has its advantages: people are forced to think whether they are doing a useful job. It also has its disadvantages, in that it splits the organization into divisively competitive elements.

The transfer of budgets to the customer side of the transaction changes the power relationships. Take the accounting function – if there is an allocation of funds to the accountants, with no accountability to line managers, they are in a strong position. Such a position is difficult to imagine in the private sector, in which an accountant arrives at a firm, announces that she has been appointed as accountant, defines what she is going to do and how much the customer is to be charged. Once the customer–supplier relationship is established and the customer has a budget for accountancy, the relationship changes. It can even change to the extent that the provider side starts to sell itself to the customers. This certainly happened in the education service. Education department employees produced glossy brochures and made sales visits to schools when the budgets for support services were devolved. Some schools were surprised when previously haughty managers transformed themselves into humble salespeople.

There are also changes in the way in which services are provided, in line with customer requirements. For example, support staff are more likely to be physically sited where the customers want them, rather than in a head office building.

Competition for whole services

A more radical step is to put a whole service out to tender. Once the customer–supplier relationship has been defined, the customer side then seeks bids from people to become the supplier. They may do this because they have been told to (in the case of local government by legislation and regulations, in central government by ministerial edict) or because they see it as a way of reducing cost. The franchise approach is a variant on this. In London, bus routes were offered to bus operators by tender, as were individual train routes in the privatization of British Rail.

When a whole service is put out to tender, there is a sudden-death competition in which the in-house team is given a single chance to keep their jobs. If they have already been through the processes we have just seen, the next step is to see whether they can reduce their cost to the likely price of the competitive bid. Since most services are labour-intensive, this often means reducing staff costs. While the European Union regulations that protect workers' conditions when their work is transferred to a new employer limit the extent to which companies can reduce staff terms and conditions after winning a bid, there is still competitive pressure on prices. While the competitors' likely prices are not known, at least the first time, the in-house team do have access to published accounts from the organizations whose work they are bidding for and are likely to reduce costs.

The search for cost reduction may involve finding different ways of providing the service. For example, Capita provide council tax collection services on a series of centralized computers, rather than each council having its own. In-house teams have to try to find their own ways of matching such changes in service design if they can.

Sometimes the in-house team decides that the constraints on its operations and its costs are such that it is unlikely to compete successfully. The only way to win is to make a management buy-out and put in a bid for the work as a new entity. An early example of this was a company called MRS which was established by managers at Westminster City Council to win the bid for refuse collection. An alternative is to find a 'host company', already established in the field, to employ the in-house team. This happened in local government, especially, as a way of avoiding going through the competitive tendering process. Tendering was compulsory only if the council wanted to do the work using its own workforce. Once the work was privatized, the rules no longer applied. Similarly there were examples of local education authorities contracting out the management of their departments in advance of being ordered to do so by the Department for Education and Employment.

Complete choice of suppliers for individual purchasers

At the extreme, all budgets are moved to the customer side of the relationship and there is neither a commitment to the internal supplier nor a periodic tendering process. Budget holders simply choose where to spend their money on each occasion on which they need services. The devolution of budgets from education authorities to schools has this effect. Once the purchasers have complete freedom, they may choose to exercise it by entering long-term contracts, but how to purchase is their decision.

Fragmentation of services

One impact of the competition process is that the organization is divided into discrete parts, each operating to its own contract. This has two effects. First, it is difficult to operate any corporate policies on matters such as redundancy or pay policy: each case is determined by the price and conditions in the contract. The second is that the contracting process reduces flexibility and responsiveness. For example, in emergencies such as floods, a workforce used to be able to be found to deal with damage from a variety of sources: road workers, refuse collectors and so on. Under a contracting regime such flexibility is much more difficult.

Conversely, dividing organizations into accountable units with very specific tasks can make the managerial task easier. Before privatization, London Buses was divided up into accountable units. Individual garages were managed by individual managers, and functions such as maintenance engineering were managed separately and accountably. Much of the performance improvement in London Buses can be attributed to this change, rather than the subsequent privatization. There was a plan to split up the management of the London Underground into separate contracts in a similar way but this was opposed by the Mayor of London. Since there had been derailments on the rail network that were in part attributable to the contracting arrangements, the Mayor won the argument and in January 2001 the government decided to retain unified management of the underground network. How it is maintained and improved is discussed in detail in Chapter 11.

In other words, dividing activities into parts which are easily seen and for which people can be held accountable is a positive result of the process of defining work for competition. Taken to excess, fragmentation occurs and flexibility is lost.

Competitive strategy

Managers have had to decide how to compete. Porter[8] has shown that there are three generic strategies in competitive markets. Companies have to compete on price if there are no special features of their product or service which would persuade customers to pay a higher price. The second strategy is the process of making one product or service appear more valuable to the customers, and is called 'differentiation'. This strategy could be adopted for part of the product range, while competing on price in the rest of the range. The third strategy is described as 'focus'.

Managers have had to decide whether to compete on price or differentiation and whether there are some areas where only price competition is appropriate. The rules about competition usually allow decisions to be taken on the value for money offered by the different bidders, but the differentiation has to be demonstrable. If there is a detailed specification, against which the bid has to be made, it is difficult to show in advance how one organization might perform better than another. The more mechanical the work, the harder it is to make the case for higher quality. In services which have a high level of personal contact, such as leisure services or homecare, it is easier to argue the case for high quality service justifying a higher price. However, there were cases where working practices did not make the service quality as high as it could be. The times at which services were available were often restricted by the working hours of the staff, for example. Such practices had to be changed if quality was to be used as a criterion for selecting the winning tender.

When local authorities wanted to retain their existing workforce, there were ways of organizing the tendering process which would make the in-house teams more likely to win. Some private sector competitors believe that local authorities favour their own workforces in the bidding process. One-third of those firms that had grounds for complaint said that the local authorities favoured their own workforce. The strategy of protecting jobs for local people on reasonable pay and conditions is attractive to local authorities, especially in areas of high unemployment, such as the North East or East London. Transferring jobs to companies who may not employ local labour can have a damaging effect on the local economy and local people. These matters may be as important to local politicians as the short-term effect of a reduction in the price of services. The Department of Transport, Environment and the Regions and auditors may take a different view of the relationship between competitive tendering and economic policy: demonstrable value for money is a higher priority than policies towards the local workforce. Such practices were made more difficult by the Best Value rules and inspections after 1999 that were designed to make it easier for alternative suppliers to compete.

If the in-house team decides to compete on price, they take a series of actions to reduce their costs, including staff reductions, changes in employment contracts, reduction of assets and changes in working practices.

Competition and privatization

In addition there have been cases where competition and competitive pressure was used as part of a process of preparation for privatization, whether explicitly or implicitly. Sometimes, competition simply made organizations more ready for privatization. Post Office Letters was restructured and reorganized into more autonomous local units under the management of Bill Cockburn, who then pressed for privatization of the Post Office and resigned to take up a post in the private sector when this did not happen. The reorganization could be seen as a preparation for privatization. London Buses Ltd was similarly restructured into smaller companies which were made relatively autonomous. This made the process of privatization simpler, although it was not an explicit objective. London Buses' privatization was completed at the end of 1995, raising £218 million net for the Treasury.

Another example was the government scientific laboratories, which were first made to compete for work, rather than having budgets allocated to them automatically. Competition then caused many to reorganize, 're-engineer' their processes (literally) and make themselves more efficient and competitive. Some were then offered for sale either to private companies or to their own management. The National Engineering Laboratory, in Scotland, was sold to Assessment Services Ltd, part of Siemens. In fact it was sold for a negative price of £1.95 million, the sum which was given to Siemens to take over the laboratory. The Transport Research Laboratory was sold to Transport Research Foundation, a not-for-profit group formed by members of the laboratory and representatives of the transport industry.

Improved management as a preparation for privatization is a confusing activity for workers and managers. There may be a public service ethic, in which the public good is the main criterion. Once privatization is mentioned, the managerial effort is being made for the benefit of the new owners, who may be the managers themselves or an unknown group of shareholders.

Implications for public services

Cost and quality

Surveys of the impact of compulsory competitive tendering suggest that the introduction of competition produces a single reduction in cost. In a comprehensive review of the studies of costs before and after competition, Walsh[9] concluded that competition produces a reduction in direct service costs, especially in relatively simple, repetitive services such as refuse collection. The results vary by service but figures of 20% reduction in the cost of refuse collection were common. This is probably because refuse collection crews were reduced from five people to four and the four had to do the work of the missing crew member. Where it is less possible to make people work harder physically, such cost reductions are less easy to achieve.

The market testing exercise in the Civil Service was mainly for clerical and technical work. Departments were given targets for savings, which they mostly met. It was difficult to discover whether the cost reductions represent a cut in unit costs or a cut in volume. However, it is probably safe to conclude that some unit cost reductions were made. Whether they could have been achieved simply by cutting budgets, rather than an expensive tendering exercise, is another matter. During the first round of competitive tendering in local government, managers had an idea of the level of cost reduction which the private sector would be likely to offer and those figures became a cost reduction target. A similar target could come from a simple budget reduction.

However, reduction in expenditure does not necessarily produce a reduction in unit cost: budget cuts can simply lead to a reduction in volume or quality of service. This is the view expressed by the Parliamentary Ombudsman:

> Reductions in staff numbers, organisational changes and new working practices will continue for some time to place individual civil servants under stress. There is a risk that fewer staff will lead to slower service and to more mistakes because civil servants will have less time for thought to enable them to pursue considered and prudent action.[10]

The main difference between budget cuts and competition is that the process of competition forces people to define services and volumes. Budget cutting may change volumes and quality but perhaps in ways which are never made explicit, other than by the number of complaints and mistakes which result.

Customer orientation

In some ways, contracted-out public services are less responsive to the public than directly provided ones. Once a contract is signed, with a specification attached, it is difficult to change the service. This is probably not important for services such as refuse collection and street cleaning, while for services such as homecare or nursing, the details of the service are a result of the relationship between the service user and the provider which cannot be described in a detailed specification.

Public accountability and democracy

Accountability to the public can only be achieved in a limited way through the contracting process. As John Stewart has argued,

> Governing is more than the provision of a series of services on a well-defined pattern. Government is the means for collective action in society, responding to and guiding change that is beyond the capacity of private action. It involves both learning of change, adapting to change and promoting change. The nature of government does not exclude the use of contracts, but places limits on the extent to which the governing process can be reduced to contracts.[11]

The argument is that contracting makes accountability narrow, concerned only with service delivery performance, rather than with responsiveness to changing needs and preferences. It is also narrow in the sense that responsibility for employment practices, environmental concerns and other matters is irrelevant to the contract and therefore beyond the influence of elected representatives. At the same time, the process of learning which occurs when elected representatives are involved in the supervision of service provision is lost when contracts exclude representatives from contact with users of services.

The growth of public service companies

There is a growing market for companies operating in the public service sector as countries contract out services. Early players include those French companies which were established to provide water and other public utilities in the nineteenth century. US companies are also active in the United Kingdom, as are some home-grown ones. The Department of the Environment (1995) published a survey of 220 companies operating in the local authority sector in building clean-ing, refuse collection, catering, sports and leisure and vehicle and ground maintenance. It found that one-third of them were large, with a turnover of £10 million-plus, a third had a turnover of £1–10 million and a third were small. Of the refuse collection companies, 20% were owned outside the United Kingdom and one in six also operated in other countries. Meanwhile, some UK companies such as Serco have expanded overseas as well as by taking public sector contracts in the United Kingdom. The Labour government tried to make it easier for such compa-nies to get access to public sector contracts.

Central government contracting for computer services has given a large volume of work to companies such as Electronic Data Services and created a high degree of dependency on those companies in areas such as tax collection. The government's view is that functions such as computing are peripheral, not part of the 'core' busi-ness of government. In practice computing is at the heart of tax collection, benefits payments and vehicle registration. Changes in the way these functions are carried out imply changes to computer systems. For example, one of the Treasury's argu-ments against the introduction of local income tax has always been that the computers could not cope with it. As computing is privatized, it will be the com-puting companies who have to assess the feasibility of alternatives, since the exper-tise has mostly been transferred to them. In these circumstances, it would be rational for companies to argue for systems and procedures which suit them.

Patrick Dunleavy [12] warned that radical contracting out to large companies could result in governments losing their expertise and being unable even to purchase services intelligently. Faced with companies operating in many countries, states would have a reducuced role, acting as mediator between citizens as consumers and companies. This argument is convincing in those areas in which government has quickly reduced its own capacity among directly employed people as it has done in the case of information systems. The deteriration of the railway after privatization was the result, among other things, of the loss of expertise on track and signals in Railtrack, as we will see in Chapter 11.

The workers

Competition based on price has affected the income of workers, whether the in-house team or a company that wins the contract. This applies especially where low-skilled work is involved and where women are employed in areas such as catering and office cleaning. The effect is not always on pay rates but can affect conditions of service such as holiday and sick pay. For example, women working as school cleaners used to be paid during the school holidays and are now generally employed on contracts only during school terms. The result can also reduce the numbers of people employed and the remaining employees have to do more work.

Conclusions

Managers have responded to the need to operate in markets according to how the markets have been established. Where there has been competition they have tried to control and reduce costs. Where public sector managers have lost in competition with the private sector, this has resulted in greater private sector involvement in public services. Companies have responded either by growing or by moving into the United Kingdom from their home countries, especially France and the United States of America.

The other consequences have been to weaken the influence of the trades unions, as wage bargaining was affected by the amount of money available for wages in the contract price. Unions have generally been keen to preserve their members' jobs, although in some cases they have been able to retain members who transferred to private employers.

The other consequence has been that services and organizations have been fragmented: individual services are provided by different companies or by fragmented units of the public organizations. While this may improve the way in which managers can concentrate on a single task, it also makes co-ordination of services more difficult.

When services are subject to competitions or market transactions without competition, they have to be managed through a series of contracts. In the next chapter we look at the nature of the contracting process which this implies.

Notes

For weblinks relevant to the issues discussed in this chapter see www.sagepub.co.uk/flynn.

1   Rudolf Klein, *The New Politics of the NHS*, 4th edn (Routledge, London, 2000).
2   See Cabinet Office/Citizen's Charter Unit, *The Citizen's Charter: Second Report*, Cm 2540 (HMSO, London, 1994), p. 93.

3 See J. Oughton, 'Market testing: the future of the civil service', *Public Policy and Administration*, 9, 2.

4 *Better Quality Services: Guidance for Senior Managers* (Cabinet Office, London, 1997)

5 Audit Commission, 'Taking Stock: Progress with Community Care', *Community Care Bulletin* No. 2, December, (HMSO, London, 1994), p. 11.

6 Ibid., p. 22.

7 Department of the Environment, Transport and the Regions, *Modernising Local Government Finance – A Green Paper* (HMSO, London, September 2000).

8 Michael Porter, *Competitive Strategy* (The Free Press, New York, 1980).

9 K. Walsh, *Public Services and Market Mechanisms: Competition, Contracting, and the New Public Management* (Macmillan, Basingstoke, 1995).

10 (Quoted in *The Times*, 21. 3. 96).

11 John Stewart, 'The limitations of government by contract', *Public Money and Management*, (July-September 1993), pp. 10–11.

12 P., Dunleavy, 'The Globalization of Public Services Production: Can Government be "Best in World"?', *Public Policy and Administration*, 9, 2, 1994.

10

Managing through contracts

Introduction

In the previous chapter we saw that many of the services provided by the public sector are delivered through contracts, which are either internal or with private and voluntary organizations. People have had to learn how to write contracts and specifications for services and how to make sure that services are delivered according to those contracts.

In this chapter we look at how contracts have developed and how they affect the delivery of services. First we find that there are different sorts of contracts in the different parts of the public sector, including the contract period, whether they are let after a competitive bidding process, how detailed the specifications are and how punitive are the default clauses.

We then try to explain why these differences occur. Explanations include the law and regulations surrounding the contracting process, the structure of the markets in which contracts are made, managers' ideas about what sort of contract is likely to produce efficiency and quality, and the political attitudes of those making the contracting policy. The fact that there are wide variations implies that managers have some discretion. We then look at how that discretion is being exercised. For this we use a framework developed by Mari Sako,[1] who looked at business-to-business contracting in the United Kingdom and Japan. She analyses contractual relationships according to a series of dimensions and proposes two archetypes, an Obligational Contractual Relationship and an Adversarial Contractual Relationship. Her dimensions are used to compare public sector contracts. As well as the nature of the contract, we then consider the nature of the specification, what it contains and who writes it.

Different forms in different sectors

Different parts of the public sector have adopted different sorts of contracts. In the case of local authorities which were compelled to use competitive tendering, the contract forms have necessarily reflected the competition process: sealed bids are invited; there can be little chance to establish a relationship with the supplier before the bidding process; apart from checking credentials and references, everything required must be specified at contract stage; the authority must protect its interests with strong penalty clauses and default procedures. At the same time, contracts are for relatively long periods (three to five years for most services) and therefore a relationship with the suppliers has to be developed during the contract period.

In the NHS, contracts were initially for one year between the purchasers and the providers, but there were long-established relationships, the purchasers and providers having been in the same organizations before they were split into the purchaser and provider sides. Despite the short-term nature of the contracts, there was not a great use of penalty clauses and destructive default procedures in the early days of contracting. There was, however, great recourse to details about the processes to be carried out under the contracts, as if the purchaser side did not trust the providers. There were not normally competitions for large blocks of work. There was tendering for some services, but generally trusts did not have to bid for the bulk of their work against other trusts. This lack of bidding would imply the need to establish trust, although the details in the contracts and specifications suggest that this has not necessarily been the case. It is not clear why this was so, but it may simply have been the result of people being put into a new position, that of purchaser, when previously they were managers or planners. We will see later that people tend to try to reproduce older styles of management relationships when they are put in the position of purchaser.

There are some doubts about whether what were called contracts in the NHS were really a contractual relationship at all in a commercial sense. It has long been known that internal contracts are not legally enforceable, because there is only one legal entity.[2] Pauline Allen[3] pointed out that there were several fundamental differences between a contract and the contractual arrangements within the NHS, where there was no freedom not to enter a contract (purchasers and providers were compelled to trade with each other), terms were imposed by a higher authority in the event of a failure to agree, and disputes were resolved by internal administrative procedures rather than recourse to the law or the terms of the agreement. She argued that the NHS contractual arrangements were in practice a series of administrative procedures, rather than a set of contracts, because of the control exercised.

She also argued that there was a potential value in using internal contracts to improve performance, but that improvements would have had to be made to the process. These improvements included that the administrative resolution of disputes should be clarified, that clinicians should be more involved in defining services and allocating resources, that the consequences of Trusts 'failing' needed to be spelled out so that they would know how their actions could influence clinicians, and finally that the accountability to end-users (patients) needed to be formally established.[4] When the Labour government cancelled the internal market in the NHS it was not making a strong statement about its lack of faith in markets and contracts. Rather it accepted that there had been no market in any conventional sense and that the administrative arrangements needed to be changed to give more real power to those commissioning health care services.

In the Civil Service, different procedures were adopted in different parts of the organization. Negotiations, rather than a strict sealed bid approach, preceded the outsourcing of the major computer contracts, implying the development of a close relationship between the departments and the computer suppliers. Market testing in other areas was done with a bidding process and a series of specifications. The major agreements between the Department of Employment and the TECs started as very detailed and punitive contracts but grew into more trusting arrangements as the years progressed.

Influences on the type of contract

There is a variety of influences on the type of contractual relationship which people adopt within the public sector and between it and the private and voluntary sectors, including legal requirements, the structure of the market, managers' approach to quality and efficiency, and politics and the administrative rules under which contracting is done.

Law and regulations

A major determinant of the nature of transactions and contracts is of course the rules established by the government. Britain does not have administrative law, as such. There are laws, such as the Competition Act 1982, which apply to public authorities as much as to companies, and European Union laws and regulations and directives on business transactions and on the procurement of goods and services by the public sector in member states, which generally promote competition and therefore mitigate against the development of long-term and less competitive relationships. While European regulations apply to all sectors, the way in which the contracting process has been organized in Britain has not been consistent across the sectors with regard to the bidding process, the length of contract or relationship, the mechanisms used for monitoring or the actions to be taken in case of default.

In the public services, there are those who believe that contracting is a matter for the law and lawyers. This view is especially held by lawyers, who get involved in writing the contracts and therefore think that they should also be involved in determining the relationships between the parties. They apply the same principles to contracting with civil engineering companies, cleaning companies and the local branch of a charity. While the purchasing side of local authorities needs to be protected, the law is not the only answer. As a standard textbook on the law of contracts says:

> Writers of contract textbooks tend to talk as if in real life agreements are effectively controlled by the law as stated in their books. A moment's reflection will show that this is not so. There is a wide range of transactions where the sums at stake are so small that litigation between the contracted parties is exceptionally unlikely ... in substantial areas of business, contractual disputes were resolved by reference to norms which were significantly different from the theoretical legal position. The most important single reason for this seems to be that, in many business situations, the contract is not a discrete transaction but part of a continuing relationship between the parties and that insistence on certain legal rights would be disruptive of that relationship ... In other areas of business, strict insistence on legal rights is common.[5]

It would seem, then, that the law and legal obligations are not the whole explanation for contract forms or sufficient guide to how to contract, except in cases where there are specific legal requirements which they cannot avoid.

Quality and efficiency

More recent work on contracting has suggested that there are other factors beside these structural market determinants which can influence the way in which organizations make transactions with each other. For example, Sako found that even where there is a large number of potential suppliers, purchasers may wish to develop a long-term relationship with a small number of them. They do this because of the potential for improved quality and a more economical long-run series of transactions.

Politics

The third influence is politics. There is a reasonably close relationship between companies supplying public services and government. For example, the process of developing competitive tendering in local government was informed by advisers drawn from the companies which wished to compete for the local authority work. As well as advisers, working parties were established to allow companies to say how they would like the process to be organized. On the other hand, there were local authority members who did not want to contract with the private sector to carry out functions previously done by directly employed labour. These included Labour-controlled authorities, but there were also Conservative authorities whose members resented being told how to run their affairs by the

Department of the Environment. In a survey,[6] contractors complained that some councils deliberately organized the contracting process in such a way as to frustrate competition. Even among those who had won local authority contracts, 25% were fairly and 11% very dissatisfied with the process (p. 92). The reasons for dissatisfaction were that councils did not want private contractors, the documents were too complicated and the procedures too difficult. On the other hand, in central government, frequently work has been awarded to private contractors without a bid from the current employees.

'"New" Institutional Economics'

Once economists started to realize that the real world exhibited few of the features of the theoretical world of perfect knowledge and perfectly rational choices in a perfectly competitive market, the problem arose: how to explain market behaviour when these conditions do not apply. This problem is important in the context of government contracting, since only rarely do conditions of perfect competition arise in the field of government procurement: in relatively trivial purchases, such as stationery or vehicles, there may be a highly competitive market with many alternative suppliers competing, in which it is possible for governments to gather sufficient information and have the capacity to make well-informed, optimal decisions.

In the procurements that typically absorb large amounts of public funds, such conditions do not apply. Markets for the supply of such things as military hardware and big computer systems are characterized by a small number of suppliers and complicated products and services, about which the buyer will have less knowledge than the supplier. Local governments are often faced with small numbers of suppliers of services, especially in expensive services such as secure accommodation for difficult children in care or rehabilitation for drug abusers. It is likely that governments will not find it possible to collect, absorb and analyse sufficient information to make an optimal choice, even when there is a compulsory tendering system in operation.

The arrangement between a government or government department and a contractor is subject to the same pressures as any other contractual arrangement: each side wants the best outcome for themselves and will use whatever advantages they can to achieve them. Both sides will try to minimize the risk attaching to themselves from entering the contract. The contract will reflect the balance of knowledge and power between the parties and the nature of the relationship between the two.

There has been a body of economics concerned with the contractual relationships between parties in the real world (as opposed to the theoretical world of perfect information and large numbers of willing buyers and sellers beloved of economic theory). This branch of economics is sometimes called 'The New Institutional Economics', although by now it is no longer new. The underlying questions of this branch of economics are:

- Why do firms sometimes choose to buy their inputs in the market place and at other times decide to make the inputs themselves?
- When is it best to organize production through the market and when is it best to organize it through a hierarchy of employees?

More broadly,

- why do organizations exist, and what determines the boundary between one organization and the next one?

These questions were first asked by Ronald Coase in 1937.[7] Oliver Williamson[8] developed Coase's work further to look systematically at the problems posed by the fact that markets are not perfect. In a book published in 1975 he looked at the question: when is it better to purchase goods and services in the market and when is it better to produce them yourself, using your own employees?

This is essentially the question for government: when should they write a contract with an independent body for the supply of services and when should they provide them using their employees? Under conditions of 'bounded rationality' not all information is known, or it is impossible to take account of all information in the decision process. The conditions in the market that Williamson considered were:

- *Complexity*: the transaction is so complex that it is not possible to consider all the options.
- *Uncertainty*: not all possible futures can be predicted, so it is not possible to write a contract that takes them all into account.
- *Language*: it is not possible to specify everything in language that both parties to contract can agree on.
- *Small numbers*: where there are very few suppliers, those in the market can engage in opportunistic behaviours to the disadvantage of the purchasers.
- *Information 'impactedness'*: where one side to the transaction has more information, especially about costs, than the other.
- *First-mover advantages*: by which winners of a contract gain information that puts future competitors at a disadvantage and reduces the impact of competition in all future transactions.
- *Atmosphere*: the moral stance that parties to the transaction take, which may not be perfectly economically self-seeking.

Williamson usefully draws these elements into a framework, which he calls the 'Organizational Failures Framework', which is illustrated in Figure 10.1.[9]

We can use this framework to interrogate the way contracting has developed between government and companies.

In most markets, people involved in transactions are not normally able to make completely optimal decisions: they do not have perfect knowledge; they do not have the capacity to process all the available information for every transaction.

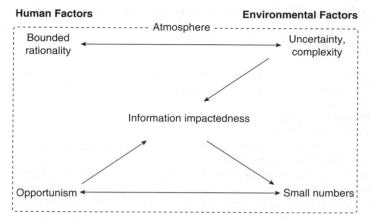

Figure 10.1   The organizational failures framework

Even if they had the information and capacity, there remains the problem in any transaction of trying to ensure that the person from whom one party is purchasing delivers what is expected, and is motivated and enabled to do so in all the possible circumstances that might arise.

Solutions to 'bounded rationality'

A contract that covers all possible events or contingencies is called a 'complete contract', which would be written in such a way that both parties know exactly what would be the consequences of every possible event. In practice, such contracts are very rare and can be written only for very simple transactions. Complicated transactions make the costs of writing complete contracts too high under conditions of bounded rationality.

The existence of bounded rationality results in the possibility of 'opportunistic behaviour' through which one party to the transaction tries to take advantage of the other. One way that one side can get an advantage is to know more than the other side, or to keep secret 'private information'. The fact that information is not perfectly shared (known as 'information asymmetry') leads to 'adverse selection' and 'moral hazard', both forms of self-interested misbehaviour made possible by imperfect knowledge.

The problem for governments is: how should we organize the procurement process when complete contracts are not feasible?

It is especially difficult in the case of services, as opposed to products, in that the characteristics of the service are technically difficult to design. It is also the case that, in many public services, the specification of the full range of possible contingencies is impossible to write in advance.

Paul Milgrom and John Roberts describe one set of solutions to the problem of bounded rationality in the world of real contracts that can never be complete.[10] These solutions are:

1 relational contracts, through which long-term relationships are developed
2 implicit contracts, where shared objectives make detailed explicit contracts unnecessary
3 developing commitment
4 ex-post renegotiation
5 dealing with specific assets, which the contractor has bought solely for the purpose of fulfilling the contract
6 the 'hold-up' problem, whereby the buyer is completely dependent on a single contractor
7 private information and pre-contractual opportunism, whereby the contractor cheats the purchaser
8 measurement costs
9 adverse selection, where contractors only choose contracts, or parts of contracts, that can make big profits, leaving aside the rest
10 signalling, screening and self-selection.

The question for governments can now be reformulated: 'How can governments ensure that contracting with the private sector avoids the dangers identified in the New Institutional Economics literature?'

The first way suggested by Milgrom and Roberts was the establishment of 'relational contracts', by which they mean a relationship between the buyer and the seller that does not rely entirely on the contract for the supply of a particular good or service at a particular time but involves the establishment of expectations on both sides that a longer-term relationship will develop in which the two sides behave in mutually beneficial ways. Later in this chapter we look in more detail at how such relationships require contracts that differ from those appropriate to 'adversarial' relationships, in which there is very low trust and heavy reliance on the contract itself to manage the delivery of the good or service.

For managers, therefore, there are no simple answers to the question of how to establish and manage contractual relationships. On the one hand, there are market structure considerations and efficiency and effectiveness considerations which would provide some guidance as to the most effective way to do things. In some cases, these might lead to a preference for long-term contracting, in others for short-term. The nature of the market may lead to a desire to establish long-term close relationships with suppliers, or may lead to frequent competitions to keep prices down. Overlaid on these influences on practice are the legal considerations. The law itself and the regulations may force people to behave in a particular way, even though they know that the results will be less good than if they behaved in other ways. There are also more local legal influences. Legal advice may itself lead people to behave in ways which they do not think make managerial or contractual sense. Lawyers accustomed to caution may be more interested in generating apparently detailed and enforceable contracts which professionals know cannot be enforced in practice. Politics can also determine managerial decisions. While managers may know that it would make more sense to keep a service in-house, they are not able to exercise that choice. The opposite can also be true: managers may wish to contract out but are instructed to retain directly managed provision.

However, there is still some discretion. In the rest of this chapter we look at the elements of the contracting process and ask what would be the best approach to each of these elements in different circumstances.

Obligational and adversarial contracting

'Relational' contracts are sometimes referred to as 'obligational' contracts, in which the two parties have obligations to each other to make a success of their joint efforts beyond the terms of their immediate contractual relationship. 'Obligational' contracts are contrasted with 'adversarial' ones in which each side is out for their own advantage from the immediate contract and is unconcerned about the success of the joint enterprise.

Sako[11] has developed a framework for understanding contracting behaviour, using these two archetypal relationships. At one extreme is the Obligational Contractual Relationship (OCR), where the two parties trust each other, work together for mutual benefit, share risk and do things for each other which go beyond the details in the contract. Adversarial Contractual Relationship (ACR) is at the other extreme, where there is low trust, the expectation that each side wishes to gain at the expense of the other and contracts are used to protect each side from the other. Sako breaks down the contracting process into eleven elements: transactional dependence; ordering procedure; length of trading; documentation; the approach to 'contractualism' or contingencies; contractual trust; competence trust; goodwill trust; technology transfer and training; communication channels and intensity; and risk-sharing.

Transactional dependence

If a purchaser wants to be able to switch from one supplier to another, they will have contracts with a large number of people. They can then use the threat of switching to make suppliers do what they want. On the other side, suppliers may wish to maintain contracts with a large number of purchasers to minimize their dependence. In these circumstances, the relationships are likely to be distant. Under OCR, the purchaser may wish to develop closer relationships with a small number of suppliers and offset the dependency created by fewer closer relationships.

There is a variety of experience with regard to dependency. The large computer privatizations which have occurred in the Inland Revenue and Driver and Vehicle

Licensing have made the government very dependent on one supplier in each case. Local authorities which have established contracts for items such as refuse collection have sometimes become completely dependent on a single firm, which has won the contract for the whole of that local authority area.

We would expect high dependency to result in a close relationship between the two parties. In practice, the legal constraints and lack of experience on the part of purchasers led to the development of detailed contracts and specifications with complicated procedures for coping with default. As time went on, however, both sides realized that the interdependency which comes from having a single supplier and a single purchaser allows a relationship which is closer than those implied by spot contracts or frequent switching of supplier.

Ordering procedure

The stereotype of the adversarial approach to ordering was encapsulated in the compulsory competitive tendering legislation for local authorities: competitors had to bid for the work, the purchaser chose the supplier as a result of the bid, rather than any other aspect of the bidder's work or reputation, and the price was fixed before the contract was let. The opposite, OCR, way of ordering may not involve bidding and if it does, the bid price is not the only criterion for placing an order and prices are finally settled after the decision about who will be awarded the contract. The way orders are placed has an effect on the relationship between the parties. If a long-term relationship is expected, both sides need to decide whether such an arrangement would be beneficial. This requires more than doing some pre-tender checks and then opening sealed bids. When Toyota was setting up its plant in Derby, the process it used to sign up component suppliers started with assessing the management capabilities of potential suppliers, then the manufacturing skills of the workforce. The end of the process was concerned with negotiating price.

Bidding is almost universal in the public sector, for reasons of propriety. Public accountability requires that contracts are awarded fairly, without corrupt favouritism. This is interpreted to mean that the only way to accept bids is through a procedure which keeps the two sides at arm's length. European regulations require that large public sector contracts are advertised in the *Gazette* and bids invited from companies in all EU states. These regulations imply an adversarial style of contract award, rather than the development of a close relationship.

There are occasions on which negotiation about price and quality continue after a bid has been accepted. The most notable of these was the post-tender negotiation for the Inland Revenue computer contract, much to the displeasure of the unsuccessful bidders who were not given a chance to re-tender. Local authorities sometimes negotiate with the successful bidders for building and civil engineering contracts.

In the United States of America, some public authorities have a system of 'calls for proposals'. In this process, instead of the authority writing a specification and inviting bids to carry it out, they may state a problem, give an indicative budget and ask companies and the voluntary sector how they might solve the problem. This approach has been used in substance-abuse programmes and community care. It allows the suppliers of services to show what they can do, rather than waiting for the public authority to do all the work on service design and specification. It is similar to the system of commissioning buildings in North America, where it is normal practice to specify the required performance of a building and then ask architects to design and organize its construction.

The ordering procedure sets the tone for the nature of the relationship between the two parties. If contracts are based on a quotation against a specification which is the same for all bidders, the responsibility for developing the contract and specification rests with the purchasers, rather than being a joint effort between buyers and suppliers. After the contract is let, the process of contract management is therefore concerned with ensuring conformance to the specification.

Once a contract is let, purchasers may try to develop a closer relationship than that which existed prior to the award. However, contracts are normally for a fixed term, at the end of which a new bidding process is started. The close relationships are stopped and the distancing implied by fair treatment begins again.

Length of trading

In an ACR contractual relationship, the parties expect to trade with each other only for the length of the contract. In OCR, there is an expectation that, if things go well, there will be further contracts and there will be a mutual long-term commitment between the parties. There is the possibility of 'roll-over' contracts in the public sector where contractors are allowed to continue for a further period. However, lawyers say that it is unwise to include clauses in initial contracts which imply that successful completion of a given contract would most likely result in another.

The length of trading can determine the type of company or charity with which the public sector trades. Large suppliers with a variety of contracts in the public and private sectors are more likely than small local suppliers to be able to cope with a series of time-limited contracts with any purchaser. This applies especially in community care, where small local voluntary organizations become completely dependent on their local authority for their funds. They are, in other words, dependent on the one transaction, the failure of which would result in the end of the organization. In practice, they often lurch from one short-term contract to the next.

Documents for exchange

In ACR, there is an attempt to write all the terms and conditions, including substantive conditions. Every possible item is written down. In OCR, the contracts concentrate on procedural rules which set out how problems would be resolved if they arise, and individual issues are dealt with when they occur. Contracts may even be oral rather than written.

In the public sector, contracts and their associated specifications have generally been long and detailed. In some cases, manuals of procedure which were in place when the service was directly managed were used as the basis for the contract and specification. For example, the original contracts between the Department of Employment and the TECs were the old department area office programme manuals. Hospital contracts and specifications consisted of a detailed description of existing procedures. However, people have realized that not everything can be written down and that in any case, the fact that the contract contains a long and detailed specification is no guarantee of service delivery. Contracts have become less detailed as people have learned that there are other ways of ensuring quality, such as involvement in the suppliers' quality assurance procedures or talking to the users of the services.

'Contractualism'

Sako refers to the treatment of contingencies as 'contractualism'. A contingent claims contract is one in which contingencies have to be defined, a procedure has to be established to agree whether a contingency has occurred, and the consequences of the occurrence are specified.

Most contracts have contingent elements: exceptional weather can affect highway maintenance contracts; sudden outbreaks of disease trigger health service interventions. The question is whether each possible contingency can be sufficiently defined in advance and whether the recognition of its occurrence can be spelled out in advance. The OCR option is to agree procedures by which both sides can agree on contingencies and what should be done as a result, relying on trust and an expectation that an agreement can be reached. The ACR option assumes that an agreement will not be reached or will be difficult, and that every contingency must be defined in advance. We will see in Chapter 11 that in the case of the maintenance contracts for London Undergound, neither party could predict the state of the track and had to agree on a way to define the contingencies when they arose.

There is a mixture of approaches to this question in the public sector. Attempts to specify contingencies have not always worked. For example, in the care of older people, there are 'tariffs' for the cost of care according to people's degree of dependency, from a range of physical and mental disabilities. Local authorities usually have a 'banding' system in which progressive disabilities trigger progressively intensive care, but there have to be procedures by which the purchasers of care and the provider agree the extent of an individual's difficulties.

Trust: contractual, competence and goodwill

Sako distinguishes three areas of trust: contractual, competence and goodwill. An ACR approach to contractual trust means that suppliers do not do anything without a prior, written order. In an OCR relationship, supply or changes to specification can be started as a result of an oral communication. Competence trust is concerned with the degree to which the purchaser trusts the supplier to deliver the quality of product. If there is low trust, the purchaser will inspect heavily and presume that the supplier will try to skimp. In a high trust relationship, the purchaser may be involved in the supplier's quality assurance procedures, but will not carry out much, if any, inspection. Goodwill trust refers to the degree to which each side is willing to become dependent on the other.

Trust is a very important element in public sector contractual relationships. The degree of trust depends partly on the sort of relationship established during the ordering procedure. If the order is placed on the basis of the bid price only, it is likely that the chosen supplier will be operating on low, or even negative, profit margins. In order to make a profit, suppliers have to shave the quality as close to the specification as possible, if not below it. The purchaser's main function then becomes one of trying to make sure that the specifications are met, requiring inspection and checking. If the winning contractors believe in any case that the purchaser did not wish to contract with them but was forced into it by the legislation, there is no initial basis for establishing trust, and adversarial relationships are probably inevitable.

Trust can develop during the contract period or as a succession of contracts is completed. It is natural for buyers to be wary of new suppliers until they have evidence that they can be trusted. Sometimes the voluntary sector may be trusted more than the private sector, whose profit motive causes immediate suspicion by some public sector managers.

Technology transfer and training

In an OCR relationship, the purchaser is willing to help the supplier develop the best technology and skills. This may involve helping the supplier to organize training or allowing them to join in joint training, which may not be fully costed. In an ACR relationship, help is given only when it is fully costed and paid for. One area in which this is important is in the NHS. If purchasers do not fund the development of new technologies, research and development has to be funded in other ways. In practice, since prices are supposed to be equal to cost in NHS contracts, there is no surplus available for research, which is funded through a separate mechanism.

In community care, this is not the case. Providers have to make sufficient surplus from their contracts to fund research and development. This problem was recognized in the joint statement by the Association of Directors of Social Services and National Council for Voluntary Organisations, but there is no compulsion on purchasers to price contracts in such a way as to allow innovation:

> ADSS and Voluntary Organisations jointly recognise ... that VOs may include in the costs of service provision reasonable allowance for indirect costs properly associated with the maintenance and development of a cost effective quality service, as well as the direct costs of service provision.[12]

It is unlikely that there would be much transfer of technology and training in the mainly adversarial relationships which have developed: public accountability for funds, which pushes the relationship in an adversarial direction, makes it unlikely that free funding of development would occur, as a routine part of a long-term contractual relationship.

Communication channels and intensity

In ACR, the communication channels between the two contracting parties are specified in the contract. Nominated officers on each side are allowed to speak about technical and financial matters, according to their individual competence. In an OCR relationship there are multiple channels of communication as each side tries to understand the other. As with other aspects of the relationship between public organizations and contractors, frequent contact is treated with suspicion, especially informal contact. Lunches are frowned upon as corruption. While there may be some basis for suspicion, it is unfortunate that the need for propriety stops beneficial exchanges between the two sides.

The National Audit Office found that joint working and good communication improved the contracting process in the NHS:

> The National Audit Office surveys of regions and trust monitoring outposts ... showed that both felt that health authorities and hospitals were still mainly concerned with achieving their own distinct objectives rather than coming to a jointly beneficial agreement. Both groups surveyed considered that forming joint long-term strategies and providing comprehensive and timely information as well as maintaining regular communications between chief executives, were most important in achieving good relationships.[13]

Risk-sharing

In OCR relationships, risk is shared, based on principles of fairness. In ACR, risk may not be shared but the acceptance of risk is defined in advance. There are three aspects of risk in public service contracts: risk of price changes, of changes in the volume of demand, and the risk that arises from suppliers making innovations.

With relatively low inflation, the risk of price changes turning out to be much different from that predicted at the time of signing the contract is small. However, there are prices which may fall suddenly, because of technical changes. For example, the introduction of keyhole surgery, or much cheaper computer processing, may produce a 'windfall' increase in profits for a supplier. A risk-sharing approach would lead to such windfalls being shared between the supplier and the purchaser.

The second type of risk refers to the possibility that the volume of work predicted will not be forthcoming. The supplier sets up an operation to provide the predicted volume and incurs costs which are not recouped. Again, a risk-sharing approach would involve sharing a proportion of those costs. One way of doing that is for the purchaser to guarantee a certain volume of service will be purchased, even though it may not be required.

The third element comes from innovation; a supplier may invent and offer a new way of providing a service, which turns out to be unsuccessful. Without such innovation, the contracting process will stop the development of new services, as all specifications are based on already accepted practice.

Private Finance Initiative projects and Public–Private Partnerships are based on the premise that the contract can allocate the risk between the private and public sectors and the contract can be formulated to reward risk taking. In the case of unpredictable costs, this can provide incentives for the contractor to contain costs. In the case of unpredictable volumes, such as on a toll road or bridge where the revenue to the contractor depends on traffic volumes, the risk avoidance cannot be achieved by changing contractor behaviour.

The specification

Inputs, process and outcomes

Sako's work dealt mainly with the supply of components, which could be specified in physical terms. The purchase of services can be more complicated. First, it may be difficult to specify the result required from the service in an unambiguous way. Even in relatively simple, physical services such as grounds maintenance, the results of the work will be hard to describe: what is a well-maintained cricket pitch, or an attractive flower bed, when the answer to the question determines whether a contractor gets paid or not? Attempts to answer such questions have resulted in elaborate schemes of measuring the length of grass and counting the numbers of flowers.

In other services, the problem can be more acute. What is the satisfactory outcome from a process of treating a patient with mental illness, or looking after an elderly person in a residential home? There are ways of defining these things, but if specifications are to be used as the basis for a legal contractual obligation, they are more difficult to define and measure than material things, which can have measurable characteristics and tolerable deviations from them.

Because of this, many specifications rely on describing the processes by which services are provided. If the cricket pitch is mown ten times each summer and rolled before each match, it is assumed that it will be in a good state for cricket. If a patient receives diagnosis, drugs and nursing of a specified quantity, that is enough to ensure that the bill will be paid. If the processes cannot be described in detail, then the specification may rely on the inputs used: the number of hours of a gardener's attention or a psychiatric nurse's visits. The description of the input may include the qualifications and skills of the staff: increasingly National Vocational Qualifications are being used for this purpose.

What is quoted in the specification has a big impact on the relationship between a purchaser and a provider of services. In general the provider has a professional or technical expertise which they are offering as a part of the contract. If that expertise is usurped by the specification, the purchaser has to have all the skills required to write the specification and monitor performance against it to ensure that a good job is done. If the purchaser has to specify the nursing ratio, for example, there is no discretion for a director of nursing services to decide what is appropriate and manage his or her resources accordingly.

In the case of the London Underground, contracts were based on outcomes, of matters such as the availability of trains and the level of amenity of stations. Once agreed measures are established, the idea is that the contractors find the best way to achieve the outcomes.

The use of outcomes as the basis for a contractual agreement has two implications for the relationship. It assumes that the providers have the expertise to decide on the appropriate inputs and process required to produce the outcome. It also implies that the purchaser trusts the provider to make those decisions in the interests of arriving at the outcome, rather than in the interests of the provider or their profits. The higher the degree of trust, the more possible it is to use outcome specifications.

However, in low-trust environments, the use of inputs and processes as the basis for the contract produces problems of its own. How will the purchaser stay up to date with the best procedures? In services such as building cleaning, for example, technology changes. New chemicals and machines increase efficiency and change working practices: some of the early specifications for floor cleaning in hospitals specified what was meant by mopping floors, complete with diagrams indicating mop direction. In care services, there are developments in best practice for helping, for example, elderly mentally infirm people. Such things as whether doors should be locked or not, or what degree of choice of food people can or should make, have an impact on people's well-being. If contracts for this type of care specify exactly the routines and never change them, best practice cannot be adopted.

As time goes on the purchasers have less direct experience of services. While they may be appointed to a post of purchasing manager with recent relevant direct experience, inevitably they become detached from it over time. As their expertise deteriorates relative to that of the providers it becomes less easy for them confidently to specify inputs and processes.

Who should write the specification?

Therefore, the question 'what is in the specification?' implies another question: 'who should write the specification?' If technical and professional expertise is heavily weighted towards the provider side, then it is sensible that they should at least be involved in writing the input and process part of the specification, the purchasers becoming increasingly involved in specifying the required outcomes.

This brings us back to the beginning of the argument. If the purchasers are to allow the providers to specify the inputs and process, with the intention of providing the best possible outcomes for the money available, this implies a high degree of trust. If the providers are only to be trusted as far as to carry out the letter of the contract, then that letter must contain enough detail to reassure the purchaser that they are getting a good deal. If they are to be trusted to make an impact on the service user and left to decide how to achieve that, then there has to be a high degree of goodwill between the two parties.

There are two separate issues here, which are frequently confused. The first is whether the purchasers have the technical competence to write and monitor an input- and/or process-based specification. The second is whether the purchaser has sufficient trust in the provider to do their best to produce the desired outcomes and therefore has the confidence to write an outcome-based contract. We will see that one of the reasons for the collapse of the contractual arrangements on the railway was that the contractors specified the maintenance requirements and the owners of the track and signals, Railtrack, had insufficient expertise to verify either the problems or the work done to solve them. Lack of trust was a product of uneven knowledge and profit-maximizing behaviour on the part of the contractors.

Learning to manage through contracts

People have learned that adversarial contracting is unproductive and expensive to maintain. The Department of Health began to worry, towards the end of 1995, about the costs which contracting imposed on the administration of the NHS. Contractors for local authorities have complained about over-complicated paperwork and procedures. Local authority social services departments are trying to establish more collaborative relationships with the voluntary sector for the provision of community care services.

However, people have also realized that there are constraints on the development of obligational relationships. Legal requirements to follow procedures put purchasers and providers at a distance from each other and emphasize the elements where interests are opposed.

While the number of actual and potential suppliers varies among sectors, there seems to be a relationship between market structure and contracting style: monopolies or near monopolies in health and employment services have led to the development of longer-term relationships, less reliance on detailed inspections and other aspects of ACR relationships. In the relationship between local authorities and their contractors there are still signs of adversarial relationships.

If there is an underlying suspicion of the private sector, it is likely that contracts will remain adversarial. The implication is that there will be a continuation of detailed contracts, harsh penalty clauses, heavy inspection and generally poor relationships.

Expensive failures

The contracting system that was imposed through the imposition of internal markets and enforced outsourcing improved as people, especially in local government and health services, learned how to manage through contracts. Central government has less satisfactory experiences. Defence procurement was one case in which costs got out of hand and delays were sometimes measured in decades rather than years. The Public Accounts Committee investigated 25 major defence procurement contracts that produced £2.8 billion of overspending. The average slippage was 43 months, or 27% of the projects' lifecycles. Some were very overdue, such as the Brimstone anti-armour weapon ten years delayed, and Bowman, a tactical communications system, 6 years delayed by 2000. One solution to these overspends and loss of control was to commission a Defence Electronic Commerce Service from Cap Gemini Ernst and Young at a cost of £45 millions over ten years.[14]

The other was the sad case of information technology contracting. This is a complex area and may be best understood by following through some examples. The biggest contracts concerned large systems to collect national insurance and taxes and to pay out benefits through the Post Office.

Benefits Payment Card project

In May 1996 the Benefits Agency and the Department of Social Security and Post Office Counters Limited jointly awarded a contract to Pathway, a subsidiary of the ICL computer services group. The Benefits Payment Card project (called 'Horizon') was intended to replace by 1999 the existing paper-based methods of paying social security benefits with a magnetic stripe payment card, and to automate the national network of post offices through which most benefits are paid.

The project was large and complex and estimated to cost £1 billion in payments to Pathway. The contract was awarded under the Private Finance Initiative, under which the contractor designs, builds, finances and operates an asset and is paid for the provision of a service only as it is successfully delivered. Risk was supposed to be transferred to the contractor by the government. The business case for the project was the reduction in fraud in benefits payments.

By October 1996 a trial version of the system was used to deliver child benefits in ten post offices. It was estimated at the time of signing the contract that 24 benefits in 19,000 post offices would be delivered by the new system within ten months. This stage was not reached when the contract was terminated three years later. In February 1997 the project was replanned and all parties agreed to delay the project by three months and each party would cover their own costs.

Although Pathway delivered intermediate releases of the software, by 21st November 1997 they had not completed a live trial as agreed. The purchasers served a breach of contract. Pathway denied liability and asserted breach of obligations by the purchasers. In July 1998 an independent panel of experts concluded that the project could deliver the required results but that it would take until the end of 2001.

In May 1999 the card element of the scheme was dropped and other aspects of automation continued, including the automatic transfer of benefit payments to bank accounts, to be completed by 2005.

The National Audit Office report[15] found:

- The project was high risk. It was feasible, but probably not fully deliverable within the very tight timetable originally specified
- The procurement method was innovative and since the risk was transferred to the supplier the purchaser was not concerned with the supplier's internal arrangements
- The department (Social Security) and the Post Office had different objectives for the project
- The department's business case did not adequately assess the risk and costs of serious slippage
- The purchasers identified most of the risks of the project, but were less successful in assessing their probability and impact
- When the contract was signed, key parts of the detailed specification had not been finalized
- More rigorous demonstrations by the bidders might have better highlighted the risks to deliverability and the extent to which new software had to be developed
- Pathway submitted narrowly the cheapest bid but the purchasers ranked their proposal third on eight of the eleven technical and management criteria
- A decisive factor in the selection of Pathway was their acceptance of greater risk, making their bid compliant with the Private Finance Initiative
- The purchasers found monitoring and controlling risks difficult.

Their conclusion was that the project did not fail because of the complexity and scale but because:

- The project was run by two organizations
- Insufficient time was spent on the specification and on demonstrations by the bidders
- There was not a shared, open approach to risk management
- Government does not learn from previous mistakes in IT procurement.

The National Insurance Recording System ('NIRS2')

The Contributions Agency employed 5,000 people and collected £45 billion per year in national insurance contributions, about one-third of national government revenue. The recording system at the heart of the process was a 1960s batch-based mainframe system. In May 1995 Anderson Consulting were awarded a contract to take over the old system, design a new one to provide an on-line enquiry and update service, and run it over the contract period to 2004. Anderson chose to design a new system rather than modify the old one, using a client/server system set up on a Sybase database and Hewlett–Packard servers. The first phase was completed on time in February 1997. The October 1997 release was delayed until January 1998 to reduce the risk of transferring all the work at one time. The April 1998 phase was delayed until July and Anderson paid compensation for late delivery. It then considered that it had fulfilled its contractual obligations.

The National Audit Office estimated that by the end of December 1998 there were still 1,900 problems with the system. At the end of January 2000 one million claims from unemployed people had to be processed with no information, together with 300,000 claims from disabled people. Incorrect calculations resulted in claimants being paid more than £35 million in compensation by March 2000. NIRS2 became fully operational by June 2001, about three years behind schedule.

In October 2000 the Inland Revenue was given permission to write off more than 1 million tax records from 1997–98 because there was insufficient information to process the tax demands. A *Computer Weekly* investigation showed that there were 7 million records in the NIRS2 system with missing data.

Anderson spent £120 million developing the system for a fee of £19 million. It hoped to recover its investment by selling the system to other national governments. Anderson retains the Intellectual Property Rights since it contracted to deliver a service using the software, not to deliver the software. Ownership of the IPR enabled it to put in a low bid, valuing the rights at £100 million.

The Public Accounts Committee concluded that:

- Departments should examine and research the costs, benefits and risks underpinning decisions on ownership of Intellectual Property Rights in major government systems
- The commercial risk ... has not sufficiently shifted to the private sector, and has left the government wholly dependent on the contractor.

Electronic Data Systems and the Inland Revenue

In 1994 the Inland Revenue entered a 'Partnership' contract with EDS to provide all its IT services. The contract did not specify in detail all the work to be done, nor was the price fixed. It was a large example of IT outsourcing and transfer of 1,900 staff from the employ of the government to EDS. The contract was for ten years and currently is forecast to cost £2.4 billion over that time.

The National Audit Office has judged the contract to be successful:

> Partnerships like the one between the Inland Revenue and EDS, rely on trust and understanding between two organisations, qualities which are particularly important as requirements change and develop. Management of the risks associated with new work is therefore a challenging area for value for money. Much has already been achieved, and the Department must ensure that it retains the capability to manage the relationship and keep its options open for the future. (Auditor and Comptroller General, John Bourne, 29 March 2000)

The areas specifically addressed were:

- Retaining sufficient independent capability in the Department to assess projects objectively, so as to avoid becoming locked in the partnership and restricting options to change suppliers at the end of the contract.
- Increasing the rotation of staff in specialist units working in partnership with EDS, to address the risk of important skills and knowledge being concentrated in a few key people
- Exploring how to obtain reliable evidence to enable it to extend its benchmarking of the services offered by EDS.

In October 1999 EDS was awarded the contract to outsource the Department of Social Security's IT services, taking on 1,600 staff.

Conclusions

The eagerness of governments to contract out large parts of the work required to deliver public services has sometimes run ahead of the capacity to make contracting succeed. There are some structural reasons for this. First, a contract between a government and a contractor is not equivalent to a joint venture between two or more companies collaborating to make a project or business venture successful: in most cases the revenues to the company come from from public funds, not from customers who are attracted to the product of the joint venture. The cash available is finite, subject to renegotiation as costs rise, rather than subject to success in the market. Companies' profits will come only from getting more money from the government buying their service than the services cost to produce, rather than from jointly making the service profitable.

Second, there is an almost inevitable information impactedness. Whatever the sector, whether Information and Communication Technology, or the internal arrangements in the NHS, or the transport system, the expertise is likely to be with the contractor rather than the purchaser: that is where the best returns to individuals are and where the greatest professional satisfaction is. Given the first condition, that there is a finite amount of money and therefore a zero-sum game, the fact that the expertise is likely to be concentrated in the provider side of the transaction is very likely to lead to opportunism.

In the next chapter we will see how these issues have been approached in the capital intensive sectors that rely on expensive networks: railways, power, water and sewerage, and big capital investments: prisons and hospitals.

Notes

For weblinks relevant to the issues discussed in this chapter see www.sagepub.co.uk/flynn.

1 M. Sako, *Prices, Quality and Trust* (Cambridge University Press, Cambridge, 1992).
2 I. Harden, *The Contracting State* (Open University Press, Buckingham, 1992).
3 P. Allen, 'Contracts in the National Health Service Internal Market', *The Modern Law Review*, 58, May 1995.
4 Ibid., pp. 341–2.
5 M.P. Furmston, *Cheshire, Fifoot and Furmston's Law of Contract* (Oxford University Press, Oxford, p. 24).
6 Department of the Environment, *CCT: The Private Sector View* (DOE Local Government Research Programme, Ruislip, 1995).
7 Ronald Coase, 'The Nature of the Firm', *Economica*, vol 4, 16, pp. 386–405, 1937.
8 Oliver Williamson, *Markets and Hierarchies* (The Free Press, New York, 1975).
9 Ibid., p. 40.
10 Paul Milgrom and John Roberts, 'Bounded Rationality and Private Information', Chapter 5 of *Economics, Organization and Management*, (Prentice Hall, Englewood Cliffs, 1992).
11 M. Sako, *Prices, Quality and Trust*.
12 Association of Directors of Social Services and National Council for Voluntary Organisations, 'Community Care and Voluntary Organisations: Joint Policy Statement' (ADSS/NCVO, London, 1995) para 14e, p. 7).
13 National Audit Office, 'Contracting for Acute Health Care in England, Report by the Comptroller and Auditor General, (HMSO, London, 1995), p. 19.
14 *Engineer*, 10.8.00, p. 10
15 Comptroller and Auditor General, *The Cancellation of the Benefits Payment Card project* (National Audit Office, London, August 2000).

11

Privatization, regulation and public–private partnerships

Introduction

In the previous chapter we discussed the principles of contracting and looked at some examples, including ones where the contracting method was not adequate to the task. Here we look at services that are provided in whole or part by the private sector. The use of Public–Private Partnerships to provide and manage both infrastructure and services is a special case of outsourcing, with its own set of relationships between government and contractor. There are two other, very large, examples of the use of the private sector, the railway and London Underground, both of which are special cases and which illustrate the problems and solutions of large infrastructure development and maintenance using contractual arrangements. Water, sewerage and power are provided by companies, with some exceptions in the case of water, operating as profit-seeking enterprises with some government regulation to ensure supply and prevent monopoly exploitation.

Privatization and regulation of 'public utilities'

The supply of gas, electricity, water and sewerage services in the UK were all originally in private companies' hands, then 'municipalized' as local authorities took them over in the interests of public health and universal access, then 'nationalized' as central government took management and control to itself, before being privatized.

Privatization of nationalized industries and public services began as soon as the 1979 Conservative government could organize the process. The first sales were Cable and Wireless and British Aerospace in 1981 and some of the shares in British Petroleum in 1983. The first of the privatizations of public services was the sale of British Telecom in 1984. Motivations were mixed. Privatization proceeds were a source of income or (in the definitions used in public accounting) negative expenditure that were a welcome alternative to taxation or borrowing. The Thatcher governments, along with other right-wing governments including the New Zealand

Labour Party and the Republican Party in the USA, had an ideological aversion to state involvement in any avoidable activities. There was also a growing faith in the market as the best organizing mechanism for goods and services.

The privatization of British Telecom, the telephone service run by the General Post Office, provided a test-run in the sale of a state monopoly service. Rather than regulating the prices charged to customers, a competitor, Mercury, was promoted and encouraged to compete with the privatized telecommunication provider, without price controls. The only price control was on the agreements between companies for the use of the physical network. Thereafter competition, rather than direct controls, was to be the preferred regulatory mechanism of the privatized public services. The model of competition, rather than price controls, was the preferred option and was used where possible after the other privatizations.

Water, sewerage and power were at the core of the definition of the 'public utilities', a combination of the idea that certain services are more than a commodity to be bought and sold, but entail some notion of rights, and the idea of a 'natural monopoly', where it makes sense to have a single supplier because of the economies of scale in the provision of the infrastructure. Access to power is less clearly a right, but access to light and heating are seen as a basic human need. For these reasons, privatization was accompanied by some price regulation.

Prior to privatization there were British Gas, a Central Electricity Generating Board and a series of Regional Water Authorities. When the Conservative government decided to privatize these public utilities it was faced with the question of how much control the government should retain and which mechanisms to use, once they were in private hands. If they were natural monopolies, how could the consumer be protected from predatory behaviour? If they were not, how could competition be organized to make sure that profits were not excessive? If there were some element of 'public good' or externalities, how could government ensure that water quality and the absence of pollution of the rivers were not sacrificed in the interests of profit? On the other hand, the government wanted to get the best possible price for these public assets when it sold them. If there were to be no profits, investors would not buy the assets.

A further consideration was the state of the infrastructure: successive governments since 1975 had squeezed public capital investment, as we saw in Chapter 3, and the water and sewerage networks reflected the years of neglect, with large losses of water from old and badly-maintained pipes and polluted rivers and beaches from untreated sewage. How could the private owners be persuaded to rectify this history of neglect?

The regulatory frameworks varied across the sectors and across the countries that make up the UK. In the case of power, initially the government regulator set the retail prices and later, from 2001, the regulator acted like a competition regulator, trying to make sure that there was enough competition to keep prices down. In the case of water, the regulation of price, assessment of water quality and river and sea pollution were carried out separately. Different regulatory régimes and ownership structures emerged in the different countries, according to local physical and political circumstances, and allowed some degree of comparison of the results of the different arrangements.

Water and sewerage

In the case of water and sewerage, there are 'externalities' whereby access to supplies of water and sewage services are good for the community at large as well as the individuals who benefit directly from them. Neither service was started as a state activity but in the nineteenth century concerns about public health and monopoly led to the development of municipal organization of these services. While in the middle of the nineteenth century only 10% of households were connected to piped water, by the middle of the twentieth century 90% of households were connected, mainly because of the efforts of the municipal water undertakings. The Public Health Act of 1875 gave responsibility to the local authorities for ensuring an adequate supply of water. The services were financed by a 'water rate', a property tax based on the 'rateable value' of domestic properties and charges for industrial users. For domestic water users, this method of charging represented a subsidy for poor consumers whose charges were determined by the value of their house rather than the volume of water they consumed. The water companies would never have made profits from a universal supply to all, including the very poor.

The water industry was nationalized in 1974, the municipal water enterprises in England and Wales being taken over by ten Regional Water Authorities, their boundaries determined by the natural water catchments. The government controlled the Water Authorities' capital programmes, and capital spending halved between 1974 and 1982 as part of the general cuts in public spending.

When the water supply and sewerage services were privatized in 1989, they were in poor shape. Pollution incidents were rising, there was proportionately more raw sewage being discharged into the sea than in any other European country, 3,000 km of rivers were so polluted that no fish survived in them, and the EU were legislating for drinking and bathing water quality.

Four models of ownership and three regulatory régimes were employed, based on the overall idea of dividing the industry among regional companies that were given 25-year monopolies. In England and Wales they were to be regulated by three bodies; price was to be controlled by the Office for Water Services ('Ofwat'); water quality by the Drinking Water Inspectorate and pollution by the Environment Agency.

Water and sewerage supply and services in England are provided by a collection of private companies: ten water and waste companies and 13 water-only.[1] Like other private companies they have a history of business decisions, including mergers, acquisitions and diversifications, some of which have been more successful than others. An example was Southern Water, a company that after privatization diversified unsuccessfully into a variety of businesses before it was taken over by Scottish Power. Scottish Power got into financial trouble in its operations in the United States of America and needed cash, so put the business up for sale. After the Competition Commission blocked the sale to Vivendi,[2] it was bought by a company established for the purpose, Southern Water Investments, whose ownership is shared by Southern Water Capital (80.1%) and Veiola. Thames Water, one of the biggest suppliers of water in the UK, was bought by the German firm RWE in 2001 and together they have become one of the world's large companies in the water industry.

In Scotland, since April 2002, water is supplied by Scottish Water, a nationalized industry created out of the old East, North and West of Scotland Water companies. Its investment programme is run through Scottish Water Solutions, a company set up for the purpose of implementing most of Scottish Water's capital programme and owned 51% by Scottish Water, 25% by United Utilities, the rest by a consortium of companies called the Stirling Water consortium. The Scottish Executive established an independent Water Industry Commission to act as regulator.

In Wales, privatization produced a company called Welsh Water, which went in for a spree of acquisitions, including the electricity company Swalec. It soon ran into financial problems and was bought by Western Power Distribution, who soon in turn put it up for sale again. This time a not-for-profit organization was formed to buy the water part of the business, Glas Cymru, running the water business through wholly-owned Dŵr Cymru/Welsh Water. Dŵr Cymru has a small staff and operations are outsourced to United Utilities (which used to be called North West Water), while capital investments are outsourced to a variety of partners. The process through which the company provides water is by raising loan finance and organizing a series of contracts at all points along the value chain. This process is similar in some ways to the way that London Underground relates to its PFI contractors for works on the infrastructure while maintaining public ownership of the operation: the water operation is similarly split between the not-for-profit organization and its operational and engineering contractors.

In Northern Ireland, water is supplied by the Northern Ireland Water Service, a government department, funded through taxation. This is the last remaining 'traditional' publicly-owned water and sewerage service run as part of government.

Ofwat regulates water prices in England and Wales, while the Environment Agency monitors environmental quality. Scottish regulation is carried out by a Water Commissioner who reports to the Scottish Executive, and environmental standards are regulated by the Scottish Environmental Protection Agency. European regulations and standards on water quality are a major determinant of investment in sewage treatment. Regulation in Northern Ireland is done by the Water Management Unit, within the Environment and Heritage Service.

Colin Mayer has suggested that water privatization and regulation occurred in three phases.[3] The initial privatization was designed to get the Water Authorities out of government hands and secure infrastructure investment 'at almost any price'. The price was quite high: while the flotation raised £5.2 billion, there was a debt write-off of £4.9 billion and a cash injection of £1.5 billion.[4] In this first phase there was easy money to be made. Prices were set to allow rates of return well above the cost of capital to the companies.

The privatized monopolies in England and Wales had their prices set at periodic reviews for five years. Prices in England and Wales were set in 1990, 1994, 1999 and 2004 (with a revision in 2005). While they invested around £3 billion per year, these companies achieved very good returns on their capital. The average domestic water bill rose from £166 in 1989 to £242 in 1998–9, an increase of 46%. At the end of the first period of price setting the average return on 23%, the highest return being 31% for the company supplying Manchester's water. Profit margins by 1998 included 59.7% for Southern, 51.6% for South West and 46.7% for United Utilities. Total pre-tax profits for the ten companies grew by 142% between 1989 and 1998. These returns were very high by comparison with other countries' private water industries[5] but the investment produced improvements in water quality and environmental quality of the rivers.

In 1997 the newly-elected Labour government called a 'water summit', partly in response to public concern about rising prices and big profits for the water companies. One result of the change of policy towards the industry was that the water companies were charged a 'windfall tax' that cost the industry £1.65 billion. In 1999, Ofwat declared that water bills should be cut by 12.3%, after an average increase since 1990 of 30% for domestic water users without a meter (and 19% for those with a meter). Share prices in the water companies fell by 50%, reducing the market value of the companies to less than the value of their assets.

One consequence of this change in profitability was a series of 'leveraged buyouts', financed by borrowing, as shareholders sold their equity in the water companies, seeing that the days of easy high returns were over. The capital structure changed from 20% debt in 1989 to 50% debt in 1999. The other consequence was that there was now pressure on the companies to control their costs. The only source of profits, once prices were fixed, was to increase operating efficiency. This was Colin Mayer's second phase: a period during which managerial efforts were directed towards the efficiency of the operations, and cutting running costs. The third phase is one of pressure on capital efficiency, making better use of the assets. The progression was from a regulatory régime in which both the firms and the regulator were committed to high levels of investment and high rates of return, to one of control, where the regulator forced the companies to become more efficient. The change in the capital structure reflects the desire of investors to have an exit strategy, once the days of easy money were over.

However, the 2004 review announced an 18% price rise for the next five years, soon to be superseded by an announcement of an 11.8% rise for 2005/6. At the same time the Scottish Executive announced that domestic water prices in Scotland would rise by 0.5% less than inflation. It is not possible to conclude that a regulated privatized monopoly (England and Wales) produces big price increases while a regulated nationalized industry (Scotland) produces no real-terms increases in price, because the physical conditions of water and sewerage systems may be different. It is hard, however, to believe that average domestic water bills in England and Wales are more than twice the level that they are in Scotland only because of the physical infrastructure and the nature of the water capture and distribution systems. The actions of the regulator in England and Wales, allowing big price rises again, seem to be in response to the change in capital structure and a desire to continue to promote investment in infrastructure for the industry.

The lesson from the case of the water and sewerage industry is that the companies respond quickly to changes in the regulatory regime: when prices are left to rise and there is a monopoly, consumers have to pay both for the investment in infrastructure and the shareholders' dividends. When prices are held back, investors flee and share prices fall. As a mechanism for generating investment, privatization depends on regulation allowing the companies to collect revenue from the consumers. Without competition, consumers have no choice but to pay up. For the companies, strategy depends on what the regulator does: incentives to invest, or to cut costs, or to exit the industry are all determined by what the regulator decides.

Power

Since electricity privatization in 1990 (England and Wales), 1991 (Scotland) and 1992–3 (Northern Ireland), the government has attempted to create a competitive market in Great Britain in the generation and distribution of electricity and the distribution of gas. Electricity has a supply chain that stretches from *generation*, the production of electricity in power stations, through *transmission*, carrying high voltage electricity from the power stations, *distribution*, delivering from the high-voltage system to the low-voltage regional redistribution system, to *supply*, buying electricity wholesale and selling it to end-users.

At privatization the old Central Electricity Generating Board, a nationalized industry, was split into three generators, National Power, Powergen and Nuclear Electric. Transmission was handed to the Independent Transmission System Operators (TSOs), and the 12 Area Boards were sold as privatized Regional Electricity Companies to become the suppliers.

TSOs in both gas and electricity are not allowed to get involved in buying and selling power in the wholesale or retail markets. However, there was no restriction on companies in the generation business from buying the retail suppliers, and generators now own all the retailers, effectively bypassing the wholesale market for electricity. By 2000, all the Regional Electricity Companies were owned by generators.

The regulator of the power industries in Great Britain,[6] the Office of Gas and Electricity Markets (Ofgem), works through issuing licences and by being a competition authority, working in parallel with the Office of Fair Trading. Retail prices are controlled by competition among suppliers, rather than price-setting for domestic consumers.[7]

The retailers compete for customers on price and service levels, and domestic customers are free to switch suppliers. At the network level, prices are fixed by the regulator, using a formula of Retail Price Index–X, usually for a period of five years. Companies can make profits by reducing their costs below the formula, while still delivering specified outputs. Having several distributors allows the regulator to compare costs and set challenging 'X' levels based on the performance of the more efficient distributors. Network operating costs fell under this regime, by 30% in real terms, between privatization and 2001.

The energy market operates through British Energy Trading and Transmission Arrangements, which allows for 'spot' trading of energy in half-hour segments. Competition in the energy market is the main mechanism for determining price and improving efficiency. The National Audit Office reported that the régime produced a 20% reduction in wholesale prices in the year after the introduction of the scheme[8] and that the system had produced a 40% reduction in wholesale prices between 1998 and 2003.

There is a debate about the extent to which the price reductions can be attributed to the market and regulation arrangements that were established. Steve Thomas[9] has two reservations about the competition arrangements and their impact on the prices. The first is institutional: he argues that there are confidential long-term contracts rather than a real spot market, and that the only real market is at the retail level where consumers can switch their suppliers, and that there is not enough switching to affect the price. His second argument is that there were other factors at work to bring about the price reductions: that prices were artificially raised (by 7% more than the industry needed) prior to privatization to make the privatization more attractive to investors; the removal of the nuclear subsidy reduced prices by 10%; high-priced coal contracts ended in 1998; the creation of over-capacity as new generation plants were added after 1997; the cut in distribution costs; the price regulation calculations were based on incorrect asset valuation at privatization; the world price of fossil fuels fell over the period of wholesale price reduction.

As Dieter Helm said, the internal competitive arrangements within the energy industry are not the main determinant of the price outcomes: 'Energy is now about the big oligopolists and their relationships with the upstream oil and gas companies in the emerging liquefied natural gas and international gas markets.'[10] The regulatory arrangements have no influence over those markets.

Public–Private Partnerships

We saw in Chapter 3 that capital investment by the public sector was chronically neglected and big backlogs of maintenance had accumulated. The Private Finance Initiative seemed to offer a way to restore investment without increasing capital spending. Essentially PFI, later called Public–Private Partnership (PPP), was a leasing arrangement: a private company or a consortium of companies would undertake to finance and build an asset, and in some cases run the asset and provide the services associated with it, in exchange for an annual fee under a long-term contractual arrangement. The asset could be transferred to public ownership at the end of the contract period. The arrangement was applied to a variety of assets, including roads, the Skye road bridge, school building and refurbishment, hospital building, office developments for ministries and other public bodies. In this chapter we will also look at two special cases, the railway network and London Underground system, which did not fit the standard PFI/PPP pattern.

There are three elements of a PFI/PPP deal: the financing arrangements; the construction or refurbishment phase, which is a type of building and civil engineering contract; the provision of services to keep the asset in use. For the companies in the PPP industry, there is a fourth phase in which they can sell the contract for the future revenue stream to a third party and take the profit.[11] While the government has raised a levy on these profits, the deals are not otherwise relevant to the running of the services. The sale of contracts, apart from being very profitable for the companies that signed the original PPP deals, were also a consequence of the fact that companies that were skilled at the construction phase were not necessarily the right people to manage the services associated with the assets. The three elements of PPP deals solved three problems for government. The financing arrangement postponed payment to future years. The construction element, based on a specification and performance contract, removed the problem of the management of capital projects from the public sector. The ongoing contracts transferred the problem of running the assets to the company that provided them. Potentially, the transfer of the problems seems also to allow the risk to be transferred to the private sector, or at least shared between the public and the private.

The Private Finance Initiative was introduced in the Autumn Statement in 1992 when Norman Lamont was Chancellor of the Exchequer. Essentially the idea was that instead of borrowing money for capital expenditure, the government would contract with a private-sector firm to provide the services associated with a capital asset and pay a fee for them. So, for example, a road could be designed, financed, built and operated by an engineering company who would then receive an annual fee for doing so. The advantage to the Treasury was that they would not have to borrow the money and that the capital spending would not appear as public expenditure, thus keeping borrowing and spending low in the year in which the deal was done.

Table 11.1 *Number and Value of PFI schemes by year 1987–2004*

Year	Number of signed projects	Capital value (£m)
1987	1	180.0
1988	0	0.0
1989	0	0.0
1990	2	336.0
1991	2	6.0
1992	5	518.5
1993	1	1.6
1994	2	10.5
1995	11	667.5
1996	38	1560.1
1997	60	2474.9
1998	86	2758.0
1999	99	2580.4
2000	108	3934.2
2001	85	2210.8
2002	70	7732.5
2003	52	14854.1
2004	45	2809.8
N/A	10	64.6
Total	**677**	**42699.4**

Source: HM Treasury website

The scheme was embraced enthusiastically by the incoming Labour government in 1997, which commissioned a report on the scheme from Michael Bates within two months of the election. Table 11.1 shows the number and total value of PFI schemes by year.

While the scheme was formalized in 1992, deals using similar formulae had been in place previously.[12] Health had the largest number of projects, with 136 deals over the period, and Education and Skills had 121. By value, transport was the biggest user of the scheme, with £21,432.1 million worth of contracts, including the London Underground and the Channel Tunnel Rail Link. While playing an important role in procurement of assets and services, PFI amounted to only about 11% of government investment (Fig. 11.1).[13]

Financing

It was not entirely clear what were the financial reasons behind the government's enthusiasm for PFI. Once the accounting treatment of capital expenditure was changed to reflect the use of capital rather than the cash expended on it, the impact on the published public expenditure figures was reduced. The 'golden rule', as we saw in Chapter 3, that current public expenditure should be covered

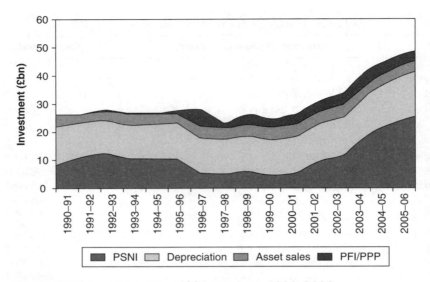

Figure 11.1   Total investment in public services, 1990–2006

Source: HM Treasury, PFI figures indicate deals signed to date and report capital investment expected under signed contracts in the year investment takes place

by current receipts over the economic cycle, is not affected by whether capital spending is financed conventionally or through PFI: public borrowing would be classified as investment, not current spending. What PFI does to the public accounts is to accumulate future liabilities: once long-term contracts are entered, there is no cheap way of exiting. Whereas routine decisions on public spending are made on a three-year cycle, PFI commits budgets for 30 years, or whatever the agreements are. Since the investments are made by the contracting companies, all public expenditure on the use of the assets appears as current, rather than capital spending.

The other self-imposed financial rule was that public sector net debt should not exceed 40% of GDP. During the first Labour government net debt was reduced from 42% in 1997/8 to 31% in 2000/1, so there was no great pressure from this rule to transfer capital spending from the public to the private sector.[14] In any case, as we saw in Chapter 3, the new government had reversed previous policies of cutting public sector capital spending as a matter of principle.

The arguments put forward in favour of PFI and later PPPs were that they might produce better value for money than traditional financing and management and that they could transfer risk from the public to the private sector. Value for money was to be tested by making a comparison with a real or hypothetical

Public Sector Comparator and by introducing some competition for the right to participate in a PFI deal. Risk was to be transferred explicitly by calculating the value and likelihood of various contingencies.

The government's position, argued at length with various accounting and professional bodies, was that PFI deals were contracts for the purchase of a stream of services, not for the lease of an asset. If a road, hospital or school were built by the PFI contractor, this was an action prior to the provision of a stream of services which is all the public sector is interested in. This has implications for the control of the asset, which remains in the contractor's hands, and for the accounting treatment in that the value of the asset does not appear on the government's balance sheet. There were arguments about the accounting treatment, the Accounting Standards Board arguing that the asset and the service stream could be separated and therefore accounted for separately, but the Treasury prevailed and PFI schemes remain off balance sheet for the government.

There were also arguments about the question of value for money. In general governments can borrow at lower rates of interest than companies. Hence borrowing directly to purchase an asset should be cheaper than leasing the asset (and its associated stream of services) from a company that has to pay higher rates on its borrowings. In addition the company has to make a return to its owners. For a PFI scheme to provide better value for money means that the difference in efficiency between the private management and its public equivalent, plus the value of the transferred risk, outweighs these cost differences. When the argument was applied to the health sector it was found that PFI deals reduced the number of hospital beds available.

For managers the presumption that PFI should be considered for any capital investment scheme implies that the financing method drives the way projects are managed. Since it is generally (not universally) the case that PFI schemes bring with them staffing as well as the building, then outsourcing of basic building services is implied.

Second, the PFI schemes lock up the expenditure for the period of the agreement, which may be up to 60 years. Options to replace or change the service arrangements over that period will be limited by penalties incurred to cancel the service agreements. There is also the question of the extent to which risk is in practice transferred. As we saw in Chapter 6, while IT contracts in principle transferred risk from the government to companies it was the taxpayer who eventually paid for the dire failures.

PFI/PPP as management tools

While the financial advantages seem slim and the accounting impact on public borrowing was reduced by the introduction of Resource Accounting, the government's enthusiasm for PPPs remained strong. One reason was that the PPP contracts seemed to offer an effective way to manage certain aspects of public service delivery. If a company signed a contract for a hospital building, for example, the 'housekeeping' aspects of management, building maintenance and possibly catering, could be managed through the contract, with some leverage over non-performing companies.

The PPPs could go further than simple building maintenance and include the core service as well: the PPPs in the Prison Service, for example, were designed to include the custodial functions, with prison officers directly employed by the PPP companies and managers reporting directly to the Prison Service hierarchy. In the case of London Underground the PPP was designed to achieve a defined level of service.

London Underground

The London Underground PPP was designed to deliver service quality improvements through an output specification and a régime of bonuses for performance above the benchmark and 'abatements' for poor performance. The PPP deals, signed in 2002, were split into three contracts with two infrastructure companies (Infracos), Tube Lines and Metronet. Management of operations remained with London Underground Limited, while the Infracos were responsible for maintenance, upgrade and replacement of trains, stations, signalling, track, tunnels and bridges. Operations and infrastructure each cost around £1 billion per annum. Revenues are split between fares collected, about £1 billion, and grant from the Department for Transport of £1.1 billion.

The PPP is based on a set of performance contracts that include measures of the time and cost of work done, but more importantly of the results, or 'outcomes', of that work. The underlying principle of the PPP is that the companies should have incentives to produce the required outcomes for the travellers on the system, measured in the time spent in delays. For the rolling stock, the main measure is 'average mean distance between failures',[15] a measure of how far an item of rolling stock travels before it breaks dowm.

Figures 11.2 and 11.3 show lost customer hours and engineering overruns, 2003–4 to 2004–5; details of average distance between failures over that period are set out in Figure 11.4.

These figures illustrate three of the measures used in the PPP contracts with the Infracos. Lost customer hours are a measure of outcome: the impact of engineering work on the delays to customer journeys. Overruns are a measure of management performance, and are aggregated into a 'points' system that affects the amount of fee the companies receive.

Transport for London, the regulatory body for the London Undergound, was able to identify the causes of lost customer hours:

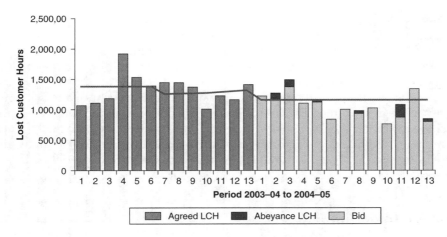

Figure 11.2   Lost customer hours, London Underground, 2003–5, attributal to Infracos

Source: Transport for London, London Underground and the PPP: the second years, 2004–2005, p. 14

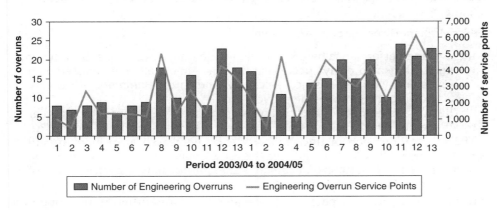

Figure 11.3   Engineering overruns, London Underground, all Infracos

Source: Transport for London, London Underground and the PPP: the second year, 2004–2005, p. 29

Rolling stock failures remain the primary cause of lost customer hours. Asset performance is assessed according to the mean distance a train travels between failures (MDBF) and the average duration of related disruption. Across the entire LU fleet MDBF improved by 25%, from 5,382 km in 2003/04 to 6,741 km last year. This represents an improvement of 17% compared to

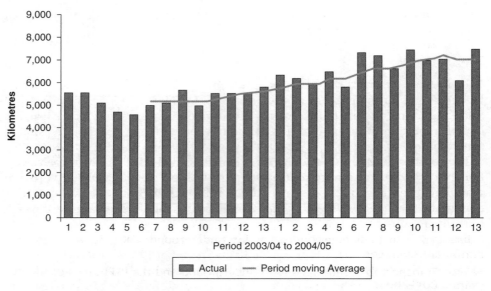

Figure 11.4   Average mean distance between failures in service, all Infracos' rolling stock

Source: Transport for London, Annual Report

the average performance before the PPP. In addition, the average duration of rolling stock related delays decreased by 16%. Almost all lines registered an improvement, with the District, Piccadilly, and Circle/Hammersmith & City fleets showing the strongest improvement.

The average number of track failures decreased by 32% over the last year to an average of 47 incidents per four-week period, down from around 70. The average duration of track related delays decreased even more significantly, down 53% with average delays over 30 minutes only recorded in one four-week period of 2004/05 compared to eight the previous year. (para 4.3)

Transport for London, a part of the Greater London Authority, was opposed to the use of PPP as a vehicle for investment in the underground railway. Based on the experience of the privatized railway, the Mayor and his advisers thought that the complexity of the contractual arrangements and the leakage of public funds to the shareholders of the Infracos presented too great a risk. The government's argument was that the risk of underperformance by the existing management of London Underground was greater than the risks from contracting. In the event, the PPP was forced on Transport for London and the payment of the £1.1 billion annual subsidy was conditional on a PPP being entered into. The contractual arrangements were innovative, in that they are partly based on outcomes. The review of the second year of operation of the contracts, reported above, indicates some improvements in performance over the first year, and over the situation that prevailed before the PPP started.

The railway

The surface railway[16] presented a problem similar to that of the London Underground: an inheritance of underfunding for maintenance and renewal of track and trains, and a lack of government confidence in the ability of the existing management to produce the results required, even with a big capital investment programme.

The solution for the railway was not formally called a PPP, rather a privatization, but it had features in common with partnerships: private capital invested in what had been a public asset; overall control by government with day-to-day operations managed by the companies; continuing public expenditure through the railway subsidies.

British Rail, the nationalized industry that ran Britain's railway from nationalization in 1947, was privatized through the Railways Act of 1993. The structure set up to run the privatized railway contained a variety of mechanisms to try to make the trains run. First, ownership and control of the track and signals were separated from all other parts of the railway business. A new company, called Railtrack, was floated to own the network, organize maintenance and improvements and lease the network to the people who ran the trains. The physical work of maintaining the network was contracted initially to 13 Infracos, soon whittled down through mergers and acquisitions to 4 companies. In turn they subcontracted to about 1,000 individual companies. The government initially paid about £1.3 billion annual subsidy to this disparate set of companies to keep the infrastructure running.

Passenger train services were allocated by franchise bidding. Companies could bid for services organized geographically. While there was competition for the franchises, the layout of the railway meant that once franchises were allocated there was little competition for passengers for particular journeys, with very few exceptions. Competition was a periodic event organized by the Office of Passenger Rail Franchising, which was replaced from February 2001 to April 2005 by the Strategic Rail Authority. As with the Infracos, the Train Operating Companies (TOCs) were soon reduced in number by merger and acquisition and by some being more successful at winning franchises. By 2001 70% of passenger revenue went to four groups, mostly companies in the bus industry. With franchise prices fixed for the period of the contract, leasing costs fixed and fares regulated, the main way that companies could improve their profits was to attract more passengers and cut the costs of running the trains. This mostly meant cutting the numbers of staff, with unforeseen consequences for reliability.

These companies leased their trains from a third set of companies, the three Rolling Stock Companies, the Roscos, set up for the purpose. Two, called Eversholt and Porterbrook, were created as management buy-outs by former

British Rail employees. The third, Angel, was a consortium. Within a few years all the Roscos had been sold to banks (HSBC, Abbey and Royal Bank of Scotland), incidentally making multi-millionaires of the management buy-out staff.

The total public subsidy to this collection of organizations rose to £3.8 billion in 2003–4, compared with a subsidy of £1.3 billion in the last year before privatization. If privatization had been seen as a way of reducing the government's expenditure on the rail system, it clearly did not have this effect.

It was a big task to co-ordinate all of these companies, over 100 main players, and well over a thousand if all the maintenance subcontractors were included, to run trains to a timetable, maintain and improve the track and run the stations and ticketing system. The mechanism chosen was licensing and incentive-based contracts. The Office of the Rail Regulator issued licenses to everybody in the system, apart from the Roscos. The TOCs had a contract with Railtrack to use the tracks. If track problems caused delays, their fee to Railtrack was reduced. If trains caused delays by blocking the tracks, they paid a fine, by the minute of delay. This was all organized through the Train Running System (TRUST), with 2,900 'reporting points' and 1,300 'delay attribution points' designed not to make the trains run on time, rather to apportion blame when they were late. Some companies collected more money in compensation payments from Railtrack than their total operating profit.

Maintenance was organized by a cascade of contracts from Railtrack to the Infracos and from them to the subcontractors. These contracts were unusual in that the contractor rather than the client mostly specified what needed to be done, since Railtrack had little engineering expertise or up-to-date knowledge of the condition of the network. Since the contractor had more information and expertise than the client it should not have been surprising that the contractor was able to operate in its own interests.

While passenger numbers continued to grow after privatization[17] the complexity of the contracting system and its incentives led to a decline in reliability[18] and safety. Railtrack's contracts with the TOCs, having to compensate for lost time, meant that they had an incentive not to close tracks for repair and upgrading. The Infracos, with their combined job of specifying the work necessary as well as carrying it out, had no financial incentive to create a safe and reliable network.

Three crashes causing multiple fatalities, at Southall, Ladbroke Grove and Hatfield (in 2000) brought the problem to the attention of those people who had not already noticed the deteriorating state of the railway. After Hatfield, Railtrack imposed speed restrictions and closure on many tracks to 'export the risk' of another accident and the whole system slowed down and became more unreliable. The government replaced Railtrack, handing over the ownership of the tracks and stations to a new not-for-profit company. The government effectively re-nationalized the network by transferring the assets to Network Rail, after cutting Railtrack's funds and effectively bankrupting it. While the government defined Network Rail as a private, not-for-profit company, its revenues consisted of government subsidy and its borrowings were all backed by the Government, so in effect the company and its assets were publicly owned. The new company took over the assets in October 2002.

The White Paper published in July 2004[19] found five main structural problems:

- a complex and confusing public sector structure, with too many overlapping responsibilities and no clear command of strategy;
- a regulatory system and contractual structure which do not give the Government direct control of the level of public funding for the railways;
- an over-complex private sector structure, with Government often far removed from the impact of the decisions that it takes;
- a relationship between track and train companies based on false and sometimes perverse market incentives, that in many cases do not reflect customers' needs;
- a lack of operational leadership in the private sector, with no-one clearly accountable for the delivery of improved performance and reliability. (p. 13)

In addition the White Paper brought maintenance work back in-house to Network Rail. 'This will allow it control over the work carried out, reducing management duplication and overheads ...' (p. 20) The Strategic Rail Authority was wound up and its powers taken back to the Department of Transport.

The White Paper pointed to the failure of the relationship between the TOCs and Network Rail and proposed a new franchise contract, that would be awarded on the basis not only of cost but past records of reliability and 'provisions on train and crew availability, which are by far the largest factors in delays attributed to train companies, and are clearly within their control.' (p. 47)

The story of the railway provides several lessons for public management. First, the replacement of hierarchical command structures by contractual relationships requires care. The relationship between Railtrack and the Infracos was always uneven, since Railtrack lost most of its expertise and knowledge. There was no capacity for Railtrack to be an intelligent client, however much such capacity was needed to make the contracts work. The contracts between the TOCs and Railtrack focused everyone's attention on blame, rather than making the system work.

Second, the main objective of the privatization was to reduce the public subsidy to the railway, transferring the commercial risks to the companies with the assets and reducing public responsibility. Not only did this not occur, but the subsidy grew rather than shrank. The Roscos took very little risk, letting contracts to match the franchise periods, and yet the original owners were rewarded with very large profits when they sold the businesses, eventually to the banks. These profits were not a reward for risk-taking.

Third, despite the continuing and growing public liability, the government lost control of the railway. Taking strategy back in-house and virtually renationalizing the infrastructure were eventually seen as the only way to get the railway back under government control.

There are differences between the arrangements put in place for the privatization of the railway and the PPP for London Underground. The most obvious is that while private companies operate and maintain the Undergound system, the ultimate control is with Transport for London and the Department of Transport, a situation that was not the case with the railway, at least while the track and signals were in private hands.

The nature of the contracts is also different, in that the underground railway contracts have an emphasis on outcomes, although in both cases there was a low level of information about the state of the infrastructure and the amount needed to be spent on it.

PFI prisons

The National Offender Management Service (previously the Prison Service) provides an example of PFIs that include not only the construction and/or maintenance of the physical infrastructure, but also the core service, of incarceration and management of the prisoners in the PFI prisons. There has been a series of competitions for control of the prisons between the (then) Prison Service and a small number of private sector providers, with both sides having some success. At the time of writing there are nine PFI prisons.

Prisons are variously governed: publicly owned and run with or without Service Level Agreements, privately owned and run, and PFI prisons. The PFI prisons are subject to contracts containing 30–40 performance measures, about 40 performance targets and 61 prison service standards. The contracts, both within PFI and within the Service Level Agreements (SLAs) with the public providers, tend towards the 'adversarial' end of the contracting spectrum. There is an attempt at as complete a contract as possible, with specifications for prison régimes as well as some obvious outcomes, such as escapes. One aspect of the 'adversarial' nature of the contracts, as defined in Chapter 11, is that they are subject to periodic formal competitive bidding. Another is that there are penalty arrangements in the contracts that can result in payments being withheld for poor performance.

The National Audit Office reported[20] on the operational performance of PFI prisons in 2003. While the report points out that prison performance is affected by many variables other than the governance arrangements, such as the category of prison and prisoners and the age of the buildings, it was able to reach some conclusions about the impact of PFI management arrangements on the operational performance.

One conclusion concerns the rigidity built into the prison régime by a long-term contract:

Prisons constructed and managed under PFI contracts, like those built and funded conventionally, may not be sufficiently flexible in design and operation to respond to changing penal priorities. Negotiating changes through a PFI contract or SLA adds a further level of complexity to this process. For example, there is now a greater emphasis on education and rehabilitation rather than employment in prison workshops, which was a priority when the earlier PFI contracts were let. (p. 6)

In general, the auditors could attribute neither good nor bad results to the PFI arrangements, showing that there were good and bad prisons under each of the governance mechanisms. The fact of competition has, however, had an impact on standards as both public and private prisons respond to the targets in the management contracts. Otherwise the main impact was on recruitment and the use of technology:

The use of the PFI has brought innovation, mainly in the recruitment and deployment of staff and use of new technology; however, there appears little difference in terms of the daily routines of prisons. (p. 9)

The report's overall conclusion was non-committal:

The use of the PFI is neither a guarantee of success nor the cause of inevitable failure. Like other forms of providing public services, there are successes and failures and they cannot be ascribed to a single factor. This report shows therefore what we should expect. A relatively new procurement method such as the PFI is associated with encouraging and disappointing results and that performance will improve over time. But a general verdict that the PFI is either good or bad in the case of prisons, or more generally, cannot be justified. (p. 9)

If the Auditor General's conclusions are accurate, this may suggest a general conclusion about the use of PFI as a way of managing services, as distinct from a way of financing them. The prison case seems to suggest that a system of service level agreements with internal providers, and a periodic market test, in this case a real competition, is as effective in producing good (or not so good) management as the use of PFI. The PFI arrangement is not demonstrably better than the internal contract, backed by some external comparisons.

PFI hospitals

As we saw in Chapter 3, the Blair governments made a big increase in spending on the NHS, including a programme of new hospital building. From 1997 onwards, nearly all major hospital schemes – either complete hospitals or major extensions – have been financed and built under PFI. In 2000, the Government set a target of delivering over 100 hospital schemes by 2010. By 2005 68 were either built or underway, with PFI accounting for 64 of those projects. The boom in PFI-financed rebuilding stalled in 2006 when plans for new buildings for St Bartholomew's and Royal London Hospitals were delayed by the Secretary of State because of the cost – at around £1.1 billion. One reason for this hesitation was the change in NHS funding from block contracts, guaranteeing NHS Trusts' revenues to 'payment by results', where trusts are paid for work done under a national average cost formula.[21] PFI funding requires a risk-free revenue stream to make it attractive to private finance companies.

The building programme in the NHS has transformed the estate. In 1997, the average age of buildings in the NHS was older than the NHS, founded in 1948. By 2005 fewer than a quarter of NHS buildings were built before 1948.[22]

The use of PFI for building and running hospitals has been controversial. The first area of dispute is whether conventional financing and building would have provided better value for money than PFI-built hospitals. There are three elements to the argument: the cost of finance for the private schemes is higher than the cost of government borrowing; the transaction and financing costs of PFI-funded schemes are higher than conventional funding arrangements; the comparisons between Public Sector Comparators and PFI only favour the PFI after allowance is made for risk transfer. The first two elements are a matter of arithmetic and there is no doubt that higher costs arise from the financing method. The controversy is over whether those additional costs are more than cancelled out by the extra efficiency afforded by using private contractors to manage the building work. This is a hypothetical question, since during the hospital building boom, there have been no large schemes financed and managed by conventional means. The National Audit Office report on public building[23] in general indicated that PFI schemes are more likely to be delivered to time and budget than 'conventionally' managed projects, based on past experience.

The third element, the use of risk transfer as a balancing factor in the comparison between the two methods, has two aspects: how robust is the estimate of the value of the risk transferred? To what extent is risk actually transferred to the private sector when contracts are written guaranteeing payment for a 25 – 40-year period? Allyson Pollock and her colleagues at University College London have studied the results of PFI schemes since the beginning. In one analysis[24] they check the risk valuation with the difference in costs between PFI and the public sector comparator in a selection of PFI schemes (Table 11.2).

As Pollock et al. say, 'the table shows that the value of risk transferred to the private sector is remarkably close to the amount needed to close the gap between the public sector comparator and the PFI.' (p. 1207). The coincidence seems even more remarkable when they point out that the value of risk as a percentage of the total capital costs ranges from 17% in Swindon to 50.4% in South Tees. At the time of writing it is not clear what will be the impact of the change in the NHS funding

Table 11.2   *How risk transfer closes the gap between the net present costs of a publicly funded scheme and those of a PFI scheme*

Trust	Cost advantage to publicly financed scheme before risk transfer (£m)	Value of risk transfer to the PFI scheme
Swindon and Marlborough	16.6	17.3
Kings Healthcare	22.9	23.8
St George's Healthcare	11.9	12.5
South Durham	6.1	9.1
Hereford Hospitals	14.4	21.9
South Tees	28.8	67.8
West Midlands	8.4	13.5
University College London Hospitals	36.5	48.5
West Berkshire	36.3	41.8
Northumbria Healthcare – Hexham	3.2	4.8

Source: Pollock et al.[25] Table 4, p. 432

régime on the revenue streams of PFI hospitals. If Trusts running PFI-funded hospitals are to be allowed to fail, then the PFI contracts will presumably also be allowed to, and the risk will be seen genuinely to have been transferred to the PFI contractors.

Another feature of contracts for hospitals is their long term. As in the case of prisons, policy about the nature of the service changes with technology and with priorities. The hospitals constructed under PFI reflect policies towards the volume and nature of hospital care, reflected in the number of beds, the configuration of the wards, the location of the buildings, that will be fixed for the term of the contracts.

Hospital PFIs have generally had a good record in the construction phase of the deal. The NAO looked, for example, at the experience of the Middlesex Hospital.[26] It found that the building phase of the contract had worked well and the trust had achieved the best possible deal for the redevelopment of the hospital. While not all schemes were as straightforward, the controversy over PFI in the NHS is not mainly concerned with the relative merits of one building contracting method over another. The controversies mainly concern the actual value for money achieved, once account was taken of the value of the risk transfer and the cost of capital to the PFI provider compared with government as borrower. In cases such as Durham General Hospital, the number of beds provided in the replacement hospital was smaller than in the hospital to be replaced, to enable the scheme to be financed through PFI. If costs are in practice higher under PFI than they would have been under conventional financing, the policy is in conflict with the other policy of making NHS Trusts more responsible for keeping costs down. Conventional financing was strongly discouraged during the hospital building boom of the early 2000s.

Conclusions

While privatization solved the government's financing problem for the renewal of the water and sewerage networks, it transferred the problem to the consumers, the same people who would have paid for tax-funded investment. The differences between the two funding methods are the incidence of the tax or charges and the cost of capital. Unmetered domestic consumers pay for water at a tariff based on the value of their property, in the same way as the Council Tax. Neither is a progressive tax in the way that income tax is. The cost of capital is higher for the water companies than it would be for government, because interest charges on borrowings are higher and because shareholders need a rate of return higher than the return on government bonds. If we look at water privatization from the point of view of who pays and who benefits, it was a redistributive process, from less well-off to better-off people.

In the case of power, the policy principle was that competitive markets would provide incentives for investment and efficiencies at all stages in the process of supply. While there never has been a perfectly competitive market since many contracts are set in secret and for long periods, there has been some competitive impact on the price to the consumer. However, the world market for oil and gas is oligopolistic. Domestic competition among producers or distributors does nothing to protect consumers against prices set by the oligopoly bargaining processes at the global level.

The regulatory régimes in the water and power industries face new challenges. Periods of reduced rainfall emphasize the vulnerability of parts of Britain to water shortages. Plans for expanded house building in the South East of England depend, among other environmental issues, on adequate water supply. Conservation of existing flows, by better water management and reduced leakages, requires continuing investment. In turn, this means that consumers will have to pay higher prices to enable the water companies to make a return on their investments.

In the case of energy, the challenge is to confine dependency on a small number of gas suppliers, and to contain energy demand by promoting more energy efficiency. At the same time, agreements on emission reductions imply an investment in cleaner energy production. The regulator régime, operating through competition and price controls, uses fairly blunt instruments to achieve these policy goals.

Private Finance Initiative/Public–Private Partnerships have been used to meet a number of government objectives. They have been seen as a solution to the problem of delays and cost overruns in public building and a solution to the 'principal–agent' problem of service provisions, that was sketched in the Introduction to Part Two, since they incorporate various forms of performance contracts and incentives. They have also been seen as a solution to the fiscal problem caused by a big backlog in capital spending on infrastructure, since they apparently transfer funding to the PFI/PPP contractors.

As a funding mechanism, PFI/PPP has been successful in the sense that businesses have, so far, been willing to arrange finance for the contracts on offer. The secondary market in these contracts shows that the earnings streams that they generated were attractive to the initial investors as well as to the secondary market. Whether they can be declared successful as a financing method depends on a comparator: we have seen that the Private Sector Comparators have relied heavily, in the case of the NHS, on the valuation of risk transfer to make PFI/PPP look like better value. The extra cost of capital for the private sector, imposed by higher interest rates on loan capital and the need to provide shareholders with a return on their equity investment higher than a return in the bond markets, would suggest that purely as a method of financing, PFI/PPP should be higher than direct public procurement.

As a way of getting buildings constructed, the method has also had reasonable success, when compared with older experience of direct public provision through building contractors, according to the Auditor General. Not all projects were successful. The first PFI contract to be terminated before completion was that for the building of the National Physical Laboratory, in 2004. Delays and overruns led to the building being taken back from the PFI contractor, Laser, and the services contract terminated.[27]

Unlike selling off state assets and ceasing government subsidies, as in the case of British Airways, the electricity industry or any of the other early privatizations, PFI/PPP does not transfer the responsibility for the service to the private sector. PFI prisons are still the responsibility of the National Offender Management Service; the NHS is still responsible for the provision of health care. The government undertakes its obligations through a series of contracts for building, maintenance, service provision. The success of these contracts in PFI/PPP and in the special case of the railway has been mixed.

Clearly, the contracting system on the railways was bad, literally leading to disaster for the victims of the train crashes. Adversarial contracting and the construction of an elaborate system of blame attribution and accounting, combined with conflicting incentives, brought the railway close to a standstill. The new arrangements have been modified to some degree to try to correct these failures.

Early experience on London's underground railway has been better, with improvements in service standards resulting from maintenance programmes. It remains to be seen how well the contracts, and the contractors, perform in the major improvements to the network and the stations.

The contracts for running PFI prisons, according to NAO, have been no better, and probably no worse, than the other contractual arrangements and performance régimes in place in the publicly owned and run establishments. Companies have not avoided performance penalties, there have been cases of prisons taken back into public control, and there is no marked difference in performance that can be attributed to the existence of the PFI.

PFI has been the main vehicle used for the biggest-ever hospital building programme since the NHS was founded, the contracts confined to the construction and maintenance of the buildings. Here, doubts about contracts as a management mechanism centre on the rigidity of the services provided, rather than the success of the building and maintenance contracts themselves, compared with other available methods.

Notes

For weblinks relevant to the issues discussed in this chapter see www.sagepub.co.uk/flynn.

1 The structure of the industry changes as mergers and acquisitions and divestments take place. For up to date information check: http://www.thewaterplace.co.uk/
2 'Veiola', briefly known as 'Vivendi' and 'Vivendi Environment', was previously 'Compagnie Générale des Eaux', the company that has 50% of the French privatised water market.
3 Colin Mayer, 'Commitment and Control in Regulation: The Future of Regulation in Water', in Colin Robinson (ed.) *Governments, Competition and Utility Regulation*, (Edward Elgar, Cheltenham, 2005).
4 Karen J. Bakker, 2003, *An Uncooperative Commodity: Privatizing Water in England and Wales* (Oxford University Press, Oxford, 2003).
5 Mohammed H.I. Dove, Joseph Kushner and Klemen Zumer, 'Privatization of Water in the UK and France – What Can We Learn?', *Utilities Policy*, 12 (2004), pp. 41–50.
6 In Northern Ireland the Office for the Regulation of Electricity and Gas, in the Northern Ireland Authority for Energy Regulation. At the time of writing there was only one electricity supplier, Northern Ireland Electricity, which was privatized in 1992 (power stations) and 1993 (the rest of the business) and discussions had started about opening up the market.
7 The regulator set retail prices until 2001, after which competition was to be the main determinant of price.
8 It was called the National Energy Trading Arrangements when it was introduced without Scotland in 2001: see National Audit Office, *The New Energy Trading Arrangements in England and Wales*, HC 624, Session 2002–3, 9 May 2003.
9 Steve Thomas, 'The British Model: Failing Slowly', *Energy Policy*, 34, March 2006.
10 Dieter Helm, Editorial, *Utilities Journal*, vol. 8, March 2005, p. 1.
11 The government imposed some rules on the share of the profits from refinancing, making the companies pay some of them back.
12 The so-called 'Ryrie rules' set out in 1981 criteria under which private finance could be introduced to the nationalized industries. They were revised in 1988 to extend the

process to other sorts of private/public joint activities and introduce the possibility of paying a premium to the private sector for accepting risk.

13 HM Treasury, *PFI: Meeting the Investment Challenge* (HMSO, London, 2003).

14 For a discussion of the relationship between the Chancellor's fiscal rules and the PFI, see Grahame Allen, *The Private Finance Initiative*, House of Commons Research Paper 01/117, December 2001, House of Commons Library, pp. 23–25.

15 Material on the performance elements of the London Underground contracts comes from: Transport for London, *London Underground and the PPP: the Second Year, 2004/2005* (TfL, London, 2005).

16 The description of the railway story is mostly based on Andrew Murray, *Off the Rails – the crisis in Britain's railways* (verso, London, 2001) and Department of Transport, *The Future of Rail* (White Paper CM 6233), HMSO, London, July 2004.

17 The White Paper says that the number of passenger journeys grew by 26% between 1996/7 and 2004.

18 In 1992–3 British Rail achieved nearly 90% of trains on time; the system achieved 80% in 2002–3.

19 Department of Transport, 2004, *The Future of Rail*.

20 Comptroller and Auditor General, *The Operational Performance of PFI Prisons*, HC 700 Session 2002–3: 18 June 2003, HMSO, London.

21 Payment by results was introduced for acute inpatient procedures in April 2004, and for elective surgery in April 2005. See Chapter 4 for a summary of changes in payment methods in the NHS.

22 King's Fund, *An Independent Audit of the NHS Under Labour (1997-2005)*, (King's Fund, London, 2005), p. 66.

23 NAO, 2003, *PFI Construction Performance*, HC 371, Session 2002–3, 5 February 2003.

24 Allyson Pollock, Jean Shaol and Neil Vickers, 2002, 'Private finance and "value for money" in NHS hospitals: a policy in search of a rationale?', *British Medical Journal* 324 (May), pp. 1205–9.

25 Ibid.

26 National Audit Office, *The PFI Contract for the Redevelopment of West Middlesex University Hospital*, HC Session 49 2002–3 (National Audit Office, London, November 2002).

27 National Audit Office, *The Termination of the PFI Contract for the National Physical Laboratory*, HC 1044, 2005–6, (NAO, London, 2006).

Conclusions

We have seen that governments have struggled with the problems of performance, productivity, service quality and customer satisfaction in the public services over a period of at least three decades if not since the establishment of the institutions of the welfare state six decades ago. Such a large array of principles, approaches, and management techniques have been used that it is hard to think of many that have not. When visitors to the UK look at the apparently continuous process of change in the public sector they often ask, 'What can we learn about what works and does not work?'

Performance against targets

To answer this question, we start by looking at a range of targets and the degree to which they were met. In Appendix 1 there is a selection of targets and performance measures, mostly in graphic form, from Education, Home Office, Health, Customs and Excise (before the merger with Inland Revenue) and Work and Pensions.

In the case of Education, there tends to be a step improvement soon after the introduction of a target, followed in most cases by flatter lines showing some slow continuing improvement, in some a slight deterioration in performance. The English and maths results for 11-year-olds show improvement from 1996, then a period of levelling out, with maths level 5 results declining slightly after 2001. Schools where fewer than 65% achieve level 4 and above at KS3 fell from 6,500 to 2,500 and then stayed constant.

What is not shown in the overall data is the performance of the Academies, the government's flagship, sponsored schools that were destined to transform poorly performing schools in deprived areas, and the model for trust schools. When 14 Academies published their results in 2006, they had achieved an improvement of 1.3% in GCSE English grade C and above, against a national average of a 1.7% improvement. One of them was declared a failing school by its inspector, while one managed to reduce from 15% to 11% its proportion of children achieving 5 or more GCSE grade Cs.[1]

The Home Office has a small number of reported targets, performance mostly going in the right direction. The majority are about categories of crime and their incidence as measured by the British Crime Survey.

The Health indicators mostly show improvement, as targets concentrate efforts towards their achievement. The health targets are of three kinds: measures of service, such as waiting times and numbers of people waiting, outcomes, such as deaths from certain conditions, and measures of patients' satisfaction. The priority targets were waiting times, and the data in Appendix 1 show that the number of people with a six-months wait for inpatient treatment fell from over 250,000 to 60,000. The outcome measures for deaths from cancer and coronary heart disease are both going in the right direction.

Customs and Excise targets are about the impact of their activities on the drugs and illegal goods markets. It is too early to say whether they can demonstrate the direction of performance.

The Work and Pensions targets are mostly showing positive results, except in the case of the service provided by the Child Support Agency, the child maintenance target. The reported performance reflects the CSA disaster we described briefly in Chapter 4.

Overall this selection of performance measures shows, using the indicators chosen by government, that there has been modest improvement in performance in many cases, but that there have been no dramatic shifts in performance, save perhaps some step changes at the introduction of the performance management system.

Productivity

In the Introduction to Part Two we saw that there is a problem of falling productivity in the public sector. Increases in spending can produce rising salaries and prices of inputs, which can dampen the impact of the increase in spending on the production of services. The fall in productivity was not dramatic, and is shown in Table C1:[2]

What seems to have happened is that as spending increased, productivity fell. Pritchard, the constructor of these statistics, does not explain the causes. What is clear, though, is that all the controls, measurement system, contracts and targets did not produce a productivity improvement over this period.

There is another example, from the NHS. With NHS published data it is possible to construct a crude index of productivity, based on the Finished Consultant Episode (FCE), a measure of activity used inside the NHS that represents a discrete item of treatment (Table C2).

What Table C2 shows is that, using this simple measure of productivity, total staff productivity fell by 7.6% between 1998 and 2002, while the productivity of clinical staff fell by 6.2% and of 'infrastructure' staff by 5.3% (not all staff are included in these two categories). In other words, all increases in 'outputs' (FCEs) were the result of increasing staff numbers and output did not increase even in line with the increase in numbers, despite a long-term planning assumption of an increase in productivity, and budgets that presumed productivity

Table C1 Volume of government output, volume of government input and annual productivity change indicative estimate

£ million

	1995	1996	1997	1998	1999	2000	2001	%Change 1995–2001
All functions								
Volume of government output at 1995 prices	141,031	142,702	142,779	144,991	149,419	152,524	156,361	
Annual change (percent)		1	0	2	3	2	3	*11*
Volume of government input at 1995 prices	141,031	142,388	141,371	142,785	149,441	153,877	160,320	
Annual change (per cent)		1	–1	1	5	3	4	*14*
Annual productivity change: indicative estimate (per cent)		0	1	1	–2	–1	–2	

Source: Pritchard, 2003, Table 2

Table C2 *NHS staff and output 1998–2002.*

	Staff	Clinical	Infrastructure	FCEs	FCE/staff	FCE/clinical	FCE/infrastructure
1998	765,900	441,000	139,500	11,983,893	15.6	27.2	85.9
2002	882,100	500,300	158,000	12,757,656	14.5	25.5	80.7
2002/1998 %					92.4	93.8	94.0

Source: Pritchard, 2003

improvements. A study of productivity in the NHS carried out by National Statistics used ten different ways of measuring productivity and found that productivity fell from 1995 to 2003 by somewhere between 3% and 12%: 'Over the period 1995 to 2003 NHS output (not allowing for quality change) has grown by 28 per cent and NHS inputs have grown by between 32 and 39 per cent.'[3]

In other cases productivity did increase. The increase in numbers of students in further and higher education, for example, was not matched by increases in resources or staff numbers, probably to the detriment of quality.

Disasters

Some of the events described in this book can only be defined as disasters. The biggest was probably the railway: a privatization followed by increased subsidy that produced such poor infrastructure and such a loose set of government controls that it took the deaths of passengers in train crashes to provoke a change to the system. The failure, as we saw in Chapter 11, could be attributed to the contracting and management mechanisms that were installed. Too many contractors, agents doing the work of principals, incentives to blame but not to improve, all contributed to the deterioration of the network.

The spectacular IT failures can also be described as disasters. The National Insurance Recording System 2 cost huge amounts in wasted cash and uncollected revenues. The Child Support Agency failure cost taxpayers and single parents millions of pounds, as well as causing distress to parents.

The prison system is a more hidden disaster. The UK has the highest proportion of its people in jail of any European country and yet its standards of detention, rehabilitation and care in many prisons are abysmal, as reported by successive inspectors.

Is there a common pattern to these disasters? The railway and the IT failures have some common characteristics. In the case of the IT disasters the purchasers, the departments responsible for buying the IT systems, had inadequate knowledge of the requirements for the specified systems, the process changes necessary to implement the computer systems and the management of large IT projects. The companies involved have their share of the blame, whether through greed or incompetence. Some of these issues have since been addressed and a more close relationship is developing between purchasers and suppliers of large, expensive and complex systems. There remains, though, an 'information asymmetry' between government departments and suppliers of information technology, as well as defence equipment and other complicated pieces of kit. In the case of the CSA, the problem was not confined to the computer system: the policy of means testing, in detail, non-resident parents who are in many cases unwilling to divulge their incomes was unlikely to have very high success and accuracy rates.

In the case of the railway, the problem was similar, in that the people responsible for the track and signals knew less than the contractors about what needed to be done, although the contractors were not fully informed. This problem has been addressed to some extent by the new arrangements on the train network and in the contracts on London Underground. These recognize that nobody has complete knowledge of the state of the track, signals and stations and therefore what needs to be done and the contracts are based on outcomes.

The prison case is not the same. Here there is a hierarchy stretching down from the Home Office and a set of performance targets and measures, expressed through Agreements with directly employed managers, contracts with private providers and PFI contracts with PFI prisons. According to the various audit and inspection reports, none of these works better, or worse, than others. More to blame than the management arrangements, at the heart of the failing prisons is prison policy and prison funding. Increasing prisoner numbers without matching increases in capacity leads to overcrowding and low quality. In these circumstances, keeping order and preventing escapes is as much as some prisons can achieve, at the expense of meaningful activity, education and rehabilitation.

What works?

Financing methods and financial control

There have been three main changes in financing methods: the separation of revenue and capital budgets through resource budgeting and accounting; the use of private capital rather than borrowing for capital financing; the devolution of financial control. In addition, changes in the rules such as being allowed to carry over some money from one financial year to the next, and the introduction of three-year financial plans, have been designed to improve management.

The main purpose of resource accounting and budgeting was to make clearer to managers the distinction between investment and running costs. In the civil service the separation of running cost budgets and other payments (departmental expenditure limits and annually managed expenditure) was a further help to financial decision-making.

What conditions are necessary to create positive results from these changes in the financing arrangements? The most obvious is that once budgets can be broken down sensibly into capital and recurrent, managers are able to make choices between the two. Continuing capital controls, through borrowing approvals and business case tests, carried on separately from budget decisions about recurrent costs and especially payroll expenses, diminish the value of the changes.

PFI/PPP is a special case. Here, capital expenditure, or what would normally be counted as capital expenditure since it involves the acquisition of an asset, is paid for as part of recurrent expenses, for the contract period. As PPP deals accumulate, a growing proportion of recurrent budgets is committed in advance, giving less rather than more financial freedom to managers.

The devolution of financial control to individual units, such as police Basic Command Units, schools, hospitals or prisons, is designed to shift the decision-making to where it can be done most effectively. There are three conditions required to make this effective. First, the people making the decisions have to be equipped with the financial information, in time and accurately, to make financial decisions both at budgeting time and throughout the financial year. They also have to have the time and skills to make good decisions.

Second, they have to be given real discretion to make financial decisions over a reasonable period. As we saw in Chapter 3, in any financial year unless there are big increases in the resources available, most spending is committed before the budget is constructed. A shift in the use of resources requires longer-term decision-making and planning. While the Treasury produces three-year spending plans, these are rarely transmitted as three-year plans for individual units.

The third condition is that there should be some scope for error and rescue if things go wrong. If a manager is faced with an unexpected contingency, there should be a method of reallocation of resources from an under-spending unit to bail her out. This is not because the system should reward poor forecasting but because if everyone has to cover every contingency, a large amount of funds will be held in reserve against such contingencies. The opposite condition, where everybody always get bailed out, is not a solution. Consistent overspending is not a sign of good management.

These conditions have sometimes been met and sometimes not in the UK reforms. As a generalization, the centralization and tight control of finance has countered the tendency to devolve financial decision-making to units. There is a genuine dilemma: if all units are allowed financial freedoms with no checks until the end of the financial year, the whole public sector could overspend; on the other hand if every decision has to be referred upwards, no quick or effective decisions will be made.

Whether PFI/PPP can be said to 'work' depends on what the schemes are expected to achieve. At their most basic, they get capital spending off the books of government and transfer costs to future times and future generations. As a way of getting infrastructure built, they seem to work, in the sense of getting things built to time and to budget, although there are some doubts about the quality of some products, especially schools. Whether they represent value for money depends on a judgement of the value of risk transfer. Many PFI/PPP schemes only appeared to be better value than the public sector alternative if a high value was attached to the risk transferred. If risk was genuinely taken on by the private sector at the valuations made in the comparisons, then there was value for money. From much of the evidence from NHS schemes, this seems unlikely.

Collaboration

The first Labour government placed great emphasis on 'joined-up government', both in policy making and service delivery. Institutions were established to bring about collaborative working, notably in regeneration services, the policy towards child poverty and the criminal justice system.

It is difficult to judge the impact of collaboration on regeneration, since collaboration was compulsory for all schemes if they were to attract funding. We do know from experience that collaboration works best when certain conditions prevail, including the development of shared values among the collaborators, a willingness to sacrifice individual organizational interests and a willingness to pool resources. There is some evidence of these conditions prevailing, but at the same time organizations are under pressure to produce results in their main activities. This is another dilemma for managers: performance targets for individual activities compete with performance targets for collaborative activity.

Structural change

Public services are mostly delivered to people through relatively local, small service delivery units. There are exceptions, with centralized state pensions administration, call centres such as NHS Direct and centralized or physically remote tax collection. But General Practitioner services, hospitals for all but the most specialist services, primary and secondary schools, waste collection and street cleaning, consumer protection, planning controls, public health, sport and recreation, road maintenance, parking controls and all the other services that people have regular contact with, are all local, visible and carried out by small groups of people under direct supervision.

What happens 'above' those people in the hierarchy can be less important than what they do every day. Your local primary school may or may not have its own budget and a line management relationship with the education authority. Your GP may be an independent practitioner or an employee of the Primary Care Trust. Your secondary school may have trust status or not. A council employee or the employee of a French conglomerate working under contract might empty your bins. Does any of this make any difference?

In principle, any structural arrangement should be able to accommodate a set of management arrangements to achieve the goals of the services. A change from direct employment to contract with the private sector should not be necessary to make an incentive scheme for people to empty bins well. Managerial autonomy at school level and central policy direction are not the only arrangements to have an impact on what happens between the teacher and her class.

According to this argument, much used by people working at the front line, management structures and arrangements at high levels, with their accompanying targets, strategic plans and visions, are very diluted by the time they reach the interface between the service provider and the service user. Professional ethics and training outweigh managerial instructions. Only where tasks are routine and mechanized can process designs and controls affect the way people work.

Governments have been activist in their approaches to the structure of the public sector. As we have seen, the NHS is in a constant state of reorganization, tiers of management created and abolished, funding methods invented, scrapped and reinvented, governance structures established and re-established, targets set and changed with such frequency that the ever-growing management staff spend a good proportion of their time on organizational arrangements, reporting, preparing for the next change, rather than concentrating on resource management for patient care. This activity is complemented by a constant stream of directives and guidance flowing down from the top of the organization in its various forms.

The first ten years of Labour government brought eight Education Acts. Schools have been told that they are more managerially accountable and autonomous but are tightly managed by a very time-consuming régime of tests, reports, inspections and assessments that have the effect of weakening local authority influence and strengthening central government controls. Secondary schools dare not stand still for fear of being left behind by the latest initiative attached to funding. They must specialize, find sponsors, join partnerships and collaborations, or they will be condemned as bog-standard and left stranded as the next wave of reforms washes over them and passes them by.

In the field of criminal justice, the Probation Service was first centralized and reorganized, then merged with the police forces under NOMS. The police were broken down into BCUs and then a series of mergers was hastily proposed to make them into bigger forces.

The civil service has not been immune from reorganization as a solution to a range of apparent problems. The Deputy Prime Minister's office accreted functions from other ministries, The Ministry of Agriculture, Fisheries and Food was abolished after various disasters, HM Customs was merged with the Inland Revenue, the agencies in Work and Pensions were merged. The inspectorates, a very important part of the government's control mechanisms, were merged, decreasing from 11 to four. And devolution was a reorganization on a grand scale, creating new institutions in Scotland and Wales.

It is difficult to isolate the effects of structural changes on performance. It is apparent, though, that big organizations do not necessarily perform better than small ones. For example, the Home Office is a conglomerate of functions but some of the most intractable problems requiring co-ordinated (or 'joined-up') policies and action are located within it and do not get adequately dealt with.

Competition and contestability: responding to incentives

Governments have been on a constant search for ways of controlling public services. They have ranged from privatization and the lightest regulation relying on competition, in the energy sector, to a series of ever-tighter performance contracts in a strict hierarchy, in the directly provided services. These two elements, competition and contestability on the one hand and a hierarchy of contracts on the other, have been applied in various combinations throughout the development of public management in the UK. Competition was introduced into local authority services at the beginning of the 1980s, while the explicit use of contracts started at the beginning of the 1990s.

Faith in hierarchical management is based on this proposition: if there is an integrated performance system, stretching down from high-level outcome targets through a PSA or PFI agreement to individual incentives, then people will all work towards the agreed targets. The evidence in favour of this view is the way that performance measures have mostly moved in the desired direction. The evidence against is the way that the productivity data, although also limited, show a decrease in productivity when all the targets are calling for improvement.

The owners of the water companies clearly respond to incentives: if they are allowed to make very large returns they will come up with the investment; cap their prices and they will drop their shares. As we saw, the regulator is in a position to determine the incentives, although there was leakage of cash from infrastructure investment into excessive dividends, once big price rises were allowed.

Outsourcing companies are apparently willing to bid for as much work as the government wants to give them. Their response to the contract régime is a combination of compliance and challenge. Failures of performance are as likely to result in renegotiated contracts at higher prices as in contract re-assignment. There are probably enough examples of regulation and competition to start to make a judgement about whether competition and contestability 'work'. In the simplest case, a competitive tendering process for a relatively simple service such as refuse collection or street cleaning, there seems to be a one-off reduction in cost at the time of contract letting. Once the service, or its outcomes, is more complicated, the result may be less successful. The case of school catering is interesting, in that competition was based almost entirely on price while quality and nutrition fell to health-threatening levels and contracts had to be renegotiated in the interests of pupils' health. Competition may have cut prices but did not produce desired outcomes.

Competition within the NHS produced adverse results, according to those in control, and price competition was stopped, in favour of a form of competition based on quality and choice. It remains to be seen whether this will produce the desired results and whether they will be more valuable than the detrimental loss of stability and predictability in the financial part of the control system.

Competition for students by universities has not resulted in price differences, as no university opted to do without top-up fees when offered. Competition is based on quality league tables and public assessment of quality or prestige. The league tables are both official, based on an assessment of research quality and quantity and teaching competence, and informal, based on indices constructed by journalists. Students can make their choices based on these indicators, or even more informal assessments about where they want to spend their student years. Whether such competition enhances overall performance of all universities is not known.

Under what conditions does competition and contestability produce positive results? The most obvious set of conditions is the structure of the market: oligopoly competition can result in high prices and low quality. In the main industry that is regulated by competition, the energy sector, there are global oligopolies in gas and oil supplies. Public transport, especially passenger train operation, is an oligopoly, where the small number of companies bid for franchises to operate services. For the high-cost items that government purchases, especially information technology and defence equipment, there is oligopoly. In the other outsourced services in local authorities, council tax collection, refuse collection and street cleansing, leisure management, there are a few large players and a reasonable number of smaller competitors. There is a small number of actual and potential prison management companies, and a large number of private and voluntary agencies offering services in the provision of non-custodial punishment and rehabilitation.

Especially where there are few, powerful, providers the achievement of a reasonable balance of cost and quality relies on the second condition for success, a well-informed, intelligent and strong purchaser. The purchaser is in a weak position if there is no option to switch suppliers, either because there are no credible alternative companies or because the contracts are very long. The option to bring the services back in-house from the outsourcers can provide a useful alternative.

Internal markets and contracts

Internal markets are run through contractual relationships without the contestability. The hierarchy of targets, stretching down from the Treasury, are a form of contract, with incentives and punishments. Under what conditions are these arrangements successful?

The first condition, as we saw in Chapter 5, is the degree to which the achievement of targets can be attributed to managers. The array of performance targets shown in the Appendix includes some that are susceptible to management actions and some that depend on many other variables. While the under-18 conception rate may respond to campaigns, advice and education, it is largely up to the under-18s whether they get pregnant or not. Many of the health service targets can be achieved through better management and more resources, while others, such as deaths from cancer, are subject to many aspects of the environment and individuals' behaviour. One of the Foreign and Commonwealth Office's targets, not listed in the Appendix, is the quantity of poppies grown in Afghanistan, a target that is influenced by the relative strength of the warlords and the occupying forces, not entirely under FCO control, and a target whose achievement is, so far, getting more remote.

The second part of this condition, whether performance is attributable to managers, is the degree to which they have control over their resources. Freedom to manage to aim for targets is not just a matter of having authority over individuals; it also means having control over finances, investments and physical resources. The drive towards PFI for major capital projects takes away managerial discretion over assets, both the means of acquisition and the use of those assets during the contract period.

The second condition is that the targets contribute towards the overall goals of the organization or unit. If targets are badly chosen, they can distort effort towards the target and away from what is important. The classic example concerns the sale of school playing fields to achieve education authorities' and schools' financial targets, resulting in more unfit and obese school children. Targeting grades A–C passes at GCSE takes attention away from those pupils who need help to rise from grade E to grade D. Waiting-list targets can result in poor performance in other areas, such as hospital-spread infections.

In general, targets based on widely-agreed desirable outcomes are less likely to distort efforts adversely. The problem is that the more targets are concerned with outcomes, especially at high levels of abstraction, the less attributable they are to services or the management of those services.

The third condition is that the measurements should be reliable and not susceptible to cheating. Part of this is that the measures and targets should not be changed frequently to hide the real outcomes. There is a tendency as performance agreements develop for them to be made more sophisticated, at the expense of a long run of data.

In arrangements where there is a division between 'purchaser' and 'provider', in which the budgets are held by someone other than the people providing the service, there has to be agreement about what the targets should be. This division is an attempt at a structural solution to a performance problem. In the civil service it is represented by the split between the departments and their executive agencies, or between the Department of Health and the NHS. Lower down the NHS it is represented by the budget holders, Primary Care Trusts or Strategic Health Authorities, or in previous systems Health Authorities or GP fundholders, being separate from the hospitals and other service providers. This kind of system makes contestability easier, and facilitates the use of funds for buying from the private sector. But whether it makes the bulk of service provision, 'purchased' by the fundholders from internal providers, any better depends on how the system works. Purchasers need to be very well-informed, intelligent operators to make their decisions better than those of the people running the hospitals. The process also relies on the presumption that if money is simply allocated to hospitals to cover their costs, the professional managers will act only in their own interests, rather than those of the patients or the population at large.

These conditions contradict each other: simple, measurable, attributable performance targets may well produce good managerial results without achieving the high-level goals of the service, or a group of services. High-level targets about the well-being and happiness of the population depend on many variables, some of which are susceptible to no public body's influence. Having intelligent, well-informed purchasers deprives the service provision side of the internal market of skilled people.

The solution is to strive for a set of targets and measures that at least work in the same direction, that are susceptible to influence and have some meaning to the users of services and to citizens in general. The solution also requires, as it does in the case of buying from outsource companies, close scrutiny and collaboration between 'buyers' and 'sellers'.

Audit and inspection

We saw in Chapter 7 that audit and inspection are used for several purposes simultaneously: for assurance, for quality improvement, for the pursuit of particular approaches to management, and as an economic regulator, deciding who should be allowed and not allowed to provide services.

Management reaction to the inspection régimes varies. In the case of prisons, while individual prison governors might try to respond to assessment and criticism, the system as a whole seems to be unable to respond to quality evaluations. Conformance with inspection, as CIPFA found,[4] becomes an art in itself, divorced from any notion of service improvement. Ofsted inspections have been used to close schools and bring about their replacement by new institutions.

For inspections to be useful for their primary purpose, the improvement of service quality, the inspectors need to be aware of the possibilities for improvement as well as the existing shortcomings, and managers need to have the tools, skills, resources and authority to bring about the improvements. Continuous reports of low standards in themselves achieve very little.

Assessment of quality has to be done with the confidence of the people being assessed. If managers and service providers do not believe that the inspectors know what they are doing, or doubt that they could do better themselves, inspection becomes an empty ritual. If inspection in used as an economic regulator, its main effect on poor performers is to instil anxiety and stress until such time as their licence to practise is revoked.

Remaining dilemmas

For around 25 years, governments have placed great faith in markets, contestability and the use of the private sector as a central solution to the problems of public sector performance and productivity. In the absence of real markets, they have constructed quasi-markets and hierarchical contractual relationships, with the contracts taking the place of competitive pressure. Everywhere there is the split between 'purchaser' and 'provider', even where there is no contest. The search for the complete contract, tight targets and foolproof measurements has pushed aside the main alternative, which is to develop high-trust relationships between government and the professionals who work for it to deliver services. And yet the dilemma remains: should professionals be allowed to pursue their professional ethics and skills or should they all be subject to control through performance targets and measures, set by 'purchasers' of their services?

A second dilemma, that most recently found expression in the fashion for 'new localism', is between the big, centralized, uniform service delivery organization, such as the Pensions Agency or Jobcentre Plus, and small, local organizations, accountable to local people. Recent government moves have produced both. The argument for centralization[5] includes a desire for equity, uniformity and social justice. 'Postcode lotteries' in the availability of medical treatment are deplored. The argument for localism, is that 'customized services' are possible and desirable, that different people, groups, classes, ethnic groups, need different services and local control enables difference. It also promotes innovation. Recent government policies have pursued centralization and decentralization simultaneously, not necessarily in pursuit of clear objectives. The education reforms have been aimed at creating diversity in types of school and choice for parents and pupils, while the national curriculum, national tests and examinations and an inspection régime all pursue conformity.

As we saw in Chapter 5, performance targets promote vertical integration and hierarchical relationships. The pursuit of joined-up policy and service delivery promotes and requires horizontal integration and collaboration. As with the central–local dilemma, the government has pursued simultaneous vertical and horizontal integration. This contradiction reflects the dilemma between trying to pursue high-level policy objectives that cut across individual services and the imposition of a strict managerial control system on individual services and organizations.

The question is, how will governments deal with these dilemmas? They mainly arise from genuinely contradictory aims, one pushing in one direction and one in another. The reason that governments have pursued contradictory actions is that there are real contradictions that cannot be reconciled. The only resolution would be to abandon one of the halves of the dilemma: go for efficiency rather than policy effectiveness and centralize and vertically integrate; abandon customization and go all out for conformity and uniformity; forget the fight between government and the professions and let the professions do what they do best (or the opposite, subject them all to strict managerial control).

The other option would be to pursue one half of the dilemma differently in each case: find the contexts in which centralization and uniformity are best, decide where customization would be the best policy, where quality of the individual experience is more important than efficiency.

A third option is muddling through, pursuing different priorities at different times, whatever the context. Community care is an example of this: the systems are there for lots of choice, customization, and individual service packages. The reality is a very restrictive, rationed, controlled service offering some choice once need has been assessed, but no choice to the large numbers who need help but can't get it. The Child Support Agency is, among other things, an example of a service where assessments of ability to pay should be done by taking account of individual circumstances but in practice this was not possible. Choice of secondary school is supposed to give access to specialisms, but in practice they all pursue the national curriculum, with little extra time for the specialist subjects. Individual choice, the last fad of the third Labour government, was seen as a customer-centred solution to the dilemma of individual services and uniformity. It is likely, with the other mechanisms in place, to offer a free choice of identical services.

For people working in public services, managing within a context of contradictory pressures has become normal. At service delivery unit level, people can make their own choices about how to cope. Inspection conformance is a good example: managers can play the inspection game, making sure that the right boxes are ticked, while keeping enough discretion to respond to local circumstances. For many years NHS managers would overspend the budgets they had agreed to at the beginning of the financial year, in the interests of their patients. Good teachers conform to the régime of testing while still finding time to organize sports and performances. There is still room for imagination, responsiveness and dedication, despite the heavy burdens imposed by a highly centralized and mechanical management control system.

Notes

For weblinks relevant to the issues discussed in this chapter see www.sagepub.co.uk/flynn.

1   *Sunday Times* reporst, March 16th 2006.
2   Alwyn Pritchard, *Understanding Government Output and Productivity* (Office for National Statistics National Expenditure and Income Division, 2003), Table 2.
3   Office for National Statistics, *Public Service Productivity: Health* (Office for National Statistics, London, 2004).
4   See Chapter 7.
5   An excellent exposition of the argument can be found in David Walker, *In Praise of Centralism: a Critique of the New Localism* (Catalyst, London, 2002).

Appendix

Selected Public Service Agreement Measures

Source: HM Treasury Performance Index: http:www.hm-treasury.gov.uk/performance/index.cfm

1. Education

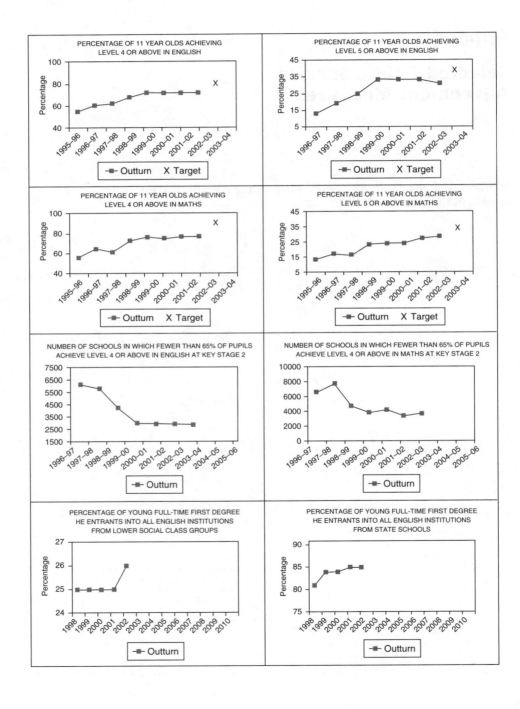

1. Education   *(Continued)*

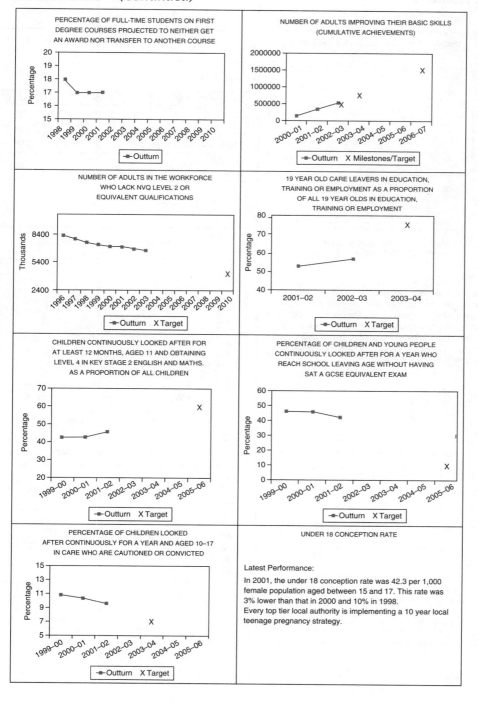

PERCENTAGE OF FULL-TIME STUDENTS ON FIRST DEGREE COURSES PROJECTED TO NEITHER GET AN AWARD NOR TRANSFER TO ANOTHER COURSE

Outturn

NUMBER OF ADULTS IMPROVING THEIR BASIC SKILLS (CUMULATIVE ACHIEVEMENTS)

Outturn   X Milestones/Target

NUMBER OF ADULTS IN THE WORKFORCE WHO LACK NVQ LEVEL 2 OR EQUIVALENT QUALIFICATIONS

Outturn   X Target

19 YEAR OLD CARE LEAVERS IN EDUCATION, TRAINING OR EMPLOYMENT AS A PROPORTION OF ALL 19 YEAR OLDS IN EDUCATION, TRAINING OR EMPLOYMENT

Outturn   X Target

CHILDREN CONTINUOUSLY LOOKED AFTER FOR AT LEAST 12 MONTHS, AGED 11 AND OBTAINING LEVEL 4 IN KEY STAGE 2 ENGLISH AND MATHS. AS A PROPORTION OF ALL CHILDREN

Outturn   X Target

PERCENTAGE OF CHILDREN AND YOUNG PEOPLE CONTINUOUSLY LOOKED AFTER FOR A YEAR WHO REACH SCHOOL LEAVING AGE WITHOUT HAVING SAT A GCSE EQUIVALENT EXAM

Outturn   X Target

PERCENTAGE OF CHILDREN LOOKED AFTER CONTINUOUSLY FOR A YEAR AND AGED 10–17 IN CARE WHO ARE CAUTIONED OR CONVICTED

Outturn   X Target

UNDER 18 CONCEPTION RATE

Latest Performance:

In 2001, the under 18 conception rate was 42.3 per 1,000 female population aged between 15 and 17. This rate was 3% lower than that in 2000 and 10% in 1998.
Every top tier local authority is implementing a 10 year local teenage pregnancy strategy.

2. Home Office

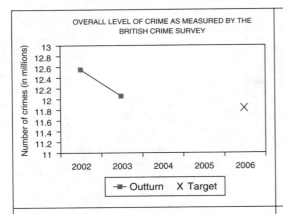

OVERALL LEVEL OF CRIME AS MEASURED BY THE BRITISH CRIME SURVEY

FEAR OF CRIME

Latest Performance:

Fear of crimes	Burglary	Vehicle crime	Violent crime
Target	Each of the level of fear is lower in the year to March 2006		
Baseline (2002)	15.2%	17.5%	21.8%
Latest outturn (Dec 2003)	14%	18%	18%

CRIME RATE IN THE HIGHEST CRIME CRPS (CRIME REDUCTION PARTNERSHIP AREAS)

Latest Performance:

The target is to improve performance overall and reduce the gap between the highest and lowest crime areas. This is assessed using the levels of recorded crime per 1000 population using the baseline of 27.1% for the year ending March 2003. The first set of outturn data is available In July 2004. Early Indications (25.8% in September 2003) are that the gap is beginning to narrow.

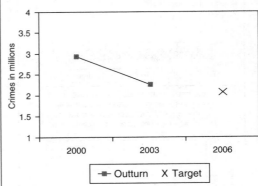

VEHICLE CRIME (BRITISH SURVEY)

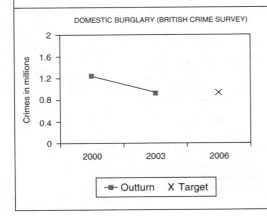

DOMESTIC BURGLARY (BRITISH CRIME SURVEY)

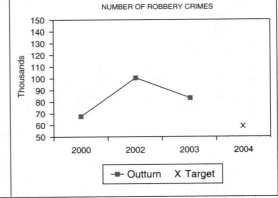

NUMBER OF ROBBERY CRIMES

2. **Home Office** *(Continued)*

REPORT OF PROGRESS ON RACE EQUALITY AND COMMUNITY COHESION

Latest Performances:

Indicator	Baseline	Latest Outturn	2004 Milactors/ Target
Confidence in public services	–Criminal Justice System: As reported through PSA target 4. –The Citizenship Survey 2001 shows that BME confidence in the other key public services (education and health) is not an Issue. Progress Indicators will be developed In due course.		
Labour market (based on Labour-force Survey)	Spring 2003: 58.3%	Due December 2003	
Community cohesion (based on Home Office Citizenship Survey Local Area Boost)	Baseline Information will be made available in June 2004.		To Improve
HO race equality employment target			
–Police	1999:		
–Overall	3.0%	3.8%	4.6 %/7.0%
–Officers	2.0%	2.9%	4.0 %/7.0%
–Immigration Service	1999: 7.0%	22.5%	7.0 %/7.0%
– Probation Services	1999: 8.3%	10.5%	8.3 %/7.0%
–Prison Service	1999: 3.2%	5.1%	4.9 %/7.0%
–Home Office London/Croydon	1999: 23.0%	31.1%	25.0%/25.0%
Number of government departments using Race Equality Impact Assessments	2003/04 to be set	Measurement to commence by April 2004	To Increase

LEVEL OF PUBLIC CONFIDENCE IN THE CRIMINAL JUSTICE SYSTEM

3. Health

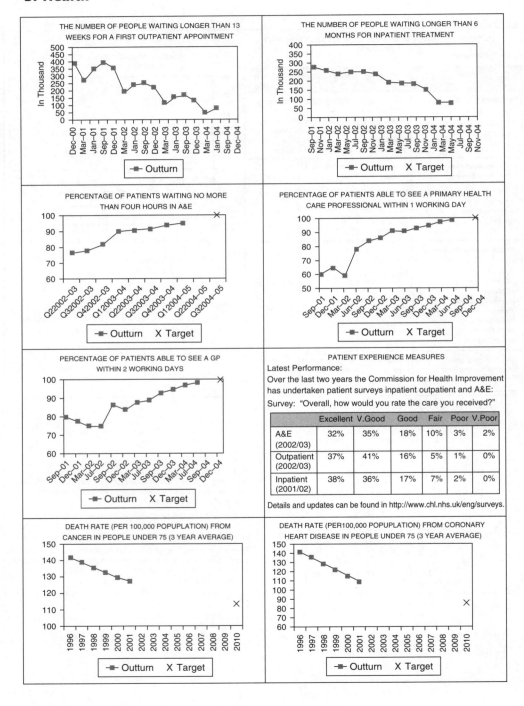

3. Health *(Continued)*

DEATH RATE FROM INTENTIONAL SELF-HARM
AND INJURY OF UNDETERMINED INTENT
(PER 100,000 POPULATION)

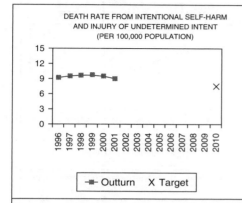

-■- Outturn   X Target

NUMBER OF PEOPLE RECEIVING CRISIS
RESOLUTION SERVICES

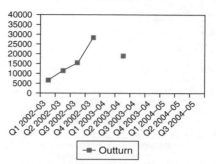

-■- Outturn

THOSE AGED 65 AND OVER SUPPORTED
INTENSIVELY TO LIVE AT HOME, AS A PERCENTAGE
OF ALL THOSE AGED 65 AND OVER SUPPORTED IN
RESIDENTIAL CARE BY SOCIAL SERVICES OR
INTENSIVELY TO LIVE AT HOME

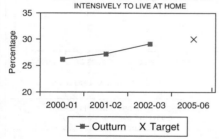

-■- Outturn   X Target

NUMBER OF PROBLEM DRUG MISUSERS PRESENTING FOR TREATMENT (PERCENTAGE CHANGE ON PREVIOUS YEAR)

Latest Outturn Information:

2003   10% (provisional)

2002   8%

Latest Performance:

The target is to increase the the number of drug users participating in drug treatment programmes by 55% between 1998 and 2004.

The achievement up to 2003 was 41%.

GAP IN AVERAGE LIFE EXPECTANCY AT BIRTH
(MALE, IN YEARS, LOWEST QUINTILE OF
POPULATION COMPARED TO ENGLAND AVERAGE)

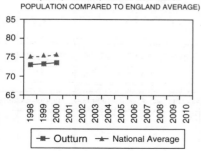

-■- Outturn   -▲- National Average

ANNUAL PERCENTAGE CHANGE IN THIS REFERENCE COSTS ADJUSTED FOR CASEMIX, UNDERLYING INFLATION AND QUALITY IMPROVEMENTS

Latest Information:

As set out in Delivering the NHS Plan, the Department have developed a better, more rounded measure of NHS efficiency. The new measure of productivity is being appraised by independent academic experts.

Performance for this target will be measured using data that is not available until the end of the financial year. As the first year of the target is 2003/04, no figures are yet available.

Taking account of the whole range of activity and investment in quality improvement, the Department estimate that productivity is increasing at the rate around 1% year, broadly based on the new measures.

4. Customs and Excise

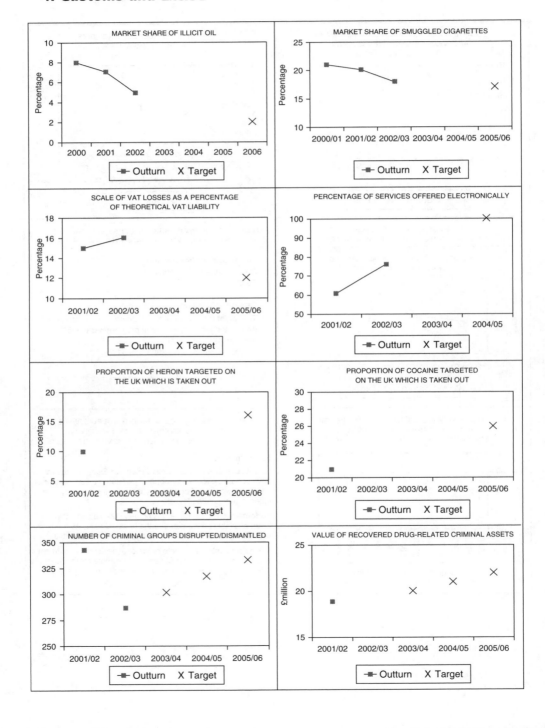

5. Work and Pensions

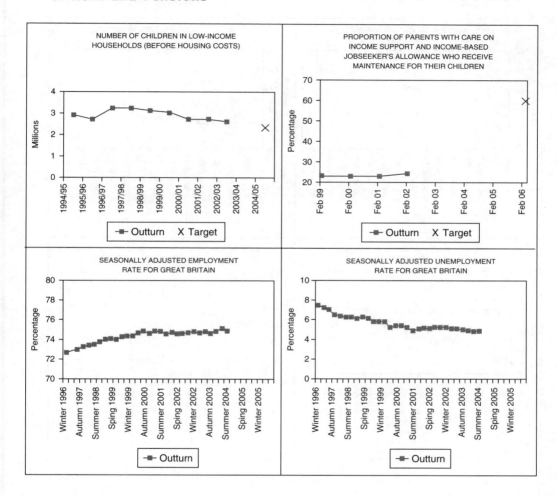

5. Work and Pensions *(Continued)*

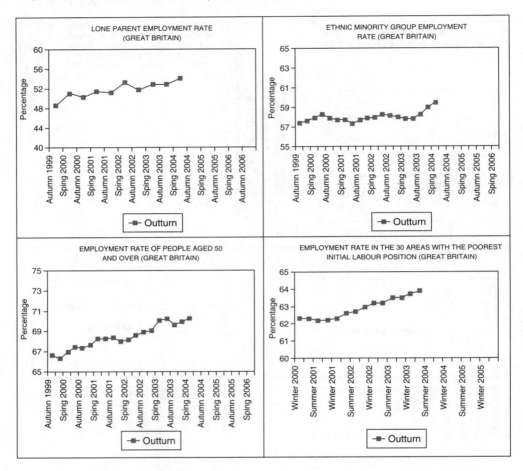

Further reading

Recommended reading is arranged by themes, since many of those listed cover material that relates to more than one chapter of the book.

Institutions

Adams, J. and Schmuecker, K. (eds) (2006) *Devolution in Practice: Public policy differences within the UK*. Newcastle Upon Tyne: IPPR.

Hennessy, Peter (2001) *Whitehall*. London: Pimlico.

Leeke, Matthew, Sear, Chris and Gay, Oonagh (2003) *An Introduction to Devolution in the UK*. London: House of Commons Library.

Pyper, Robert and Massey, Andrew (2005) *Public Management and Modernisation in Britain*. Basingstoke: Palgrave Macmillan.

Rhodes, R.A.W. (ed) (2000) *Transforming British Government*. Basingstoke: Macmillan, 2 vols.

Stewart, John D. (2003) *Modernising British Local Government: An assessment of Labour's reform programme*. Basingstoke: Palgrave Macmillan.

Stoker, Gerry (2005) *What is Local Government for?: Refocusing local governance to meet the challenges of the 21st century*. London: New Local Government Network.

Wilks-Heeg, Stuart and Atkinson, Hugh (2000) *Local Government from Thatcher to Blair*. Cambridge: Polity.

Politics of the public sector

Clarke, John (2004) *Changing Welfare, Changing States*. London: Sage.

Riddell, Peter (2005) *The Unfulfilled Prime Minister*. London: Politico's Publishing.

Savage, S. and Atkinson, R. (2001) *Public Policy Under Blair*. London: Palgrave.

Seldon, Anthony and Kavanagh, Dennis (2005) *The Blair Effect 2001–5*. Cambridge: Cambridge University Press. An assessment of the achievements of the second government under Tony Blair's leadership. Previous volumes in the series were *The Thatcher Effect* (1989), *The Major Effect* (1994) and *The Blair Effect 1997–2001* (2001).

Welfare state and individual welfare sectors

Baldock, J. Manning, N. and Vickerstaff, S. (eds) (2003) *Social Policy*. Oxford: Oxford University Press.

Barr, Nicholas (2004) *Economics of the Welfare State*. Oxford: Oxford University Press.

Deakin, Nicholas (2000) *The Treasury and Social Policy: The contest for control of welfare strategy (transforming government)*. Basingstoke: Palgrave.

Fraser, Derek (2002) *The Evolution of the British Welfare State*. Basingstoke: Palgrave Macmillan.

Hill, Michael (2003) *Understanding Social Policy*, 6th edn. Oxford: Blackwell.

King's Fund (2005) *An Independent Audit of the NHS under Labour (1997–2005)*. London: King's Fund.

Klein, Rudolf (2000) *The New Politics of the NHS*, 4th edn. London: Longman.

Malpass, P. (2005) *Housing and the Welfare State: The development of housing policy in Britain*. Basingstoke: Palgrave.

Pollock, Allyson (2005) *NHS Plc: The Privatisation of our Healthcare*. London: Verso.

Timmins, Nicholas (1995) *The Five Giants: A Biography of the Welfare State*. London: HarperCollins. A very detailed account of the development of the welfare state.

Public finance

Coombs, H.M. and Jenkins, D.E. (2002) *Public Sector Financial Management*, 3rd edn. London: Thomson Learning.

Hillman, Arye L. (2003) *Public Finance and Public Policy: Responsibilities and limitations of government*. Cambridge: Cambridge University Press.

Jones, R. and Pendlebury, M. (2000) *Public Sector Accounting*, 5th edn. Harlow: Financial Times Prentice Hall.

Citizen–Customer Orientation

Clarke, J. et al. (eds) (2000) *New Managerialism: New Welfare?* London: Sage.

Needham, C. (2003) *Citizen-consumers: New Labour's marketplace democracy*. London: Catalyst. A critical analysis of the use of markets in public services.

Normann, R. (1991) *Service Management*, 2nd edn. Chichester: Wiley. An analysis of the elements of service design.

Prior, D., Stewart, J.D. and Walsh, K. (1995) *Citizenship: Rights, Community and Participation*. London: Pitman. A review of the exercise of citizenship in public services.

Public management and performance

Bovaird, T. and Loffler, E. (2003) *Public Management and Governance*. London: Routledge.

Doherty, T. and Horne, T. (2002) *Managing Public Services*. London: Routledge.

Le Grand, J. (2003) *Motivation, Agency and Public Policy*. Oxford: Oxford University Press.

Greenwood, J., Pyper, R. and Wilson, D. (2002) *New Public Administration in Britain Today*, 3rd edn. London: Routledge.

Leach, R. and Percy-Smith, J. (2001) *Local Governance in Britain*. Basingstoke: Palgrave.

Pollitt, C. et al. (1998) *Decentralising Public Service Management*. Basingstoke: Macmillan.

Collaboration

Alter, Catherine and Hage, Jerald (1993) *Organizations Working Together*. Newbury Park: Sage.

Bardach, E. (1998) *Getting Agencies to Work Together: The practice and theory of managerial craftsmanship*. Washington: Brookings Institution.

Cabinet Office Performance and Innovation Unit (2000) *Wiring it Up: Whitehall's Management of Cross-Cutting Policies and Services*. London: Cabinet Office.

Child, John and Faulkner, David (1998) *Strategies of Cooperation*. Oxford: Oxford University Press.

Doz, Yves and Hamel, Gary (1998) *Alliance Advantage*. Boston: Harvard Business School Press.

Peters, B. Guy (1998) *Managing Horizontal Government*. Canadian Centre for Management Development, Ottawa, Research paper 21.

Audit and Inspection

Hood, C. (1999) *Regulation Inside Government*. Oxford: Oxford University Press.

Power, M. (1999) *The Audit Society: Rituals of Verification*. Oxford: Oxford University Press.

Markets in the public sector

Bartlett, W., Propper, C., Wilson, D. and Le Grand, J. (1994) *Quasi-Markets in the Welfare State*. Bristol: School of Advanced Urban Studies. A series of papers on the markets created in health, education and community care.

Walsh, K. (1995) *Public Services and Market Mechanisms: Competition, contracting, and the New Public Management*. Basingstoke: Macmillan. An analysis of the impact of markets on management of services.

Contracts

Bovis, Christopher (2005) *Public Procurement in the European Union: Case law and regulation*. Basingstoke: Palgrave Macmillan.

Harrison, A. (ed.) (1993) *From Hierarchy to Contract*. Oxford: Policy Journals. A collection of articles on the introduction of contracts in UK public services.

Sako, M. (1992) *Prices, Quality and Trust*. Cambridge: Cambridge University Press.

Private Finance Initiative and Public–Private Partnerships

Baldwin, R. and Cave, M. (1999) *Understanding Regulation: Theory, Strategy and Practice*. Oxford: Oxford University Press.

Grimsey, D. and Lewis, M. K. (2004) *Public Private Partnerships*. Cheltenham: Edward Elgar. Examples of PPPs from around the world, including the UK.

Beck, Matthias, Falconer, Peter and Dinan, William (2006) *Managing Public Private Partnerships in the UK*. London: Ashgate.

References

Allen, G. (2001) *The Private Finance Initiative*. House of Commons Research Paper 01/117, London: House of Commons Library, pp. 23–5.

Allen, P. (1995) 'Contracts in the National Health Service Internal Market'. *The Modern Law Review*, 58, May.

Appleby, J. and Rosete, A.R. (2003) 'The NHS: keeping up with public expectations?' in Park, A., Curtice, J., Thomson, K., et al. (eds), *British Social Attitudes: The 20th Report*. London: Sage.

Association of Directors of Social Services and National Council for Voluntary Organisations (1995) *Community Care and Voluntary Organizations: Joint Policy Statement*. London: ADSS/NCVO.

Atkinson, H. and Wilks-Heeg, S. (2002) *Local Government from Thatcher to Blair: the politics of creative autonomy*. Cambridge: Polity.

Audit Commission (1994) 'Taking Stock: Progress with Community Care', *Community Care Bulletin* No. 2, December. London: HMSO, p. 11.

Audit Commission (1999) *Performance Measurement as a Tool for Modernising Government: Using the PSAs to Drive Continuous Improvement*. London: Audit Commission.

Audit Commission (2000) *Seeing is Believing*. London: Audit Commission.

Audit Commission (2005) *Early Lessons from Payment by Results*. London: Audit Commission.

Audit Commission (2006) *The Future of Regulation in the Public Sector*, Corporate Discussion Paper. March 2006.

Bakker, K.J. (2003) *An Uncooperative Commodity: Privatizing Water in England and Wales*. Oxford: Oxford University Press.

Bardach, E. (1998) *Getting Agencies to Work Together: The Practice and Theory of Managerial Craftsmanship*. Washington DC: Brookings Institution.

Barker, K. (2004) *Delivering stability: Securing our future housing needs*. The Barker Review of Housing Supply – Final Report. London: H.M. Treasury.

Barzelay M. (1992) *Breaking Through Bureaucracy: A New Vision for Managing in Government*. Berkeley: University of California Press.

Blair, T. (1998) *The Third Way: New Politics for the New Century*. London: Fabian Society.

Bryson, J. (2004) *Strategic Planning for Public and Not For Profit Organizations*, 3rd edn. San Francisco: Jossey Bass.

Byatt, I. and Lyons, M. (2001) *Role of External Review in Improving Performance*. London: Public Services Productivity Panel.

Cabinet Office (1991) *The Citizen's Charter* Cm 1599. London: HMSO.

Cabinet Office (1997) *Better Quality Services: Guidance for Senior Managers*. London: HMSO.

Cabinet Office (2004) *Chartermark Standard*. London: HMSO.

Cabinet Office Agencies and Public Bodies Team (2005) *Public Bodies 2005*. Norwich: HMSO.

Cabinet Office/Citizen's Charter Unit (1994) *The Citizen's Charter: Second Report*, Cm 2540. London: HMSO.

Cabinet Office/Office of Public Services Reform (2003) *The Government's Policy on Inspection*. London: OPSR.

Carter, P. (2003) *Managing Offenders, Reducing Crime*. London: Cabinet Office Strategy Unit.

Child Support Agency (2005) Annual Report and Accounts 2004–05. London: TSO.

CIPFA (2005) *Response to ODPM Consultation on Inspection Reform*. CIPFA homepage.

Clark, T., Dilnot, A., Goodman, A. et al. (2002) 'Taxes and Transfers 1997–2001'. *Oxford Review of Economic Policy*, 18 (2): 187–201.

Clarke, J. (2004) *Citizen-Consumers: the trajectory of an identity*. Conference of the Canadian Anthropological Society, London, Ontario.

Coase, R. (1937) 'The Nature of the Firm'. *Economica*, 4 (16): 386–405.

Commission for Social Care Inspection (2005) *The State of Social Care in England 2004–05*. London: CSCI.

Comptroller and Auditor General (2003) *The Optional Performance of PFI Prisons*, HC 700, Session 2002–3. HMSO, London.

Department of Education and Skills, (2004) Statistical Bulletin: National Curriculum Assessments. London: DFES.

Department of Education and Skills (2006) Statistical Bulletin: National Curriculum Assessments. London: DFES.

Department for Education and Skills (2006) *A Short Guide to the Education and Inspections Bill 2006*. London: HMSO.

Department of the Environment (1995) *CCT: The Private Sector View*. Local Government Research Programme, Ruislip: DoE.

Department of the Environment, Transport and the Regions (1998) *Modern Local Government: in Touch with the People*. London: HMSO.

Department of the Environment, Transport and the Regions (1999) Modernising Local Government. London: HMSO.

Department of the Environment, Transport and the Regions (2000) Modernising Local Government Finance – a Green Paper. London: HMSO.

Department of Health (1997) *The New NHS, Modern, Dependable*, Cm 3807. London: DoH.

Department of Health (2000a) *NHS Plan, a plan for investment, a plan for reform*. London: DoH.

Department of Health (2000b) *Tracking Progress in Children's Services: An evaluation of local responses to the Quality Protects Programme*, Year 2. London: HMSO.

Department of Health (2003) *A short guide to NHS Foundation Trusts*. London: HMSO

Department of Health (2005) *Performance Indicators*. London: DoH.

Department of Social Security/Department of Employment (1994) *Jobseeker's Allowance*, Cm 2687. London: HMSO

Department of Transport (2004) *The Future of Rail*. London: HMSO.

Department of Work and Pensions (2006) *A New Deal For Welfare: Empowering people to work*, Cm 6730. London: HMSO.

Dews, V. and Watts, J. (1994) *Review of Probation Officer Recruitment and Qualifying Training*. London: Home Office.

Dove, M.H.I., Kushner, J. and Zumer, K. (2004) Privatization of Water in the UK and France – What Can We Learn? *Utilities Policy*, 12: 41–50.

Dunleavy, P. (1991) *Democracy, Bureaucracy and Public Choice*. Hemel Hempstead: Harvester Wheatsheaf.

Dunleavy, P. (1994) The Globalization of Public Services Production: Can Government be "Best in World"? *Public Policy and Administration*, 9 (2).

Faulkner, D. (1995) 'The Criminal Justice Act 1991: Policy, Legislation and Practice', in D. Ward and M. Lacey (eds) *Probation: Working for Justice*. London: Whiting and Birch, p. 63.

Ferguson, N., Earley P., Ouston, J. et al. (2000) *Improving Schools and Inspection: The Self-Inspecting School*. London: Paul Chapman/Sage.

Ford, J. and Wilcox, S. (1994) *Affordable Housing, Low Incomes and the Flexible Labour Market*. National Federation of Housing Associations, Research Report 22. London: NFHA.

Freeden, M. (1999) 'The Ideology of New Labour'. *Political Quarterly*, 70 (1), Jan–March.

Furmston, M.P. (2006) *Cheshire, Fifoot and Furmston's Law of Contract*. Oxford: Oxford University Press.

Glennerster, H. (1995) *British Social Policy Since 1945*. Oxford: Blackwell.

Hall, L., Torrington, D. and Taylor, S. (2004) *Human Resource Management*. Hemel Hempstead: FT Prentice Hall.

Halward, W. (1994) 'Manchester Prison: Mounting a Successful In-house Bid'. In Prison Reform Trust, *Privatisation and Market Testing in the Prison Service*. London: Prison Reform Trust.

Harden, I. (1992) *The Contracting State*. Buckingham: Open University Press.

Helm, D. (2005) Editorial, *Utilities Journal*, 8: March.

Her Majesty's Inspectorate of Constabulary (1999) *Report on Greater Manchester Police, 1998–99*. London: TSO.

Her Majesty's Inspectorate of Constabulary (1999) *Report on West Midlands Police, 1998–99*. London: TSO.

Her Majesty's Treasury (2000) *Comprehensive Spending Review*. London: HMSO.

Her Majesty's Treasury (2003) *PFI: Meeting the Investment Challenge*. London: HMSO.

Her Majesty's Treasury (2005) *Budget*. London: HMSO.

Home Office, Department of Health and Welsh Office (1992 and 1995) *National Standards for the Supervision of Offenders in the Community*. London: Home Office Public Relations Branch.

Home Office, Northern Ireland Office and Scottish Office (1993) *Inquiry into Police Responsibilities and Rewards*, Cm 2280. London: HMSO. (The 'Sheehy Report'.)

Home Office (1995) *Statistical Bulletin 20/95. Statistics of Mentally Disordered Offenders, England and Wales 1994*. London: Government Statistical Service.

Home Office (1998) *Prisons, Probation: Joining Forces to Protect the Public*. London: HMSO.

Home Office (2000) *Modernising the Management of the Prison Service: An Independent Report by the Targeted Performance Initiative Working Group.* London: HMSO.

Howard, M. (1994) *Conservatives and the Community,* the 1994 Disraeli Lecture. London: Conservative Political Centre.

Jackson, P. (1995) 'Reflections on Performance Measurement in Public Service Organisations' in P.M. Jackson (ed.) *Measures of Success in the Public Sector.* London: CIPFA, p. 4.

Jenkins, S. (1995) *Accountable to None: The Tory Nationalisation of Britain.* London: Hamish Hamilton.

Kavanagh, D. and Seldon, A. (eds) (1994) *The Major Effect.* Basingstoke: Macmillan.

King's Fund (2005) *An Independent Audit of the NHS Under Labour (1997–2005).* London: King's Fund.

Klein, R. (2000) *The New Politics of the NHS,* 4th edn. London: Routledge.

Laffont, J.-J. and Martimort, D. (2002) *The Theory of Incentives.* Princeton and Oxford: Princeton University Press.

Leishman, F., Cope, S. and Starie, P. (1995) 'Reforming the police in Britain'. *International Journal of Public Sector Management,* 8 (4).

Leadbeater, C. (2004) *Personalisation through participation.* London: Demos.

Lewis, M., Long, S. and Williams, A. (1995) 'What to do with what you've got'. *Policing,* 11 (4): 261–71.

Lipsey, D. (2000) *The Secret Treasury.* London: Viking.

Loveday, B. (1994) 'The Police and Magistrates' Court Act'. *Policing,* 10 (4).

Maddock, S. and Morgan, E. (1999) *Conditions for Partnership.* Manchester: Manchester Business School.

Major, J. (1993) *Conservatism in the 1990s: Our Common Purpose.* Fifth Carlton Lecture. London: Carlton Club Political Committee and Conservative Political Centre.

Malpass, P. (2005) *Housing and the Welfare State: the Development of Housing Policy in Britain.* Basingstoke: Palgrave, p. 193.

Marshall, T.H. (1963) *Sociology at the Crossroads.* London: Heinemann (originally published 1950).

Mayer, C. (2005) 'Commitment and control in regulation: The future of regulation in water', in C. Robinson (ed.) *Governments, Competition and Utility Regulation.* Cheltenham: Edward Elgar.

Milgrom, P. and Roberts, J. (1992) 'Bounded rationality and private information', in P. Milgrom and J. Roberts, *Economics, Organization and Management.* Englewood Cliffs: Prentice Hall.

MORI (2004) *Frontiers of performance in the NHS.* London: MORI (Market and Opinion Research International).

Murray, A. (2001) *Off the Rails – the Crisis in Britain's Railways.* London: Verso.

National Audit Office (1995) *Contracting for Acute Health Care in England,* Report by the Comptroller and Auditor General. London: HMSO, p. 19.

National Audit Office (2000) *The Cancellation of the Benefits Payment Card Project,* Report by the Comptroller and Auditor General. London: NAO.

National Audit Office (2002a) *The PFI Contract for the Redevelopment of West Middlesex University Hospital,* HC Session 49 2002–3. London: NAO.

National Audit Office (2002b) *Using Call Centres to Deliver Public Services*, HC 134 Session 2002–3. 11 December 2002. London: NAO.

National Audit Office (2003a) *PFI Construction Performance*, HC 371, Session 2002–3, 5 February 2003. London: NAO.

National Audit Office (2003b) *The New Energy Trading Arrangements in England and Wales*, HC 624, Session 2002–3, London: NAO.

National Audit Office, (2003c) *The Operational Performance of PFI Prisons*, HC 700 Session 2002–3. London: HMSO.

National Audit Office (2006) *The Termination of the PFI Contract for the National Physical Laboratory*, HC 1044, 2005–6. London: NAO.

National Consumer Council (2003) *Expectations of Public Services*. London: National Consumer Council.

Needham C. (2003) *Citizen-Consumers, New Labour's Market Place Democracy*. London: Catalyst.

Nicholas, S. Povey, D., Walker, A. et al. (2005) *Crime in England and Wales 2004/2005* (The British Crime Survey). London: HMSO, p. 21.

Normann, R. (1991) *Service Management*, 2nd edn. Chichester: Wiley.

O'Connor, D. (2005) *Closing the gap: a review of the 'fitness for purpose' of the current structure of policing in England and Wales*. London: HM Inspector of Constabulary.

Office of the Deputy Prime Minister (2003) *Evaluation of local strategic partnerships. Report of a survey of all English LSPs*. London: ODPM.

Office of the Deputy Prime Minister (2004a) *Delivering stability: securing our future housing needs. The Barker Review of Housing Supply – Final Report*. London: ODPM.

Office of the Deputy Prime Minister (2004b) *The Future of Local Government: Developing a 10-year Vision*. London: ODPM.

Office of the Deputy Prime Minister (2005a) *Local Government finance: Key Facts, England*. National Statistics 2005. London: ODPM.

Office of the Deputy Prime Minister (2005b) *Local Strategic Partnerships: Shaping their future. A consultation paper*. London: ODPM/Department for Communities and Local Government.

Office of Health Economics (2001) *Compendium of Health Statistics*, 12th edn. London: Office of Health Economics.

Office for National Statistics (2004) *Public Service Productivity:* Health. London: HMSO.

Office for National Statistics (2005) *Community Care Statistics 2004–05*. London: ONS. HMSO.

Office for National Statistics (2006a) *Average Earnings Index*. London: ONS.

Office for National Statistics (2006b) *Community Care Statistics* 2004–05. London: ONS.

Office for National Statistics (2006c) *Social Trends* 36. London: ONS.

Office of Public Services Reform (2002) *Monitoring Satisfaction: trends from 1998–2002*. London: HMSO.

Oughton, J. (1994) 'Market testing: the future of the civil service.' *Public Policy and Administration,* 9 (2).

Parasuraman, A., Zeithaml, V. and Berry, L. (1985) 'A Conceptual Model of Service Quality and its Implications for Future Research'. *Journal of Marketing,* Fall, 41–50.

Park, A., Curtice J., Thomson, K., Jarvis, L. et al. (eds) (2003) *British Social Attitudes: The 20th Report.* London: Sage.

Peters, B. Guy (1998) *Managing Horizontal Government.* Ottawa: Canadian Center for Management Development, Research Paper 21.

Pollock, A., Shaol, J. and Vickers, N. (2002) *'Private finance and "value for money" in NHS hospitals: a policy in search of a rationale?'* British Medical Journal 324, May: 1205–1209.

Porter, M. (1980) *Competitive Strategy.* New York: The Free Press.

Portillo, M. (1993) 'The Blue Horizon', speech to Conservative Party Conference 1993. London: Centre for Policy Studies.

Prescott-Clarke, P., Clemens, S. and Park, A. (1994) *Routes into Local Authority Housing: A Study of Local Authority Waiting Lists and New Tenancies.* London: HMSO.

PricewaterhouseCoopers (2000) *Report on the Evaluation of the Public Service Excellence Programme.* London: PWC.

Pritchard, A. (2003) *Understanding Government Output and Productivity.* London: National Expenditure and Income Division, Office for National Statistics.

Rowntree Foundation (1996) *The Future of Work: a Contribution to the Debate, Policy Summary 7.* York: Rowntree Foundation.

Sako, M. (1992) *Prices, Quality and Trust.* Cambridge: Cambridge University Press.

Scottish Executive (2004) *Public Attitudes to the National Health Service in Scotland – 2004 Survey.* Edinburgh: Scottish Executive.

Skelcher, C.K. (1993) 'Involvement and Empowerment in Local Public Services', *Public Money and Management*, July–September.

Stewart, J. (1993) 'The limitations of government by contract'. *Public Money and Management*, July–September, 10–11.

Stretton, H. and Orchard, L. (1994) *Public Goods, Public Enterprise, Public Choice: Theoretical Foundations of the Contemporary Attack on Government.* Basingstoke: Macmillan.

Talbot, C. (2004) 'Executive Agencies: have they improved management in government?' *Public Money and Management*, April: 104–112.

Targeted Performance Initiative Working Group (2000) *Modernising the Management of the Prison Service: an Independent Report.* London: Home Office.

Theakston, K. (1995) *The Civil Service Since 1945.* Oxford: Blackwell.

Thomas, S. (2006) 'The British Model: Failing Slowly'. *Energy Policy*, 34, March.

Transport for London (2005) *London Underground and the PPP: the Second Year, 2004–2005.* London: TfL.

Travers, T. (2005) 'Local and Central Government', Ch. 4 in A. Seldon and D. Kavanagh (eds) *The Blair Effect: 2001–5.* Cambridge: Cambridge University Press, p. 77.

Udehn, L. (1996) *The Limits of Public Choice: a Sociological Critique of the Economic Theory of Politics,* London: Routledge.

Walker, D. (2002) *In Praise of Centralism: a Critique of New Localism.* London: Catalyst.

Walsh, K. (1995) *Public Services and Market Mechanisms: Competition, Contracting, and the New Public Management.* Basingstoke: Macmillan.

Westmarland, L. and Smith, N, (2004) 'From scumbags to consumers: Customer Service and the Commodification of Policing', output from *Creating Citizen*

Consumers: Changing Identifications and Relationships. Milton Keynes: Open University.

Wilks, S. (1996) 'Class Compromise in the International Economy: the Rise and Fall of Swedish Social Democracy'. *Capital and Class*, 58.

Wilks-Heeg, S. (2001) *Urban Regeneration.* Unpublished paper.

Wilks-Heeg, S. and Claydon, S. (2006) *Whose Town is it Anyway?* York: Joseph Rowntree Charitable Trust.

Willetts, D. (1994) *Civic Conservatism.* London: Social Market Foundation.

Williamson, O. (1975) *Markets and Hierarchies. New York:* The Free Press.

Wright, K. (1995) *The Mental Health (Patients in the Community) Bill, Research Paper 95/71.* London: House of Commons Library.

Index